Object Detection by Stereo Vision Images

Scrivener Publishing
100 Cummings Center, Suite 541J
Beverly, MA 01915-6106

Publishers at Scrivener
Martin Scrivener (martin@scrivenerpublishing.com)
Phillip Carmical (pcarmical@scrivenerpublishing.com)

Object Detection by Stereo Vision Images

Edited by

R. Arokia Priya
Anupama V Patil
Manisha Bhende
Anuradha Thakare
and
Sanjeev Wagh

Scrivener
Publishing

WILEY

This edition first published 2022 by John Wiley & Sons, Inc., 111 River Street, Hoboken, NJ 07030, USA and Scrivener Publishing LLC, 100 Cummings Center, Suite 541J, Beverly, MA 01915, USA
© 2022 Scrivener Publishing LLC
For more information about Scrivener publications please visit www.scrivenerpublishing.com.

Wiley Global Headquarters
111 River Street, Hoboken, NJ 07030, USA

For details of our global editorial offices, customer services, and more information about Wiley products visit us at www.wiley.com.

Limit of Liability/Disclaimer of Warranty
While the publisher and authors have used their best efforts in preparing this work, they make no representations or warranties with respect to the accuracy or completeness of the contents of this work and specifically disclaim all warranties, including without limitation any implied warranties of merchantability or fitness for a particular purpose. No warranty may be created or extended by sales representatives, written sales materials, or promotional statements for this work. The fact that an organization, website, or product is referred to in this work as a citation and/or potential source of further information does not mean that the publisher and authors endorse the information or services the organization, website, or product may provide or recommendations it may make. This work is sold with the understanding that the publisher is not engaged in rendering professional services. The advice and strategies contained herein may not be suitable for your situation. You should consult with a specialist where appropriate. Neither the publisher nor authors shall be liable for any loss of profit or any other commercial damages, including but not limited to special, incidental, consequential, or other damages. Further, readers should be aware that websites listed in this work may have changed or disappeared between when this work was written and when it is read.

Library of Congress Cataloging-in-Publication Data

ISBN 978-1-119-84219-4

Cover image: Pixabay.Com
Cover design by Russell Richardson

Set in size of 11pt and Minion Pro by Manila Typesetting Company, Makati, Philippines

Printed in the USA

10 9 8 7 6 5 4 3 2 1

Contents

Preface

Current state-of-the-art technologies have opened up new opportunities in research in the areas of object detection and recognition of digital images and videos, robotics, neural networks, machine learning, stereo vision matching algorithms, soft computing, customer prediction, social media analysis, recommendation systems, and stereo vision. Therefore, this book has been designed to provide directions for those interested in researching and developing intelligent applications to detect an object and estimate depth. In addition to focusing on the performance of the system using high-performance computing techniques, a technical overview of certain tools, languages, libraries, frameworks, and APIs for developing applications is also given. More specifically, detection using stereo vision images/video from its developmental stage up till today, its possible applications, and general research problems relating to it are covered. Also presented are techniques and algorithms that satisfy the peculiar needs of stereo vision images along with emerging research opportunities through analysis of modern techniques being applied to intelligent systems.

Since both theoretical and practical aspects of the developments in this field of research are explored, including recent state-of-the-art technologies and research opportunities in the area of object detection, this book will act as a good reference for practitioners, students, and researchers. Briefly stated, since it is a pioneer reference in this particular field, it will be a significant source of information for researchers who have been longing for an integrated reference. It is ideally designed for researchers, academics, and post-graduate students seeking current research on emerging soft computing areas; and it can also be used by various universities as a textbook for graduate/post-graduate courses. Many professional societies, IT professionals, or organizations working in the field of robotics will also benefit from this book.

A chapter-by-chapter synopsis of the topics covered in this book follows:

- In Chapter 1, Deepti Nikumbh *et al.* present data conditioning techniques for medical imaging. Digital images have a tremendous influence on today's world and have become an essential component in the clinical medical field. Significant advancements in the processing of medical images, and improvements in diagnosis and analysis, have transformed medical imaging into one of today's hottest emerging fields for implementation and research. Image pre-processing techniques along with image segmentation and image processing algorithms are useful tools that pave the way for advancement in the medical field with wide applications such as cancer detection, fingerprint identification and many others using pattern matching, feature extraction and edge detection algorithms.
- In Chapter 2, Shravani Nimbolkar *et al.* present an analytical study for pneumonia detection using machine learning and deep learning techniques. This chapter studies different types of lung diseases and how their diagnosis can be aided using these techniques. Experimentation with different machine learning models, like CNN and MLP, and pretrained architectures, like VGG16 and ResNet, are used to predict pneumonia from chest X-rays.
- In Chapter 3, Kavita R. Singh *et al.* explore the advanced application of a contamination monitoring system using IoT and GIS. Contamination/pollution is one of the biggest challenges where environmental issues are concerned. The authors analyze particular areas that are more contaminated/polluted in Nagpur City, Maharashtra, India, by calibrating the air quality index as an IoT-based air pollution monitoring framework and plotting the data using a geographical information system. Additionally, the data analysis, which is done with the help of Tableau software and different parameters like air quality index, temperature, etc., is provided to the end user through the android application.
- In Chapter 4, Rajani P.K. *et al.* present the new area of video error concealment using particle swarm optimization. Video transmission over wired or wireless channels, such as the internet, is the fastest growing area of research. The proposed method is a novel method in the spatio-temporal

domain that can significantly improve the subjective and objective video quality. There are many algorithms for video error concealment. These optimized algorithms should be used for obtaining better video quality. Particle swarm optimization (PSO), which is one of the best optimized bio-inspired algorithms, is used to conceal the errors in different video formats. Correlation is used for detection of errors in the videos and each error frame is concealed using PSO algorithm in MATLAB.

- In Chapter 5, Nalini Jagtap explores enhanced image fusion with guided filters. She proposes the modified guided filtering approach called "novel guided filtering" to overcome blurring and ringing effects. The primary step in this approach is to design the guidance image and generate the base and complex components based on that image. The edge detection operator plays a significant role in deciding the guidance image. The focus map is generated using low-rank representation, which is based on a detailed part of the original image. The built-in characteristic of removing ringing and blurring effects using LRR helps to develop artifact-free/noiseless detail-enhanced image fusion. First, guided filters are applied on a focus map; then the guided filter output is used to generate the resultant all-in-one fused image. In this case, ringing and blurring effects are removed using guided filters in the resultant fused image.

- In Chapter 6, Tejaswini Yesugade proposes deepfake detection using LSTM-based neural network. The rapid growth of social media and new developments in deep generative networks have improved the quality of creating more realistic fake videos, which are called deepfake videos. Such deepfake videos are used in politics to create political turmoil, for blackmail, and terrorism. To reduce the harm that can be done using such methods and prevent the spread of such fake images or videos, the author proposes a method that can detect such deepfakes and a new method to detect AI-generated fake videos using an algorithm such as CNN and LSTM. This method will detect deepfakes by using ResNext50 and LSTM algorithms, which have an accuracy of around 88%.

- In Chapter 7, Kavita Shinde *et al.* present various approaches for classification of fetal brain abnormalities with MRI images. Magnetic resonance imaging of fetuses allows doctors to observe brain abnormalities early on. Therefore, since nearly three out of every 1,000 fetuses have a brain anomaly, it is necessary to determine and categorize them at an earlier stage. The literature survey finds less work is involved in the classification of abnormal fetal brain based on conventional methods of machine learning, while more related work is conducted for the segmentation and feature extraction using different techniques. In this chapter, the authors review different machine learning techniques used for the complete MRI processing chain, starting with image acquisition to its classification.

– In Chapter 8, Chinnaiah Kotadi *et al.* explore a method to analyze COVID-19 data using a machine learning algorithm. The authors analyze past COVID-19 data to raise awareness of COVID-19 second wave conditions and precautions against the delta variant. They also provide COVID-19 cases such as confirmed cases, cured patients' cases, and death rates in India. Also, by using a machine learning algorithm, the states of India in which the most cases and deaths occurred are provided.

– In Chapter 9, Manish Sharma *et al.* explore an intelligent recommendation system for evaluating teaching faculty performance using adaptive collaborative filtering. This system uses the deep learning model for the evaluation and enhancement of the performance of teachers in educational institutions. To give a recommendation framework, this work incorporates numerous elements such as student assessment, intake quality, innovative practices, experiential learning approaches, and so on. The dataset derived from an educational institute's ERP was used to train and test the proposed recommender. The performance of the proposed recommender system was evaluated using the real-time data of teachers and other stakeholders from an educational institute apart from some secondary parameters. The comparative analysis of various techniques along with the performance comparison based on accuracy, precision, and recall are well furnished.

– In Chapter 10, Manisha Blende *et al.* propose a virtual moratorium system. By using the proposed system, the banker will get all the information regarding a customer who has opted for the moratorium. The user will interact with the chatbot and submit the moratorium request and then chatbot will ask questions based on customers' responses. Rasa natural language processing (NLP) and Rasa natural language understanding algorithm will classify the intents from the user responses. Intents will be compared with predefined patterns to extract the specific data. These responses will be stored in the NoSQL (MongoDB) database, and these data will be shared with the banker, who will further analyze them. The main purpose of this study is to help the banker know whether the customer who has applied for the moratorium is genuine. With this system, both the customer and the banker will be able to save time and effort. The proposed system will allow customers to register the moratorium at any time and from anywhere using a dedicated web platform and android application as well as some social media platforms. The complete chatbot moratorium system will be encrypted with secure encryption algorithms (AES-256, SSH). This system not only contains moratorium functionalities but also has some extra features, like News and Updates, which are crawled from various genuine news platforms and official banking sites. With all of these features, REST API services are also available for further enhancements and integration into multiple platforms.

– In Chapter 11, Vandana TulsidasChavan *et al.* explore efficient land cover classification for urban planning. They propose the development of a land cover classification system that can classify images efficiently based on the land cover without any human intervention. Land cover categorization analysis for multispectral and hyperspectral pictures is evaluated. It provides a unique perspective on LU/LC change assessment and tactics at each level of the land cover classification process. The primary goal of this classification is to motivate future researchers to work accurately and to assist land resource planners, urban development managers, forest department personnel, and government officials in taking critical actions to maintain our precious planet's ecology.

– In Chapter 12, Pradnya Patil *et al.* present a study on data-driven approaches for fake news detection on social media platforms. The authors discuss the drawbacks and benefits of the increased sharing of information or news on social media and how it is becoming more difficult for social media users to distinguish between what is true and what is fake. Therefore, a data-driven analysis technique is increasingly being used in a variety of decision-making processes. Similarly, it may be used to detect fake news on social media platforms, allowing fraudulent material to be caught quickly and its lateral movement to be restricted before it reaches millions of consumers. Since it's critical to have a mechanism in place that will assist social media users and communities in identifying bogus news, this will help detect fake news in a very efficient way and categorize news into fake, real, and unclear types.

–   In Chapter 13, Suvarna Patil *et al.* present a novel method to measure distance for object detection for automotive applications using a 3D density-based clustering approach for an advanced depression detection system. It determines whether a stereo vision-based item detection system is effective. Even though this approach has a fault in that it removes areas of the image that aren't required for detection, the proposed method has been shown to provide reliable detection of potential obstacles as well as precise assessment of obstacle position and magnitude. This study proposes a method for detecting artifacts using 3D density-based clustering after deleting such regions with segmentation, in which the depth map was created by scaling the picture points to a scaled XZ plane. Then, using typical object grouping methods, the depth map can be easily segmented. The first ingenious encroachment was based on the separation of identifiable things.

–   In Chapter 14, Arokia Priya *et al.* discuss the intelligence developed for a system for estimating the depth using the connected components method. The proposed expert system focuses on using a stereo vision camera for capturing the left and right images, and finding the disparity between the objects by using blob detection instead of pixel disparity. The chapter evaluates and creates a system that finds the distance of the object placed in front of both the cameras using the disparity between two objects. It focuses on a single object with background and without background. The process is carried out both in CPU and GPU and the time complexity is analyzed apart from the accuracy of depth.

In closing, we are indebted to Martin Scrivener, for the tremendous support that he has given us since the inception of this book. It was only with the cooperation, enthusiasm, and spirit of the authors and reviewers that we could make it a grand success. Finally, we would like to thank you, the contributors, for your interest in the book and we encourage you to continue to send us your invaluable feedback and ideas for further improvement of our book.

Editors
R. Arokia Priya, Anupama V Patil, Manisha Bhende,
Anuradha Thakare, Sanjeev Wagh
May 2022

1

Data Conditioning for Medical Imaging

**Shahzia Sayyad[1], Deepti Nikumbh[1]*, Dhruvi Lalit Jain[1], Prachi Dhiren Khatri[1],
Alok Saratchandra Panda[1] and Rupesh Ravindra Joshi[2,3†]**

*[1]Shah and Anchor Kutchhi Engineering College, University of Mumbai,
Mumbai, India
[2]Loknete Gopalrao Gulve Polytechnic, Nashik, India
[3]North Maharashtra University, Jalgaon, India*

Abstract

Digital images are tremendously influencing today's world and have become an essential component in the medical and clinical field. The significant advancement in the processing of medical images and the improvements in diagnosis and analysis have transformed medical imaging into the most emerging fields in the light of the day for implementation and research. Medical scanners are used to create pictures of the human body. These pictures are used in the diagnosis of diseases. In medical imaging, contrast and image quality are the challenges being faced. For human interpretation or computer analysis, image enhancement makes the picture clear. The image enhancement process does not increase the data internal information material, but it may be used to emphasize the features of importance in order to identify the pictures more efficiently. Image preprocessing is like an operation at the lowest stage that is implemented on images. It is used to generate image data that improves the features relevant to further processing or removes unwanted distortion. Medical image processing is the technique of using various algorithms for processing medical images to obtain enhanced, restored, coded, or compressed images and gain valuable information. It has the ability to image the physiologic conditions that support tumor development and growth before it forms a sizable mass. Hence, it is very useful in detecting cancer at an extremely early stage which paves ways for effective diagnosis and treatment. Image preprocessing techniques along with image segmentation and image processing algorithms are useful tools that pave the way for advancement in the medical field with wide applications such as cancer detection and fingerprint identification using pattern matching, feature extraction, and edge detection algorithms.

*Corresponding author: deepti.nikumbh@sakec.ac.in
†Corresponding author: joshirupesh77@gmail.com

R. Arokia Priya, Anupama V Patil, Manisha Bhende, Anuradha Thakare and Sanjeev Wagh (eds.)
Object Detection by Stereo Vision Images, (1–32) © 2022 Scrivener Publishing LLC

Keywords: Medical image processing, segmentation, hyperspectral imaging, feature extraction, unsupervised learning, image acquisition

1.1   Introduction

Medical imaging can reveal both the normal and pathological functioning of the human body. It has the ability to anticipate cancer symptoms up to 10 years in advance. It does not release radiation or come into touch with the human body. As a consequence, patients do not have to go through needless testing or surgeries. As a consequence, there are no risks and no discomfort.

The motivation behind writing this chapter:

There are few opportunities to learn about this topic. Despite the author's extensive analysis, all the available information did not answer the author's most pressing questions, which are as follows:

- Why is it essential to perform image processing and preprocessing on medical images?
- What exactly is it doing in the background?
- Finally, how can anyone perform image processing and preprocessing on their own?

This chapter is a collection of all the missing puzzle pieces that have been put together to address the above questions and demonstrate the magic that occurs on images when different image preprocessing and processing techniques are applied.

The following are the objectives of this chapter:

- Describe the various types of medical images used for screening.
- State the different steps involved in medical image processing.
- Discuss preprocessing techniques of medical image processing.
- Implement OpenCV and scikit-learn python libraries and perform various operations on the image using these libraries.
- Explain image acquisition, reconstruction, and feature extraction techniques.
- Illustrate an application of medical image processing, which is a case study on detection of throat cancer.

1.2   Importance of Image Preprocessing

Preprocessing is done to enhance the picture's quality so that we can analyze it very efficiently. We can eliminate extra distortions and strengthen some features that are crucial steps done by preprocessing technique.

Both the upstream and downstream pictures are resolved at the lowest level of abstraction during preprocessing. The essence of prior knowledge is significant if preprocessing is used to correct any image degradation. The type of degradation, image properties, image noise, and certain spectral characteristics are the main features of image preprocessing. The various techniques are discussed in this chapter.

As a result of different techniques, we can increase the efficiency of programs that use those images, resulting in a more accurate result.

1.3   Introduction to Digital Medical Imaging

Medical imaging is the technique of getting photographs of internal organs for medical reasons such as defining or analyzing diseases. The term "medical imaging processing" refers to the use of a computer to manipulate images.

Every week, thousands of imaging procedures are practiced around the globe. Due to advances in image processing, such as picture analysis, augmentation, and identification, and displaying it in digital form, medical imaging is continuously improving. Medical images range from the most general, such as a chest X-ray, to the most complicated, such as practical magnetic resonance imaging.

Medical imaging is becoming a vital part of the entire healthcare ecosystem from well-being and monitoring through early diagnosis and medication selection, and follow-up medical imaging is becoming a vital part of the entire healthcare ecosystem. Medical imaging helps to diagnose disease processes and also provides a basic understanding of anatomy and organ function.

It could be used to perform medical testing including organ delineation, lung tumor prediction, spinal disfigurement diagnosis, and artery stenosis detection. To boost the quality of medical imaging, image processing techniques are used. As the volume and dimensions of healthcare records expand, novel computer-aided techniques are required to balance medical data and design effective and reliable methods. As the number of healthcare institutions and patients continues to rise, the use of computer-aided medical prognostics and decision support systems in clinical practice is now becoming particularly important.

Computational intelligence has the potential to improve the efficiency of healthcare systems (such as detection, treatment, and monitoring). Combining computer analysis with appropriate care has the potential to aid clinicians in improving diagnostic accuracy. Moreover, by combining medical images and other forms of electronic health records, the accuracy of detection can be increased and the time it takes to detect can be reduced.

Reduced processing costs, simpler networking and storage, instant data quality, multiple duplications while preserving quality, fast and inexpensive replication, and versatile manipulation are just a few of the features of data medical images.

1.3.1   Types of Medical Images for Screening

Types of medical images for screening are as follows:

1. X-rays
2. Computed tomography (CT) scan
3. Ultrasound
4. Magnetic resonance imaging (MRI)
5. Positron emission tomography (PET)
6. Mammogram
7. Fluoroscopy
8. Infrared thermography

1.3.1.1   X-rays

It is the oldest, as well as the most widely used imaging type. X-ray generally works on frequency and wavelengths that are unable to see without the naked eye. X-rays are relatively quick, low-cost, non-invasive, and easy for patients to endure [11].

1.3.1.2   Computed Tomography (CT) Scan

In a CT scanner, a motored X-ray supply fires a tiny beam of X-rays that revolves around the patient. The X-rays are picked up as they pass through the patient by special digital X-ray detectors, which are positioned directly opposite the X-ray supply. Through CT scans we can get abnormal structures [16].

1.3.1.3   Ultrasound

In medical imaging, ultrasound is among the safest forms and has a wide range of applications. During an ultrasound, high-frequency sound waves are transferred from the probe to the body via the conducting gel, and after striking various structures within the body, the waves bounce back, resulting in an image that can be used for diagnosis. It can assist in the diagnosis of several body parts, including the bones, pelvis, blood vessels, belly, kidneys, muscles, breasts, and joints [11].

1.3.1.4   Magnetic Resonance Imaging (MRI)

MRI creates images that are not visible with CT scans or X-rays. These images are created using radio waves and high magnetic fields. MRI does not use ionizing radiation. Malignancies, brain function, spinal cord injury, strokes, and aneurysms are all diagnosed by examining internal physiological components. The spins of the nucleon are aligned using a strong magnetic flux, and then, the spins of the protons are flipped using radiofrequency before being aligned again. Protons in various bodily tissues return to their original spins at varying speeds, allowing the MRI to distinguish between different types of tissue and detect any abnormalities. The molecules, on the other hand, "flip" and return to their original spin orientation, which is captured and processed into an image [11].

1.3.1.5   Positron Emission Tomography (PET) Scan

PET scan contains radioactive tracer. This tracer is either injected, inhaled, or swallowed in veins, depending on which body part is to be examined. The scanner uses the gamma rays emitted by the tracer to show images of bones and organs. Unlike other imaging types, it can catch problems much earlier and can show how different parts of the body are working. PET scan is usually painless and can be used for diagnosing, treatment of various diseases. It can check how well treatment is working and how deep the disease has spread [16].

1.3.1.6   Mammogram

In the fight against breast cancer, there are two types of mammography available: diagnostic and screening mammograms. Diagnostic mammography is used to check for cancer when a tumor or thickening in the breast is discovered. Mammograms for screening are used to detect any abnormalities.

1.3.1.7   Fluoroscopy

A fluoroscopy is like a motion picture of body function because it shows moving body parts. The procedure is generally performed using contrast dyes, which show how they flow through the body whereas all of this being done, a signal is being sent by an X-ray to the monitor. Fluoroscopies are used to analyze both hard and soft tissue, including organs, joints, bones, and vessels.

1.3.1.8   Infrared Thermography

Thermography is a diagnostic technique that uses infrared light to map the body's anatomical processes. It is based on skin surface temperature, which is determined by the blood circulation in the skin's outer millimetres. Infrared medical thermography is sensitive enough to detect any changes in skin temperature. The recording of temperature to build an image distribution on the body's surface is known as clinical thermography. It is used for determining inflammation in different areas of the body [11].

1.4   Preprocessing Techniques of Medical Imaging Using Python

The images obtained through various data acquisition methods are processed. However, due to the extreme variety of noise present in the data, the raw images captured from the scan centers are not appropriate for direct processing. As a result, it must be preprocessed before being examined. Preprocessing is a crucial process, which includes filtering, labeling, artifact elimination, enhancement, and segmentation. Python libraries like OpenCV and NumPy are used for the implementation of the various preprocessing techniques [22].

1.4.1   Medical Image Preprocessing

Image preprocessing steps are as follows:

1. Reading the image
2. Resizing the image
3. Removing the noise from the image or denoise
4. Image filtering or smoothing
5. Image segmentation

Figure 1.1 displays the steps involved in Image preprocessing along with the various techniques that can be used for performing those steps.

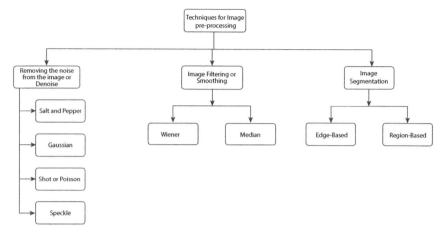

Figure 1.1 Medical image preprocessing.

1.4.1.1   Reading the Image

This is the first step in performing image preprocessing. This step reads the image which has been imported to the system for analysis.

1.4.1.2   Resizing the Image

In image processing resizing the image is a method to expand and minimize the size of a given image in the form of pixels. The image is partitioned into two types: image up-sampling and image down-sampling, both of which are required when resizing data to match a particular communication channel or output display. The clarity of an image increases with an increase in pixels. This is called up-sampling. The pixel intensities in an input image are lowered based on the sampling frequency in the down-sampling technique [3]. In Figure 1.2, the different steps of image preprocessing are implemented in python using the OpenCV library.

```
1   import numpy as np
2   import cv2
3   image=cv2.imread("img.jpg",0)
4   cv2.imshow("Original Image",image)
5   resized_image=cv2.resize(image,None,fx=0.5,fy=0.5,interpolation=cv2.INTER_CUBIC)
6   cv2.imshow("Resized Image",resized_image)
7   kernel=np.ones((2,2),np.float32)/4
8   filter_2D=cv2.filter2D(image,-1,kernel)
9   cv2.imshow("Filtering the image using 2D filter",filter_2D)
10  gaussian_blur=cv2.GaussianBlur(image,(3,3),0)
11  cv2.imshow("Gaussian Blur",gaussian_blur)
12  cv2.waitKey(0)
13  cv2.destroyAllWindows()
```

Figure 1.2 Python code using OpenCV library.

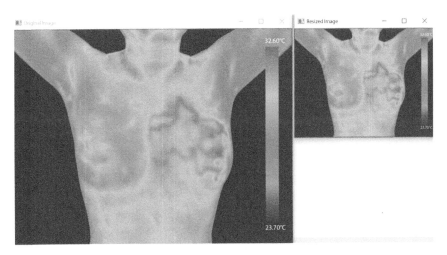

Figure 1.3 Reading and resizing the image.

In Figure 1.3, the original image on the left side is read using the image read and image show method in python. The right side of the image has the resized image resized using the resize method of OpenCV, which takes parameters such as source image, desired size scaling element along the horizontal axis, scaling element along the vertical axis, and interpolation method for resizing.

1.4.1.3 Noise Removal

Image noise is a spontaneous variation of color information or brightness in images created by medical scanners or devices. Noise is commonly described as the unpredictability of a signal caused by random fluctuations [22]. Visual noise can be seen in all medical photos. The presence of noise in a picture causes it to appear dotted, grainy, textured, or snowy. There are many forms of noise, and the most common types of noise seen in medical images are listed [8, 19].

1.4.1.3.1   Salt and Pepper

It appears as a mixture of white and black pixels on the screen. Salt and pepper noise appears in images when rapid fluctuations, such as erroneous changeover, occur [1]. It is also called spike noise or impulsive noise [19].

1.4.1.3.2   Gaussian

Noise that is random is called Gaussian noise. It is a probability density function of a normal distribution, frequently referred to as a Gaussian distribution [1]. Every individual pixel in the image is changed by a low number from its initial amount in Gaussian noise [19].

1.4.1.3.3   Shot or Poisson

The dominant noise in the lighter sections of a picture is shot noise, also known as Poisson noise [1]. Photon shot noise is the numerical quantum variations in the number of photons for a given level of exposure that are normal in imaging devices [19].

1.4.1.3.4   Speckle

It is a granular noise that generally occurs in synthetic aperture radar and active radar images and degrades their accuracy [1].

1.4.1.4   *Filtering and Smoothing*

The image contains noise, a low-pass filter is used to reduce noise in the image. Due to the noise reduction, there is a loss of accuracy, some minute features of the data are lost. There are various techniques to remove noise by filtering data very carefully, either by smoothing the image or suppressing the low frequencies. For example, adding a filter to an image to highlight some features while suppressing other images. For image filtering, there are few applications such as sharpening, reducing noise, smoothening, and edge detection [1, 4].

1.4.1.4.1   Wiener Filtering

The optimal combination of removing noise and noise smoothing is achieved by wiener filtering. Wiener filtering helps to minimize mean square error within the noise synthesis protocol and speckle noise. Wiener uses a linear estimation of the primary image [19].

1.4.1.4.2   Median Filtering

Median filtering replaces each pixel of the image with its peer's mean value, including each other [1].

It is based on a kernel, which, like other convolutions, describes the community's shape and size to be tested when evaluating the average. The most common kernel size is 3×3, but larger kernels can be used for more extreme smoothing [19].

Input images are reflected in each output pixel for the median value within the 3×3 neighborhoods around the corresponding pixel. The

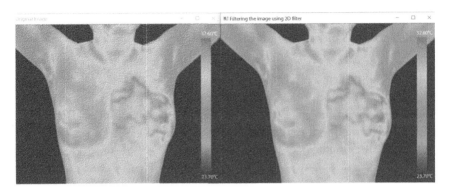

Figure 1.4 Reading and filtering the image using the 2D convolution technique.

images' margins are replaced with zeros. The filter's output is a single value that takes the place of the present pixel value at (x, y) [19].

In Figure 1.4, the source image on the left side and the right side shows the image after applying the two-dimensional (2D) convolution technique. It uses a kernel for the convolution of an image. Smoothing from the kernel accomplishes the following: a 2 × 2 window is centered on each pixel, all pixels falling inside this window are added together, and the result is then divided by 4. This is equivalent to averaging the pixel values inside that window. To generate the output filtered image, this operation is repeated for all image pixels. This is done using a 2D convolution technique that takes input parameters such as source image, depth of the filtered image, and kernel.

Figure 1.5 (left side) shows the source image and the image after applying Gaussian blur on the right side. To blur an image, a Gaussian filter is

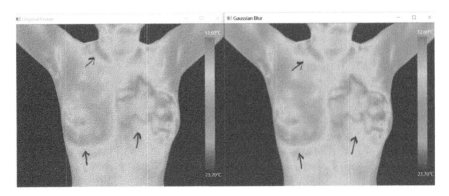

Figure 1.5 Reading and smoothing the image using Gaussian blur.

used, which is an important part of image preprocessing. This filter takes as input the width and height of the kernel, the standard deviation in the X and Y directions, as well as the mean, must be positive and odd. The kernel size is used to compute both standard deviations if they are both zeros. Gaussian blurring is highly effective when it comes to removing Gaussian noise from an image. The arrows highlight the blurred part which differentiates it from the original image.

1.4.1.5   Image Segmentation

Separation of an image into multiple parts is a methodology of image segmentation. The aim of this method is to analyse the images simpler to glance at and comprehend while maintaining their quality. Those elements reflect the entire original picture and take on characteristics like strength and similarity [21].

It significantly lowers the size of the image to be analyzed and filters out unnecessary data, leaving only the image's greatest useful qualities. Different discontinuities in gray level, color, texture, brightness, saturation, and other variables are used by edge-based segmentation algorithms to find edges in an image [21].

In image segmentation, structures of data are easily detected by humans but are difficult to specify for a computer. There are various image segmentation techniques [21].

1.4.1.5.1   Thresholding

This is the simplest but most optimized way for locating the required parts of the image. The pixels are augmented on the image's intensity by comparing their intensity to a threshold value. The threshold method has an advantage when the image's objects are believed to have a greater density than the image's backdrop [12].

1.4.1.5.2   Edge-Based Segmentation

Understanding picture features requires the ability to discern edges. Edges are regarded to hold valuable information and have significant characteristics. It minimizes the resolution of the image to be examined and eliminates small features, leaving only the image's most important architectural properties. To detect edges in the image, edge-based segmentation algorithms use various inconsistencies in gray level, color, texture, brightness, saturation, and other factors [12].

1.4.1.5.3   Region-Based Segmentation

In a region-based segmentation method, the algorithm constructs sections by separating the image into various elements with comparable features. Techniques for region-based picture separation begin by looking for certain cluster centers in the input image either smaller sections or much larger chunks. The ground levels are then further reduced or shrunk to small chunks and merged with other narrower feature vectors, or even more, pixels are added to the pixel values [12].

1.4.1.5.4   Clustering-Based Segmentation Method

Collection-based algorithms are those that divide an image into clusters that contain pixels with similar characteristics. There are two methods: hierarchical method and partition-based method. The hierarchical methods are based on the concept of trees. The root of the tree regenerates everywhere and the nodes inside re-establish the layers. Algorithms based on partitions, on the other hand, apply optimization methods repeatedly to optimize an objective function. There are numerous algorithms for finding clusters in the two methods mentioned. Clustering can be sub-divided into two categories [12]. These are as follows.

1.4.1.5.4.1   HARD CLUSTERING

Hard clustering is a straightforward clustering separation method that divides a picture into multiple nodes, with each component corresponding to just one of them. A sample of hard clustering based method is the K-means clustering technique, often known as HCM [12].

1.4.1.5.4.2   SOFT CLUSTERING

The degree of joining is characterized by feature values, and pixels are partitioned into clusters based on partial involvement, i.e., a single pixel can participate in more than one cluster. Soft clustering is exemplified by fuzzy c-means clustering [12].

Algorithm for K-Means Clustering:
The unsupervised algorithm "K-means clustering" is often adapted to differentiate the interest area from the context. Based on the K-centroids, it fragments or partitions the given data into K clusters. When there is unlabelled data, the algorithm is used. The objective is to find specific groups based on some kind of data similarities, with K representing the number of groups.

Algorithm for K-means clustering:

1. Select k as the number of nodes you want to search.
2. Assign the sets of data to one of the k clusters at random.
3. Then, figure out where the clusters' centers are.
4. Compute the difference between each cluster's center and the data points.
5. Reconfigure the data points to the clusters closest to them, based on their distance from the cluster.
6. Calculate the new cluster center once more.
7. Repeat procedures 4, 5, and 6 until the data points do not alter the clusters or until the step size is reached.

1.4.1.5.5 Watershed-Based Methods

The foundation of watershed-based models is topological interpretation. The severity in this case depicts pools with a gap in their minimum from where liquid overflows. The neighboring basins are united when the water hits the basins' border. Dams are required to maintain barriers between basins, and these dams are the fragmented region's borders. The watershed models detect the image's gradient as a topographic layer [12].

1.4.1.5.6 Partial Differential Equation–Based Segmentation Method

The non-linear isotropic diffusion filter (for sharpening edges) and convex non-quadratic variation restoration (for background subtraction) are basic two Partial Differential Equation (PDE) methods. The PDE approach results in deformed borders and edges, which can be changed with coarse operators. The fourth-order PDE technique removes noise from the image, whereas the second-order PDE strategy improves edge and boundary detection [12]. Table 1.1 summarizes different image segmentation methods along with its advantages and disadvantages.

1.5 Medical Image Processing Using Python

Medical image processing is a technique for improving image quality such that it may be easily interpreted by both machines and humans. Image processing is a technique for converting one image into another image. Hence, while the output and input images are both images, the output image has superior attributes or quality than the input image. Continuous images and discrete images are the two types of images that exist. Continuous images

Table 1.1 Different image segmentation methods [12].

Segmentation methods	Description	Advantages	Disadvantages
Thresholding technique	• It determines certain threshold values based on the image's histogram peaks.	• Prior knowledge not needed. • Method is very simple.	• It is heavily reliant on peaks, and specific details are ignored in this strategy.
Edge-based technique	• It is based on discontinuity recognition.	• It is better for images to have contrast among objects.	• It is not suitable for many corners.
Region-based technique	• It is more noise resistant since it is based on partitioning image into homogeneous regions.	• It is more noise-resistant. • It is useful when defining similarity criteria is simple.	• In terms of time and memory, it is an expensive method.
Clustering based technique	• It is based on the split into homogenous clusters.	• It is hazy and employs partial enrollment. • It is better for genuine problems.	• It is difficult to determine the membership function using this strategy.
Watershed based technique	• It is based on topological interpretation.	• The outcomes are consistent, and the identified boundaries are consistent.	• It does intricate calculation of gradients.
Pde based technique	• It is based on how mathematical models function.	• It is the rapid method. • It is ideal for time-sensitive operations.	• It has more computational effort.

are formed by optical devices that receive analog signals, while discrete images are generated by digitizing continuous images.

Medical imaging has been profoundly influenced by the advancement of computer and image technology. Medical image processing has become a major hub as the quality of medical imaging influences diagnosis and is a boon for clinical applications that want to store and fetch images for future use. With the introduction of quicker, more reliable, and less invasive devices in the last decade, medical imaging has undergone a revolution. This has prompted the development of corresponding software, which has, in turn, fueled the development of new digital image processing algorithms. Figure 1.6 displays the different steps involved in medical image processing.

The steps are as follows:

1. The process of getting image data is called image acquisition.
2. Image preprocessing is the process of enhancing the image in such a way that the processes performed on it have a better chance of succeeding.
3. The technique of breaking down a source image into its constituent sections or objects is known as image segmentation.
4. Image representation translates the input information in such a manner that it can be understood by a computer.
5. Image description is the process of obtaining features that result in measurable details of interest or features that are fundamental for separating one object type from another.
6. Image recognition is assigning a mark to an element depending upon the specifics of its descriptor.
7. Image interpretation is the method of assigning significance to a collection of objects that have been identified.

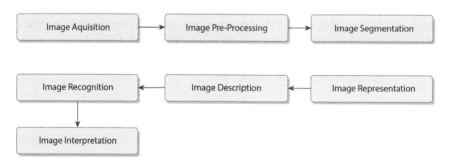

Figure 1.6 Steps for medical image processing.

In several areas of medical and laboratory science, as well as clinical practice, imaging has become indispensable. Radiologists use MRI and CT scans to categorize and analyze tumors, whereas neuroscientists use PET and functional imaging to detect brain activity. Virologists construct three-dimensional (3D) viral pictures from micrographs; radiologists categorize and analyze tumors using MRI and CT scans; biologists investigate cells and get 3D confocal microscope datasets; Computerized evaluation and visualization tools are needed for the analysis of these various image types [14].

The histogram is the most basic method of image processing. The picture quality is unaffected by the image display. The grayscale histogram takes into account the most basic type of image that is used to analyze and enhance images. The gray-level histogram shows how dark or bright a picture is. The mean pixel value may be calculated from the histogram by summing the consistent bin altitude and emitted pixel values, then dividing by the total number of pixels. Histogram equalization is a method for comparing a large number of images obtained regularly, one-dimensional (1D). The technique operates by smoothing, making consistent, and balancing the histogram.

It does not matter how many times a digital image is replicated; its originality is maintained. For doctors who moderate the quest for representative pictures, digital processing is a powerful method.

In the medical field, the applications of digital image processing are numerous. Image processing technologies like segmentation and texture analysis are utilized in medicine to detect diseases. In telemedicine, compression methods are used to transmit images over long distances. Forensic techniques include feature extraction, pattern recognition, noise removal, security, and fingerprint scanners [1]. Forensics is focused on knowledge from databases of people. To determine a person's identity, forensics compares the information entered such as (fingerprint or facial characteristic information) with the data already available. This technique is especially useful for doctors performing laparoscopic surgery to see the internal organs of the body without having to open the body.

1.5.1   Medical Image Processing Methods

Methods for image processing are as follows.

1.5.1.1   Image Formation

The process of image formation includes image reconstruction and data acquisition steps, which provide solutions to a mathematical inverse problem. Image formation comprises all the steps from capturing the image to forming a digital image matrix [6].

Image formation is a process that consists of image acquisition and image reconstruction steps.

1.5.1.1.1   Image Acquisition

In image processing, the process of retrieving an image from a hardware-based source for processing is known as image acquisition. Within the system workflow, image acquisition is the first step as no processing is feasible without an image. The image that was received is unprocessed.

By combining input electrical power with sensor material, the incoming energy is converted into a voltage that is responsive to a certain type of energy.

1.5.1.1.1.1   Image Acquisition Using Single Sensor

A photodiode is an example of a single sensor. There must be relative motion in each Y- and X-direction between the region to be photographed and the sensors to obtain a 2D image utilizing a single sensor. Linear motion gives motion in a perpendicular direction, whereas rotation provides motion in one direction. We can obtain high-resolution images with great precision control in a cost-effective manner [20].

1.5.1.1.1.2   Image Acquisition Using Sensor Strips

Single sensors are employed significantly less frequently than an inline arrangement of sensors inside a variety of sensor strips. The sensor captures images in one direction, while motion perpendicular to the strip oppositely captures images of color diseases at bed scanners; this type of configuration is common. Sensors with 4,000 or more in-line sensors can be used. In-line sensors are commonly used in airborne imaging applications, in which the imaging system is placed on an aircraft that flies over the geographical region to be scanned at a constant height and speed. One-dimensional imaging sensor element strips that recognise distinct various bands of the electromagnetic spectrum are placed perpendicular to the direction of flight. Because the imaging strip provides one line of an image at a time, its motion of the strip completes the other dimension of a 2D image. In medical and industrial imaging, sensor strips stacked in a ring shape are used to obtain cross-sectional images of 3D objects [20].

1.5.1.1.1.3   IMAGE ACQUISITION USING SENSOR ARRAY

Every single sensor is grouped into a 2D array in this method. This type of setup can be seen in digital cameras. During this time, the reaction of each sensor is proportional to the integral of the light energy directed onto its surface. It is a characteristic that certainly helps in applications where low-noise photos are required. Noise reduction is performed by enabling the sensor to integrate the input light signal over a period of minutes or even hours. Since the sensor array is usually 2D, the advantage is that by concentrating the energy pattern onto the array's surface, a complete image can be obtained [20].

1.5.1.1.2   Image Reconstruction

Medical imaging is crucial to guide the diagnosing and treatment of diseases in modern clinics. In medical imaging, medical imaging reconstruction is one of the main elementary parts, whose main goal is to attain top-quality medical images for clinical usage at the smallest risk and cost of the patients. There are two main classes of reconstruction strategies, analytical reconstruction, and iterative reconstruction. Analytical reconstruction methods are most notably used on business CT scanners, which are in the shape of filtered back projection (FBP), that uses a 1D filter on the projection knowledge before back projecting the information onto the image space: Fourier transform (FT), significantly necessary in MRI; FBP, widely utilized in tomography; and delay and sum (DAS) beamforming, a method that is integral to ultrasonography are the typical examples of analytical methods. These algorithms are sophisticated and productive in terms of needed process power and process time [24].

FBP technique is principally popular because of its computational efficiency and numerical stability. Iterations of back projection and forward projection between projection space and image space are used in the IR optimization approach. One among the foremost necessary parameters that affect the image quality is the reconstruction kernel, additionally referred to as "algorithm" or "filter" by some CT vendors. A smoother kernel produces images with lower spatial resolution, it also reduces image noise. A sharp kernel produces images with a lot of noise, but with a lot of spatial detail. Another reconstruction parameter is slice thickness, which affects the trade-offs between resolution, radiation dosage, and noise by controlling spatial resolution in the longitudinal direction. CT users must choose the most appropriate slice thickness and reconstruction kernel for each clinical application in order to reduce the radiation exposure as much as possible as per the image quality required for the examination [24].

1.5.1.2 Image Enhancement

Image enhancement is a technique for improving the features of an image. There are two types of image enhancing techniques: spatial and frequency domain techniques. A spatial technique works with the pixel value directly. These techniques depend on the histogram, logarithmic, and the power-law transforms. By applying all these techniques contrast optimizations, elimination of artifacts, noise reduction, enhancement of edges, and enhancement of other properties that are important for image analysis [6].

1.5.1.3 Image Analysis

Image analysis uses comprehensive ways that will be classified into three main groups: image registration, image quantification, and image segmentation. The quantification procedure determines properties of the related structures such as composition, diameter, volume, and other anatomical or physiological data. These procedures have a direct impact on the medical results' accuracy and the imaging data examination standards [6].

1.5.1.4 Image Visualization

The visualization method renders the image information to visually represent physiological and anatomical imaging data in a very specific type over outlined dimensions. The visualization is often performed at the initial and intermediate phases of the imaging study through direct interaction with information [17].

1.5.1.5 Image Management

The final part in the medical image process is data management, which includes a variety of systems for retrieving, communicating, and storing image data. As an example, the medical imaging technology Picture Archiving and Communication System (PACS) provides access to images from a variety of procedures as well as cost-effective storage, and therefore, the digital imaging and communication drugs (DICOM), normally, are employed for transmission and storing medical images [6].

1.6   Feature Extraction Using Python

The feature is expressed in such a manner that it computes some of the object's most significant characteristics as a function of one or more measurements, each of which defines some calculated attribute of an entity.

Feature is a method for transforming raw data into numerical characteristics that may be processed while maintaining the integrity of the actual data set. It yields better outcomes than just implementing machine learning to data that has not been processed. The amount of characteristics that may be classified is limited by feature selection. The classification task selects and employs certain features that are likely to aid in discrimination. Features that are not picked are not included. Feature extraction is critical because the unique traits made accessible for differentiation have a direct impact on the success of the classification. The extraction task yields a collection of features, referred to as a feature vector, that serves as a representation of the image [9, 10].

Each picture in the image database is analyzed for features, and the resulting feature vector is recorded in the feature directory. When a query image is given, the feature vectors of each image are compared one by one to those in the directory of features, and the images having the least function gap are found. In feature extraction, the content of a picture is defined by its structure, surface, coloration, and other aspects [5].

When you have a huge data collection and need to reduce the number of resources without losing any significant or relevant information, the feature extraction approach comes in handy. It helps to eliminate unnecessary data from a data set. The feature extraction technique seeks to minimize the complexity of classification models and shorten training time by extracting a set of features that optimizes recognition rate with the fewest number of components feasible, as well as to create similar feature sets for different instances of the same symbol. The use of a feature extraction technique increases predictive accuracy as well as the clarity and generality of the built model [15].

The extraction of features can be performed either manually or automatically. Manual feature extraction entails identifying and specifying the characteristics that are relevant for a particular situation, as well as creating a technique to extract such features. Automated feature extraction extracts features from signals or pictures without the need for human interaction, thanks to advanced algorithms and deep neural networks.

The highlights are extracted during feature extraction from images. Rather than selecting the entire arrangement of pixels, the author can select only those that are necessary and sufficient to represent the entire section. Manual intervention is used to pick the segmented image first. The picture's influenced territory can be discovered by determining the zone that connects the parts. First, the related sections of six nearby pixels are discovered. After that, the essential area properties of the information paired image are discovered. For further classification, the image's extracted portion is to be considered. The influenced area is identified. The percent zone then exemplifies the nature of the result.

Color feature extraction: Color is one of the most commonly utilized visual qualities in content-based picture retrieval since it is both flexible and easy to express.

Although texture alone cannot discover comparable pictures, it may be used to differentiate textured from non-textured photos and then coupled with another visual feature such as brightness to enhance retrieval.

Computer vision applications involving accurate representation of image features include object detection and classification, pattern recognition, image recognition, and with the use of well-established image feature extraction techniques, content-based image retrieval mammography for mass detection, iris identification, and handwriting detection are all examples of feature extraction in the medical profession.

For feature extraction, the author used the python scikit-learn module. This module is used to extract features from image datasets.

Figures 1.7 to 1.11 show the implementation of different feature extraction techniques using the different modules of Python's scikit-learn library.

```
1    from matplotlib import pyplot as plt
2    from skimage import io
3    image=io.imread("img.jpg", as_gray=True)
4    io.imshow(image)
5
6    from skimage.transform import resize
7    resizedimg=resize(image,(500,500),anti_aliasing=(True))
8    io.imshow(resizedimg)
9
10   from skimage.filters import roberts,prewitt_h,prewitt_v
11   edgemagnitude=roberts(image)
12   plt.imshow(edgemagnitude,cmap='gray')
13
14   horizontaledges=prewitt_h(image)
15   plt.imshow(horizontaledges,cmap='gray')
16
17   verticaledges=prewitt_v(image)
18   plt.imshow(verticaledges,cmap='gray')
19
20   from skimage.feature import canny
21   edgefilter=canny(image,sigma=5)
22   plt.imshow(edgefilter,cmap='gray')
```

Figure 1.7 Python code using the scikit-learn library.

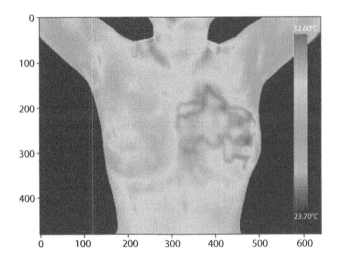

Figure 1.8 Reading the image.

Figure 1.8 reads the original image as a grayscale image.

Figure 1.9 shows an image that has been resized using the transform module's resize function, which accepts as input the source image as well as the height and width values that the image needs to be resized into.

In Figure 1.10, the horizontal edges of the image are detected using the Prewitt method of filters module, which has been given to the source image as the input.

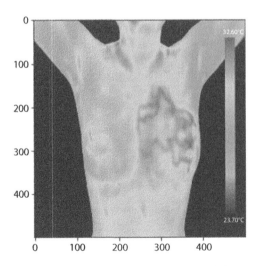

Figure 1.9 Image resized to 500 × 500 using the transform module.

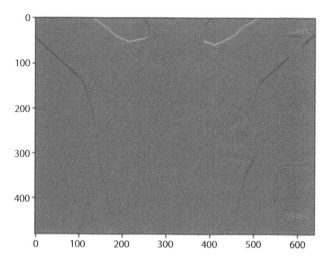

Figure 1.10 Detecting the original image's horizontal edges using Prewitt transform.

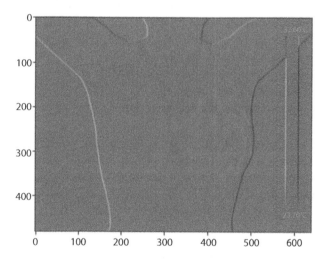

Figure 1.11 Detecting the original image's vertical edges using Prewitt transform.

In Figure 1.11, the vertical edges of the image are detected using the Prewitt method of filters module, which has been given to the source image as the input.

Canny edge detection is a method for detecting edges in an image while reducing noise. The Canny algorithm detects edges in the source image and labels those edges in the output image. For edge connectivity, the smallest value between the two thresholds is used. The largest value is used

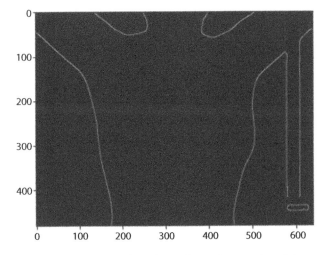

Figure 1.12 Implementing a canny algorithm to detect the image's periphery.

to locate the origin of strong edges. There are four stages in the Canny edge detection algorithm. These are as follows:

Step 1: Calculation of the gradient
Step 2: Non-maximum suppression (NMS)
Step 3: A threshold for two levels
Step 4: Hysteresis-based edge detection

Figure 1.12 shows how the edges of the picture are filtered using the scikit-learn library's canny function, which takes the original image as input and sigma as output. An edge detector is a Canny filter. The Canny technique uses two parameters to identify strong and weak edges and only outputs weak edges if they are detected.

1.7   Case Study on Throat Cancer

1.7.1   Introduction

Throat cancer is a disease that affects people all over the world, and its prevalence has been increasing in recent years. The size of the original tumor at the onset of symptoms is directly linked to the patient's survival rate. As a result, timely identification may aid in the disease's curative treatment [23].

Hyperspectral imaging is a technique for reconstructing the spectrum for each pixel by collecting a sequence of pictures in a range of nearby narrow spectral channels. By calculating the reflection and absorption of light at different frequencies, HSI may provide simultaneous results. HSI is a method of capturing a group of images in the nearby small spectral channels and reconstructing the spectrum for each image pixel [23].

1.7.1.1   HSI System

Spectroscopic pictures were captured using a wavelength scanning CRI Maestro *in vivo* scanning technology. This instrument's major feature is flexible fiber-optic lighting. A charge-coupled device with a 16-bit high-resolution, a solid-state liquid crystal filter, a spectral information configured lens, and a system the wavelength setting for image acquisition can be adjusted in 2-nm increments among 450 and 950 nm [13].

1.7.1.2   *The Adaptive Deep Learning Method Proposed*

There are four parts in the proposed adaptive deep learning system for cancer detection on HSI: preprocessing, deep feature learning, adaptive weight learning, and post-processing. After preprocessing the input hypercube, significant features are retrieved and trained for the cancer diagnosis at the start. On the basis of the pixels' performance hypothesis, the adaptive weights are calculated, and the modified hypercube is generated. In the most current hypercube, the distinctive deep functionality is learned and extracted anew. As a result, the model has been improved to be more flexible and discriminative. After that, the malignant tissue was employed in a test. In a post processing step, the adaptive model may recognize hypercubes, and the identified cancerous tissue is enhanced [13].

1.7.1.2.1   Preprocessing

To reduce the darkness influence and produce a reflectivity image, the obtained hyperspectral artifacts were stored in original form and rectification was performed using a whiteness and darkness quotation [2, 7]. The corrected image "I" is calculated as

$$I = (Ir^*Id) / (IwId)$$

where Ir denotes the raw image, Iw denotes the guaranteed reflectance obtained by defining a method, and Id denotes the depressing picture (lowest reflectance) obtained by removing the lens aperture with a white quotation board in the visual field [13].

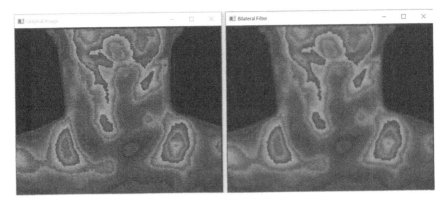

Figure 1.13 Reading the image and removing noise using the bilateral filter.

Bilateral filters can effectively reduce unwanted noise while maintaining sharp edges. However, it is extremely slow. In Figure 1.13, the bilateral filter has been used to reduce unwanted noise from the image. The original image has been placed on the left and the image after applying the bilateral filter has been placed on the right.

1.7.1.2.2   Deep Feature Learning

A form of unsupervised machine learning algorithm is the autoencoder that learns efficient and scalable coding. It has a visible input layer of 'p' units, a hidden layer of 'q' units, a layer of reconstruction of 'r' units and an activation function [18]. The autoconstruction encoder is depicted in Figure 1.14.

Based on the design of the autoencoder, we use the visual characteristics of each unit as the source data and train the network by dynamically changing the weight values to remove the deviation rate is lower bound. The decoder layer is removed, and a layer of softmax is connected to the cancer network and normal tissue isolation. The autoencoder network will distinguish between cancer and healthy pixels. The final result of cancer detection and hypothesis of pixel release can be obtained [13].

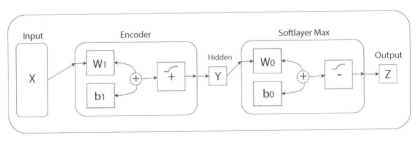

Figure 1.14 Illustration of autoencoder.

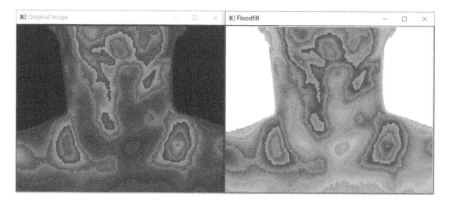

Figure 1.15 Filling the holes in the image by implementing the flood fill algorithm.

1.7.1.2.3   Adaptive Weight Learning

The tumor margin is irregular and indistinct, as seen in medical photographs. Although pixel values in tumor tissue are comparable to those in healthy tissue. As a result, any learning technique would struggle to differentiate the tumor from its surrounding normal tissue. As a consequence, based on the miscategorized pixels, we emphasize the tumor by altering its weight in two aspects adaptively. Healthy pixels that have been incorrectly classified as cancer and cancer pixels that have been incorrectly classified as healthy are the two types of miscategorized pixels. In adaptive weight learning, each pixel is rated on a scale based on the performance of the base model's hypothesis, and it can be determined [13].

1.7.1.2.4   Post-Processing

Because our method is based on pixel categorization, the tumor that is identified may have distortion and defects. To fill the gaps in the bifurcated picture, the malignant tissues flood-fill method is employed [13]. In Figure 1.15, it can be seen that the gaps in the image have been filled after applying the flood fill algorithm on it.

1.7.2   Results and Findings

The outcomes of our suggested system's quantitative assessment for 10 mouse samples are as follows: Ten mice had an average sensitivity of 95.53%, specificity of 92.26%, and accuracy of 93.188%. These findings corroborate one another. These findings support the effectiveness of our process.

Mouse ID 1: Sensitivity (99.50 %), Specificity (94.49%), and Accuracy (95.52%)

Mouse ID 2: Sensitivity (90.67 %), Specificity (92.48%), and Accuracy (95.98%)

Mouse ID 3: Sensitivity (93.85 %), Specificity (96.48%), and Accuracy (95.98%)

Mouse ID 4: Sensitivity (99.77 %), Specificity (90.89%), and Accuracy (93.13%)

Mouse ID 5: Sensitivity (93.16 %), Specificity (98.08%), and Accuracy (96.78%)

Mouse ID 6: Sensitivity (98.91 %), Specificity (95.54%), and Accuracy (96.27%)

Mouse ID 7: Sensitivity (96.13 %), Specificity (94.20%), and Accuracy (94.50%)

Mouse ID 8: Sensitivity (95.49 %), Specificity (90.03%), and Accuracy (92.28%)

Mouse ID 9: Sensitivity (99.67 %), Specificity (86.16%), and Accuracy (85.81%)

Mouse ID 10: Sensitivity (88.10 %), Specificity (84.22%), and Accuracy (85.63%)

The observed cancer area is not adequate due to noise and uneven surfaces, among other factors. The autoencoder network model, being auto adjusting focuses toward the incorrectly classified pixel values and enhances learning from the misclassified pixels, is proposed to increase the initial output and obtain a full tumor. The method is shown to have high sensitivity, specificity, and accuracy in classifying the tumor area.

By removing the valuable scripts and overlooking noise, the autoencoder trains to reduce the 251 frequencies from 450 to 950 in 2-nm amounts into a brief element. We choose one element at irregular intervals and encode its attributes using the autoencoder. It has 251 frequencies and 60 properties in its median pixel intensities for cancerous and protected tissue. The autoencoder will collect feature vectors that classify distinctive characters to successfully classify cancerous tissue from healthy cells. For early cancer diagnosis on the HSI, we compare the FCN algorithm, SegNet algorithm, U-Net method, and autoencoder and find that the autoencoder performs the best [13].

1.7.3   Discussion

In this research, the authors used adaptive deep learning on hyperspectral images to propose an automatic detection method for throat cancer. An autoencoder network is used to extract feature information from hyperspectral images and separate malignant groups of cells from their adjacent normal group of cells. The observed cancer area is undesirable due to noise and irregular texture [2]. By concentrating on the erroneously classified pixels and improving comprehension for the incorrectly classified pixels, the efficient autoencoder network model is presented to enhance the initial performance and acquire a complete tumour. The method is shown to have excellent accuracy, precision, and reliability in classifying the tumor area. Manually identifying different characteristics from the vast data is challenging since each hyperspectral image has several reflectance spectral fingerprints. Deep neural networks generate a higher group of characteristics from a lower group of features to automatically find the features necessary for cancer detection. The autoencoder aims to eliminate noise from inputs as effectively as possible by identifying discriminative features from which the original input may be reconstructed. This makes it well suited to represent hyperspectral data [13].

Using HIS, an adaptable deep learning system was proposed and validated in an animal model. To rapidly reduce complexity and identify malignant tissue, this method retrieved high-level features from hyperspectral pictures.

1.7.4   Conclusion

We may use hyperspectral image's deep features to efficiently minimize dimensionality and classify cancerous tissue in a better way [2]. In a throat cancer model, the suggested cancer detection method yielded encouraging results. The findings showed that using the HSI in conjunction with a deep learning methodology would help diagnose cancers accurately and quickly in a non-invasive manner, making it a potential tool for upcoming medical applications [7, 13].

1.8   Conclusion

In this chapter, the reader is exposed to the importance of medical images, the various steps involved in medical image processing, and the different preprocessing techniques. The usage of various functions from scikit-learn and OpenCV libraries in python for performing different operations gives the reader a better understanding of the topic. The reader also gets a brief insight into image acquisition, reconstruction, and feature extraction along with the understanding of a real-world application of medical image processing, which is the detection of throat cancer which further explains the usefulness of an autoencoder and puts light on hyperspectral imaging.

References

1. Abdallah, Y.M.Y. and Alqahtani, T., Research in medical imaging using image processing techniques, in: *Medical Imaging-Principles and Applications*, IntechOpen, London, United Kingdom, 2019.

2. Barbalata, C. and Mattos, L.S., Laryngeal tumor detection and classification in the endoscopic video. *IEEE J. Biomed. Health Inform.*, 20, 1, 322–332, 2014.

3. Barnouti, N.H., Improve face recognition rate using different image pre-processing techniques. *Am. J. Eng. Res. (AJER)*, 5, 4, 46–53, 2016.

4. Bradski, G. and Kaehler, A., Learning OpenCV, in: *Computer vision with the OpenCV library*, O' Reilly Media, Inc, Sebastopol, United States of America, 2008.

5. Choras, R.S., Image feature extraction techniques and their applications for CBIR and biometrics systems. *Int. J. Biol. Biomed. Eng.*, 1, 1, 6–16, 2007.

6. Deserno, T., Medical image processing, in: *Optipedia*, SPIE Press, Bellingham, WA, 2009.

7. Gupta, P. and Malhi, A.K., Using deep learning to enhance head and neck cancer diagnosis and classification, in: *2018 IEEE international conference on a system, computation, automation, and networking (icscan)*, IEEE, pp. 1–6, 2018, July.

8. Hambal, A.M., Pei, Z., Ishabailu, F.L., Image noise reduction and filtering techniques. *Int. J. Sci. Res. (IJSR)*, 6, 3, 2033–2038, 2017.

9. Hunter, J.D., Matplotlib: A 2D graphics environment. *IEEE Ann. Hist. Comput.*, 9, 03, 90–95, 2007.

10. Harris, C.R., Millman, K.J., van der Walt, S.J., Gommers, R., Virtanen, P., Cournapeau, D., Oliphant, T.E., Array programming with NumPy. *Nature*, 585, 357–362, 2020, https://org/10.1038/s41586-020-2649-2.

11. Kasban, H., El-Bendary, M.A.M., Salama, D.H., A comparative study of medical imaging techniques. *Int. J. Inf. Sci. Intell. Syst.*, 4, 2, 37–58, 2015.

12. Kaur, D. and Kaur, Y., Various image segmentation techniques: a review. *Int. J. Comput. Sci. Mobil. Comput.*, 3, 5, 809–814, 2014.

13. Ma, L., Lu, G., Wang, D., Qin, X., Chen, Z.G., Fei, B., Adaptive deep learning for head and neck cancer detection using hyperspectral imaging. *Vis. Comput. Ind. Biomed. Art*, 2, 1, 1–12, 2019.

14. McAuliffe, M.J., Lalonde, F.M., McGarry, D., Gandler, W., Csaky, K., Trus, B.L., Medical image processing, analysis, and visualization in clinical research, in: *Proceedings 14th IEEE Symposium on Computer-Based Medical Systems. CBMS 2001*, IEEE, pp. 381–386, 2001, July.

15. McKinney, W. and & others, Data structures for statistical computing in python, in: *Proceedings of the 9th Python in Science Conference*, vol. 445, pp. 51–56, 2010.

16. Naseera, S., Rajini, G.K., Venkateswarlu, B., Priyadarshini, J.P.M., A Review on Image Processing Applications in the Medical Field. *Res. J. Pharm. Technol.*, 10, 10, 3456–3460, 2017.

17. Obukhova, N., Motyko, A., Pozdeev, A., Personalized approach to developing image processing and analysis methods for medical video systems. *Proc. Comput. Sci.*, *176*, 2030–2039, 2020.

18. Pedregosa, F., Varoquaux, G., Gramfort, A., Michel, V., Thirion, B., Grisel, O., others, Scikit-learn: Machine learning in Python. *J. Mach. Learn. Res.*, *12*, Oct, 2825–2830, 2011.

19. Perumal, S. and Velmurugan, T., Preprocessing by contrast enhancement techniques for medical images. *Int. J. Pure Appl. Math.*, *118*, 18, 3681–3688, 2018.

20. Rafael, C. and Gonzalez, and Richard E., Woods. *Digit. Image Process.*, *793*, 70–72, 1992.

21. Sharma, N. and Aggarwal, L.M., Automated medical image segmentation techniques. *J. Med. Phys. Assoc. Med. Physicists India*, *35*, 1, 3, 2010.

22. Vasuki, P., Kanimozhi, J., Devi, M.B., A survey on image preprocessing techniques for diverse fields of medical imagery, in: *2017 IEEE International Conference on Electrical, Instrumentation and Communication Engineering (ICEICE)*, IEEE, pp. 1–6, 2017, April.

23. Xiong, H., Lin, P., Yu, J.G., Ye, J., Xiao, L., Tao, Y., Yang, H., Computer-aided diagnosis of laryngeal cancer via deep learning based on laryngoscopic images. *EBioMedicine*, *48*, 92–99, 2019.

24. Yu, L. and Leng, S., Image reconstruction techniques. *Am. Coll. Radiol.*, 2010.

Additional Reading

Aicha, A. B., & Ezzine, K. (2016, November). Cancer larynx detection using glottal flow parameters and statistical tools. In 2016 International Symposium on Signal, Image, Video, and Communications (ISIVC) (pp. 65–70). IEEE.

Aicha, A. B. (2020, September). Conventional Machine Learning Techniques with Features Engineering for Preventive Larynx Cancer Detection. In *2020 5th International Conference on Advanced Technologies for Signal and Image Processing (ATSIP)* (pp. 1–5). IEEE.

Aina, O. E., Adeshina, S. A., & Aibinu, A. M. (2019, December). Deep Learning for Image-based Cervical Cancer Detection and Diagnosis—A Survey. In *2019 15th International Conference on Electronics, Computer and Computation (ICECCO)* (pp. 1–7). IEEE.

Deserno, T. M. (2011). Fundamentals of medical image processing. In *Springer Handbook of Medical Technology* (pp. 1139–1165). Springer, Berlin, Heidelberg.

Kramme, R., Hoffmann, K. P., & Pozos, R. S. (Eds.). (2011). *Springer handbook of medical technology*. Springer Science & Business Media.

Patra, J., Moulick, H. N., & Manna, A. K. (2013). Biomedical Image Processing with Morphology and Segmentation Methods for Medical Image Analysis. *American Journal of Engineering Research (AJER)*, *2*(07), 227–244.

Sarmah, D. K., Kulkarni, A. J., & Abraham, A. (2020). *Optimization models in steganography using metaheuristics*. Springer International Publishing.

Shameena, N., & Jabbar, R. (2014). A study of preprocessing and segmentation techniques on cardiac medical images.

Key Terms and Definition

Biopsies: An examination of tissues removed from a living body to determine the presence, cause, or severity of a disease.

Diagnostic: To find out the problem that occurred.

Fluctuations: A transition, or the procedure of transitioning from one level or thing to another, particularly in a constant manner.

Hypercube: A geometric figure (like a tesseract) in the Euclidean space of a cube-size three-dimensional/computer structure in which each processor is connected to others based on a hypercube size n.

Interpolation: The inclusion of a unique element in the center of the content.

Orthogonality: Having tangents or perpendicular slopes at the intersection point.

Radioactive: Taking or engaging with power spectral density that is incredibly high.

Transients: Short-lived, occurring only for a brief period.

2

Detection of Pneumonia Using Machine Learning and Deep Learning Techniques: An Analytical Study

Shravani Nimbolkar*, Anuradha Thakare, Subhradeep Mitra, Omkar Biranje and Anant Sutar

Department of Computer Engineering, Pimpri Chinchwad College of Engineering, Savitribai Phule Pune University, Pune, India

Abstract

Lungs play an important role in the normal functioning of our body. They are one of the most important organs that facilitate the flow of much needed oxygen into the body. Studies suggest that they are prone to many life-threatening diseases. Through this survey paper, we aim to study and state different types of lung diseases and how their diagnostics can be aided using deep learning and machine learning. The paper employs experimentation with different machine learning models, to begin with, followed by the use of neural networks like CNN and MLP, and lastly pre-trained architectures like VGG16 and ResNet to predict pneumonia from chest X-rays. Unsurprisingly, CNN classifier delivered an average accuracy of 96%. The robustness and efficiency of the model are ensured by means of data augmentation and input optimization. However, further exploration and use of better preprocessing techniques can surely be expected to uplift the performance of our model.

Keywords: Lung disease, pneumonia detection, chest X-ray, machine learning, deep learning, convolution neural network, transfer learning

2.1 Introduction

Lung diseases are one of the most commonly observed diseases in India. According to a report, chronic obstructive pulmonary disease (COPD) was the second-highest cause of death in India after heart disease in 2017.

---

*Corresponding author: shravani.nimbolkar17@pccoepune.org

R. Arokia Priya, Anupama V Patil, Manisha Bhende, Anuradha Thakare and Sanjeev Wagh (eds.)
Object Detection by Stereo Vision Images, (33–56) © 2022 Scrivener Publishing LLC

These growing numbers deserve your attention and action. Some of the major reasons behind the same are increasing pollution in the environment and chain-smoking. Other reasons are infection and genetics. Chest and respiratory diseases in India are a growing concern nowadays for both doctors and patients, owing to the increased level of pollution and excessive smoking which should be dealt with as soon as possible. The lungs being an important part of the body, perform multiple functions at a single time. It relaxes and expands thousands of times each day to bring in oxygen and remove carbon dioxide. In this continuous and hectic procedure, there is always a possibility of collapse. Different types of lung diseases may affect you because of the abovementioned reasons. The following are categorized under different heads based on part of the lungs they affect. Some of the airway diseases are asthma, COPD, and chronic and acute bronchitis. Asthma, most commonly known as a breathing disorder, causes shortness of breath. This is generally triggered by pollution, infection, or allergies. COPD is a kind of lung condition in which you feel difficulty in exhaling normally. It may also cause breathing problems. Chronic and acute bronchitis: Chronic bronchitis is a form of COPD, in which excessive cough is produced. On the other hand, acute bronchitis is caused due to infection through a virus. Diseases affecting the air sacs are pneumonia, tuberculosis, lung cancer, and emphysema. Pneumonia is caused due to a bacterial infection in the alveoli. Tuberculosis is another form of pneumonia but progresses slowly and is caused due to bacterial infection. Lung cancer can be developed in any part of the lungs. Generally, it affects the main part or near the air sacs. Its treatment is determined by the location, type, and extent to which cancer has spread (stage). Emphysema disease damages the inner walls of the lung's alveoli. It causes the air sacs to expand abnormally, which leads to shortness of breathing. Interstitial lung disease generally affects the interstitium. Among various types of ILD, autoimmune disease, sarcoidosis, and idiopathic pulmonary fibrosis disease are three of them. However, interstitium can also be affected by diseases like pneumonia and pulmonary edemas. Diseases affecting blood vessels are pulmonary embolism and pulmonary hypertension. One of the major reasons for pulmonary embolism is a blood clot that travels to the lungs generally from the legs. One of the pulmonary arteries gets blocked in the lungs. This increases the risk of a heart attack. Pulmonary hypertension is a condition of high blood pressure that affects the right side of the heart, along with the arteries of the lungs. This also causes harm to the pulmonary arterioles that are tiny arteries, and capillaries as they become narrow and sometimes blocked. Diseases affecting the pleura are pleural effusion and mesothelioma. Pleural effusion involves the fluid collection in a tiny pleura space between the lung and the chest wall. This needs immediate treatment because if space becomes large and the fluid accumulates then it can cause breathing problems. Pleura cancer is another name of mesothelioma, which develops in the pleura. It gradually develops over time after getting exposed to asbestos. AI has leveraged medical assistance in diagnosing these fatal lung diseases. In this paper, we have reviewed a wide range of literature based on AI techniques proposed to aid the process of detection of various lung diseases using medical imagery like X-rays and CT scans. We studied different approaches to detect pneumonia disease using chest X-ray images. We tested a variety of machine learning (ML), deep learning (DL), and transfer learning models to classify the images and analyzed the performance of the best candidate model among them, which is the CNN model classifier. This article is further organized in the following sections: Section 2.2 covers the literature review; Section 2.3 discusses the limitations of existing methods; Section 2.4 explains different learning methods in AI; and Section 2.5 presents the experimental analysis of AI techniques, which is further followed by a conclusion.

2.2   Literature Review

Varshni *et al.* [1] discussed the usability of pre-trained CNN models for feature extraction. This paper also sheds light on different classifiers used for classifying abnormal and normal chest X - rays. Dataset used in this experiment was ChestX-ray14 by Wang, also available on Kaggle. Dataset contains 112,120 frontal chest X-ray images of 30,085 patients. Every image is labeled with at least 1 thoracic disease out of 14. The authors have proposed a model that mainly consists of three phases: pre-processing, feature extraction, followed by the classification stage. Preprocessing consisted of downsizing the images from 1,024 × 1,024 to 224 × 224, to reduce the computational complexity. DenseNet-169 was used in the feature extraction stage. This was followed by the application of SVM for the classification stage. The model resulted in an AUC of 0.8002. One of the important limitations is that the history of the selected patient is not considered in the evaluation model. Secondly, the study incorporated the use of frontal chest X-rays only. Thirdly, because the model consists of many convolutional layers, it needs very high computational power, or else it might eat up a lot of time in computations. Toğaçar *et al.* [2] discussed another approach using mRMR feature selection and ML models. The pneumonia dataset used consists of 5,849 JPEG images of variable sizes, including 1,583 normal and 4,266 pneumonia images. To balance the distribution of the samples over the classes, image augmentation was used. The proposed approach uses default parameter values in three CNNs. Each CNN model was able to analyze about 1,000 different features. The selection of the best features for every 1,000 features was carried out using the mRMR feature selection method. The last stage of the method saw the use of different classifiers for uplifting the performance. The model was able to achieve an accuracy of 99.41%. A tiny drawback of this study was that only a single dataset is used, which can lead to overfitting of the model. Hashmi *et al.* [3] proposed a high-performance model applicable to digital chest X-ray images. It introduced a weighted classifier approach, which combined weighted predictions from ResNet18, InceptionV3, DenseNet121, etc., in an optimal way. To fine-tune the models, transfer learning was used. The Guangzhou Women and Children's Medical Center pneumonia dataset was used in this study. To increase the training dataset in a balanced way, partial data augmentation was employed. The model was able to achieve a test accuracy of 98.43%. It meant an AUC score of 99.76. A major drawback of this approach was again the scarcity of available resources resulting in overfitting. In addition, this may adversely affect models' generalization ability. Moreover, the results of the DL models were not explained properly due to the lack of domain knowledge. The diagnosis of the disease requires a deep understanding of the radiological features from chest X-rays. Militante *et al.* [4] proposed a methodology that employs efficient approaches of six CNN models, to recognize and predict patients affected and unaffected with the disease, using a chest X-ray image. The models used were LeNet, VGG-16, StridedNet, GoogLeNet, AlexNet, and ResNet-50. The Radiological Society of North America (RSNA) dataset, which consisted of a total of 28,000 chest X-ray images, was used. The images were in JPEG format, having maximum dimensions of $1,024 \times 1,024$. All the images were categorized into two classes: infected and not infected. All the models attained a training accuracy of 96%–98%, with GoogLeNet and LeNet obtaining the highest, i.e., 98% accuracy for performance training. This study can also consider the optimization of hyperparameters to improve the accuracy of the model.

Defang *et al.* [5] devised to use GAN as a method to create quality-rich synthetic medical images. Then, the output of this is fed to a VGG16 network that performs classification. It attained an accuracy of 95.24, thus further signifying the importance of GAN to classify harmless and harmful nodules. The dataset was obtained from the Lung Image DB Consortium and Image Database Resource Initiative. They specifically made use of forward and backward GAN where the FGAN generates a bunch of different images and BGAN acts as a noise diminisher and makes images real and increases quality. However, the authors faced issues regarding limited availability and lack of diversity in the samples. Yuya *et al.* [6] aimed to improve classification accuracy by making use of DCNN and GAN where GAN is used for generating supplementary images and classification is done using DCNN. The network is pre-trained using the images created by GAN and then polished using actual nodule images. This process made it possible to discern between mild and lethal nodules with an accuracy of 66.7% and 93%, respectively. WGAN was used against conventional GAN where the training process was unsteady because of obstacles created by vanishing gradients. The dataset, which was obtained from Fujita Health University Hospital in Japan, consisted of 60 cases out of which 27 were harmless nodules and 33 cases were fatal. The authors stated that classification accuracy was low due to the unavailability of data. Albahli [7] specifically made use of GAN in preprocessing and the proposed model was an amalgamation of variational autoencoder and GAN (VAE-GAN) where the GAN discriminator takes place of the VAE decoder to learn the loss function. Input and attribute are fed to the encoder, which is followed by a generator that also takes additional attributes and then output is given. Dataset consisted of a total of 108,948 images of 32,717 patients. The model achieved 89% accuracy in terms of GAN-based polymerized data. The dataset was highly imbalanced, which caused inaccurate and false predictions. Ahsan *et al.* [8] proposed applying the VGG model on the chest X-ray dataset to spot if a patient is suffering from TB. The dataset used by the author consisted of 1,324 CXRs and text data from Shenzhen and 276 from Montgomery datasets. The dataset was divided into training and testing datasets with 75 to 25 ratio, respectively. The VGG-16 model was used; however, instead of using a soft-max layer, the author was prone to use a sigmoid layer as they only had two outputs. The model was able to attain 80% accuracy without augmentation and later achieved 81.2% with it. TFLearns Data Augmentation of TensorFlow was used for augmentation, which helped in the making of new images and also alleviates data overfitting in the model. The author mentioned that the low accuracy was due to partial augmentation of the dataset, and it could be improved by running the model on a high configuration system. Qjidaa *et al.* [9] made use of VGG-16 for classifying a dataset that consisted of 100 images of confirmed COVID-19 cases, viral pneumonia cases, and normal cases each. The proposed architecture consisted of three stages: first data augmentation was performed with the help of resizing the image, random flipping, scaling, and shearing; the second was feature extraction; and lastly classification. The dimensions of features before being sent to the final classification layer were reduced which discerned the author's model from typical VGG-16. It achieved an accuracy of 92.5% and 87.5% for training and testing, respectively. The dataset used was pretty small and hence the accuracy obtained may differ in the case of a larger dataset.

Naik *et al.* [10] discussed the diagnosis of different lung diseases including pneumonia using a DL approach. It uses the NIH Chest X-ray dataset, which is a large public dataset for chest radiograph interpretation, consisting of 112,120 chest radiographs of over 30,000 patients. By using a pre-trained CNN model, DenseNet121 from ImageNet achieved an AUC score of 0.765 for pneumonia detection and an overall mean AUC score of 0.843 including other ailments. The dataset is unbalanced in nature as out of the 112,120 images; most of the diseases had less than 5,000 images. Chouhan *et al.* [11] used pre-trained CNN models: AlexNet, DenseNet121, InceptionV3, resNet18, and GoogLeNet, for feature extraction and feeds them to the proposed model for training and classification. For this, the Guangzhou Women and Children's Medical Center dataset was used, which consists of 5,232 images, where 1,346 images belong to the normal category, 2,538 images belong to bacterial pneumonia, and 1,345 images depicted virus pneumonia; thus, a total of 2,538 images belonging to pneumonia class. The proposed model consists of multiple architectures (AlexNet, DenseNet121, InceptionV3, resNet18, and GoogLeNet), and the class supported by maximum architectures is produced as final output and achieved an overall accuracy of 96.39%. It was discussed that the resulting accuracy could be improved by using a larger dataset for the purpose. Rajpurkar *et al.* [12] proposed CheXNet, a 121-layer Dense Convolutional Network or DenseNet trained on the ChestX-ray14 dataset for the efficient classification of pneumonia. For evaluation, the F1 score metric was used and compared with the F1 scores of four radiologists with experience of 4, 7, 25, and 28 years, respectively. CheXNet gave an accuracy of 76.80% for the classification of pneumonia. The average F1 score of radiologists was 0.387, while that of CheXNet was 0.435. DL methods have particularly been useful in the early detection of diseases that cause severe damage to diseased people. The proposed model is tested against the diagnosis of different radiologists and can pose an ambiguity between the diagnosis of different radiologists depending on their experience level and working strategy developed from their experiences. Lin *et al.* [13] have proposed a convolutional network to detect lung tumors from CT scan images of the lungs for the early diagnosis. Additionally, the study also demonstrated the use of DCGAN for augmenting medical datasets of CT scan images, which improved the accuracy of their CNN model by 2.73% proving the effectiveness of the proposed DCGAN. In another study, Peng *et al.* [14] put forth a novel multi-scale DCNN consisting of 20 base layers of ResNet for the classification of pulmonary emphysema into four different categories, namely, centrilobular emphysema (CLE), paraseptal emphysema (PSE), panlobular emphysema (PLE), and normal tissue (NT). The proposed architecture was trained on its high-quality emphysema dataset. In addition, the paper compared and showed how the multiscale architecture is better than single existing single scaled architectures and also from other state-of-the-art methods. Like many other diseases, AI and ML have also played a prominent role in the fight against the global pandemic COVID-1. After rigorous research, many successful AI models were delivered to assist the medical specialist in detecting and diagnosing the disease. Lessmann *et al.* [15] have proposed an AI-based system. It consists of COVID-19 Reporting and Data System (CO-RADS) and CT severity scoring systems, which outputs the probability and extent of pulmonary COVID-19 from chest CT scan. The proposed system not only successfully identifies the COVID patients but also assigns them a standardized CO-RADS and CT severity score. Xu *et al.* [16] propounded a DL model for early screening of COVID-19 pneumonia, and how it differs from IAVP Influenza-A viral pneumonia) and healthy patients with the help of pulmonary CT images. The proposed model that uses the location attention mechanism in the fully connected layers is concatenated with the traditional ResNet to get better performance. The model achieved an overall accuracy rate of 86.7%. The paper also shows the comparative study of two classification models, the traditional residual network (ResNet) model and the proposed system. Moving toward cheaper alternatives than CT scans images, Brunese *et al.* [17] proposed a novel approach for detecting the COVID-19 patients more precisely. The proposed method consists of three phases for which two classifier models are built; the first phase is where pneumonia is detected in the chest X-ray; the second phase is to discern between pneumonia and COVID-19; and final phase is where regions of interest of COVID-19 presence are localized in the chest X-ray. The first model that uses a transfer learning approach is based on VGG16. It is used for the first and second phases and the second model is for the third phase. On the dataset of a total of 6,523 chest X-rays, the first and second classifiers gave an accuracy of 96% and 98%, respectively. Ansari *et al.* [18] proposed to apply the ResNet model on the chest X-ray dataset to identify if a patient is suffering from pneumonia. Two datasets were used in this paper: one is RSNA dataset and the other was taken from Guangzhou Women and Children's Medical Center Guangzhou, China. The author suggested the use of ResNet over VGG-16 and DenseNet because it was believed that VGG-16 being a small network would miss out on some features and DenseNet being a large network would degrade the accuracy. They achieved an accuracy of 96.76%. It was also suggested that the accuracy can be improved by choosing a deeper ResNet such as ResNet-101. Antin *et al.* [19] devised DenseNet-121 for the binary classification of pneumonia and non-pneumonia cases. They made use of the dataset compiled by NIH consisting of 112,120 images. Using DenseNet they achieved an AUC equal to 0.6037. The author claimed the low AUC was attributed to the minimal number of samples for pneumonia in the training dataset. In addition, the author made use of AUC for error metrics as the dataset was strongly imbalanced with only 1% pneumonia cases. The author suggested looking into class activation maps to explore DenseNet activation and may give insight into why it achieved such a low AUC.

Abiyev *et al.* [20] devised to make use of Backpropagation Neural Network (BPNN), Competitive Neural Network, and Convolutional Neural Network (CNN) to classify around 12 common lung diseases. The dataset was obtained from NIH-Clinical Center. Result obtained was as follows: BPNN had an accuracy of 80.04%, CpNN had an accuracy of 89.57%, and CNN had an accuracy of 92.4%. It has to be noted that CpNN and BPNN both attained accuracy by using only 1,000 images, whereas CNN used about 120,120 images. In addition, BPNN and CpNN achieved better accuracy when the input image had dimensions of 32×32. Moujahid [21] made use of different architectures of CNN to do a comparative study. The authors made use of VGG-16, VGG-19, RES-NET 152, NasNetMobile, and InceptionResNetV2 architectures of CNN. For the metric, they made use of RMSProp optimizer and categorical cross-entropy accuracy and proposed to initialize the weights using ImageNet. They also made use of a parameter called callback, which stops training if there is no accuracy improvement within three consequent iterations. Out of the given architectures, VGG-16 obtained the highest accuracy with 96.81% and an overall better confusion matrix as compared to other models. However, the author mentioned that the prediction accuracy could have been improved by enlarging the dataset or by improving the pre-processing technique. Tariq *et al.* [22] pointed out that the auscultatory method of listening to breathing sounds has been the easiest way to detect respiratory problems. They proposed a DCNN model to analyze the acoustic signals produced by breathing of lungs and detect any respiratory ailments. They used peak normalization, root means square, and EBU Union Standard R128 Normalization for data preprocessing. Techniques like time stretching, pitch shifting, and dynamic range compression were used for data augmentation, which resulted in producing 12 augmented audio files for each original audio file. The model receiving "normalized EBU value augmentation" gave the highest accuracy of 97% by splitting the data into 70% and 30% for training and testing, using 32 as batch size for 100 epochs.

2.3   Learning Methods

2.3.1   Machine Learning

Naive Bayes is a probabilistic approach to solving ML problems, which follows the conditional probability principle for classification. The Naive Bayes classifier assumes that the presence of one particular feature does not affect the other features. It is a simple algorithm that is also suitable for large data. It is observed that Naive Bayes perform better when given input in categorical format rather than numerical. In the case of numerical data, it assumes a normal distribution.

The decision tree has a flowchart-like structure with multiple branching leading to one of the leaf nodes resulting in some output. It falls under the category of supervised learning algorithms. However, it can also be used for regression and classification tasks. To predict a class label, it compares the value of the target variable with the value in the nodes, beginning from the root node, based on which it selects the next branch. The goal is to learn simple rules of decision-making that are inferred from the training data. The homogeneity of sub-nodes increases as we create more and more sub-nodes. The accuracy is heavily affected by the strategic splits the model decides to make. Random forests is another learning method for classification which is made out of the ensemble of decision trees. It is trained using the Bagging method, and the result is the class that is the mean or mode of speculation of discrete trees. Random forest is also used for regression tasks using its regressor. Random forest introduces randomness to the model. It selects the best features out of a random subset of features. Although the Random forest is a collection of decision trees they have few differences. For instance, the deep decision trees are more prone to overfitting than random forests. Random forests avoid this problem by making smaller trees and later combining them. However, this does not work every time as it slows the computation making affecting its efficiency. Support vector machine (SVM) is also a supervised ML model used for classification and regression both. It works by creating a hyperplane (partitioning boundary) in a high-dimensional space for classifying the observations. It consists of support vectors that are nothing but coordinates of each observation. The kernel technique is very useful when we are dealing with a non-separable problem like nonlinear separations, wherein it takes the input of low-level dimensions, which undergoes complex transformation to get converted into higher level dimensional space.

Adaptive Boosting, or AdaBoost, is a ML algorithm that is used simultaneously with other algorithms to improve the performance of the other algorithms by learning in support of those cases which were wronged by the previous classifier. It works as an extension to the output produced by the previous classifier, thus attempting to improve its performance. Quadratic discriminant analysis (QDA) is similar to linear discriminant analysis (LDA). However, unlike LDA where the measurements are assumed to be normally distributed, QDA has no such assumptions that the covariance of each class is similar to the other. When the normality is assumed to be true, then the likelihood ratio test is the one to go for testing the hypothesis that a given measurement is from a given class.

2.3.2   Deep Learning

Multilayer perceptron (MLP) is the simplest class of feedforward artificial neural network (ANN) that works on the following principle of weights and biases followed by an activation function. Any MLP model has the following steps: forward pass, calculate loss/error, and backward pass.

A CNN as shown in Figure 2.1 is an advanced version of MLP with convolutional layers, which work as filters for feature extraction from the image data, followed by an MLP classifier model.

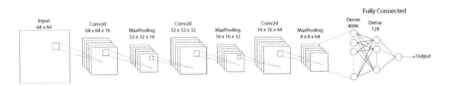

Figure 2.1 CNN architecture.

2.3.3   Transfer Learning

Transfer learning involves the use of pre-trained models for the desired classification purpose. For this study, the VGG-16 and ResNet CNN models were used.

VGG-16 as the name suggests consisted of 16 layers with an increasing number of filters where all filters are of size 3 × 3. It is handy for transfer learning and classification tasks. It is lightweight and can be used on issue with VGG is that this naive architecture is not good for deeper networks, as it becomes prone to vanishing gradients problem. More training and more parameters have to be tuned in for deeper networks. ResNet is different from VGG-16 as it is connecting not just the previous layer to the current layer but also a layer behind the previous layer. The advantage of ResNet is that we can train deeper networks with this architecture. ResNet may have different models with different layers. It has ResNet-50, which is used when we have fewer resources and we want to get faster results and the task is meager. We also have ResNet-152 which can be used for complex problems and hence require more time and resources.

2.4 Detection of Lung Diseases Using Machine Learning and Deep Learning Techniques

2.4.1 Dataset Description

For this study, the chest X-ray images from Kermany *et al.* [23] were used. The data consists of 4,273 pneumonia class and 1,583 normal class chest X-ray images. The complete dataset of 5,856 images is conveniently divided into separate folders of train, test, and validation having 5,216, 624, and 16 image samples, respectively. Figure 2.2 represents sample chest X-ray images from the dataset.

The images used in this study were resized to 128 by 128 pixels for the faster computation of the model under observation and stored as byte stream format for faster data loading as compared to loading original JPEG images.

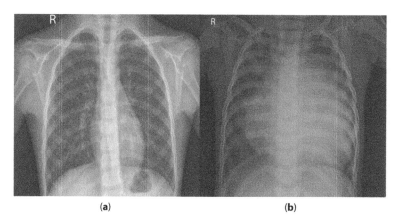

(a)   (b)

Figure 2.2 (a) Chest X-ray image of a normal person. (b) Chest X-ray image of a pneumonia patient.

2.4.2   Evaluation Platform

An Intel® Core™ i5 8th Generation processor, with NVIDIA GPU GeForce 940MX, was used as a testing server. The processing time majorly depends on the number of layers, nodes, input image resolution, etc.

2.4.3   Training Process

In our literature survey, we identified three different approaches for the detection of pneumonia using chest X-ray images; first, ML; second, DL; and third, transfer learning. We evaluated each of these approaches and compared their performance in classifying the CXR images. In the ML approach, we analyzed various supervised classification algorithms like Naive Bayes, decision trees, random Forest, AdaBoost, SVM, and QDA. Under DL, we chose the algorithms that are known to be suitable for image classification: CNNs and MLP. In transfer learning, we studied the two well-known pre-trained models: VGG16 and ResNet (residual network) architecture. We selected 10 candidate algorithms from all three approaches for the classification task. After observing the train and test accuracies of all the models, certain inferences were drawn. The train accuracies of all ML classifiers were in the range of 85%–97%. Whereas, their test accuracies got reduced to the bracket of 62%–76%. It can be inferred that these classifiers were overfitting on the benchmark dataset. Among all ML algorithms, the QDA shows the highest drop in its accuracy from train to test, i.e., 35.60%, and Naive Bayes shows the lowest drop, i.e., 14%. It indicates that the Naive Bayes classifier performs better than all other algorithms when new sample inputs are introduced to the model. VGG16 and ResNet are the two pre-trained models used in our study. VGG-16 is a 16-layer CNN. It is trained on the ImageNet database to classify images into one thousand categories of objects and animals. ResNet is another pre-trained CNN that is well known to solve the problem of vanishing gradients. It uses skip connections to expedite the learning process. We used these two famous pre-trained models to classify the pneumonia chest X-rays and obtained the training accuracy of 94.6% with VGG16 and 85.2% with ResNet. However, the testing accuracy of VGG16 plunged 8.02%. Whereas, for ResNet, the test accuracy was 82.13%. We may infer that VGG16 overfitted on the training data as opposed to ResNet. For DL, we tested two DL neural networks: CNN and MLP. The MLP used consists of one layer with hundred nodes, ReLU activation function, and Adam optimizer achieved a training and testing accuracy of 99.54% and 75.96%, respectively.

Table 2.1 Comparison of machine learning models.

Candidate models	Training accuracy (%)	Testing accuracy (%)
Naive Bayes	85.18	72.92
Decision Tree	92.48	72.92
Random Forest	99.54	69.55
AdaBoost	97.18	71.96
SVM	98.24	76.44
Quadratic Discriminant Analysis	97.05	62.5
VGG 16	94.6	87.01
ResNet	85.2	82.13
MLP	99.54	75.96
CNN	**96.95**	**94.79**

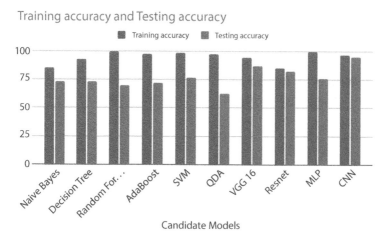

Figure 2.3 Performance comparison of different candidate classifier models.

The CNN with three hidden convolutional layers uses the binary cross-entropy loss function, three max-pooling layers, two dense layers, and one input layer, with ReLU activation function yielded training and testing accuracies of 96.95% and 94.79%. It can be observed that the MLP model is overfitting like other ML classifiers. Hence, it can be inferred that CNN is the best performing model, which can generalize better and does not overfit on the training data. Table 2.1 depicts the comparison of ML models, whereas Figure 2.3 represents the comparison between performances of the candidate's models based on their training and testing accuracies.

2.4.4   Model Evaluation of CNN Classifier

The CNN performed well among all other candidate models. Since it achieved the highest test accuracy of 94.79%, to further testify its robustness, we trained the CNN classifier on the newly augmented data as well. With the help of Keras experimental class, we augmented the chest X-ray dataset by applying transitions like random rotation and random zoom on the X-ray images of 64 × 64 resolution. Figure 2.4 shows the samples of augmented data of CXR Images. Various transitions including horizontal flip, rotation, and zoom are applied on the data.

To check the robustness of the CNN classifier, these newly augmented data were fed to the model. The classifier was able to predict the labels correctly and produced good results with training and testing accuracies of 94.47% and 94.96%, respectively. The model was able to learn from the training data and correctly labeled the newly introduced chest X-rays also. The model was not only robust but it was also time and space efficient. With a simple structure of convolutional layers, it was able to converge within 10 epochs on the training and testing data with continuously and sharply declining training and validation loss. Figure 2.4 represents CNN classifier performance on original and augmented data.

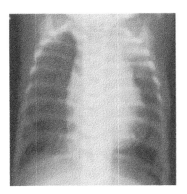 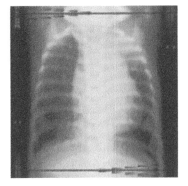

Figure 2.4 Augmented image data.

2.4.5   Mathematical Model

In purely mathematical terms, convolution is a function derived from two given functions by integration which expresses how the shape of one is modified by the other. There are several different layers like convolutional layer, pooling layer, fully connected layer, activation layer, and optimization layer. The classification task is performed in the last two layers of the network, i.e., fully connected layer and Softmax. There are three elements involved in the convolution operation: input image, feature detector, and feature map. The mathematical formula represents the working of the feature detector:

$$G(m,n) = (f * h)(m * n)$$

$$\sum_i \sum_j h(j,k)\, f\big[(m-j),(n-k)\big] \tag{2.1}$$

where h = kernel, f = image, m, and n = indexes of rows and columns of the resultant matrix.

The kernel is a small matrix of numbers also called a filter which passes over an image and transforms it based on the values from the filter. While sliding this kernel, we take each value from the kernel and multiply them with corresponding values from the image. Eventually, everything is summed up and the resultant values are put in the output feature map. The convolution of f and g denoted by $(f * g)$ is defined as the integral product of two functions. It can also be described as the weighted average of function $f(\tau)$ at the time index t, where the weight factor is given by $g(-\tau)$ shifted by amount t. The convolution function is given as follows:

$$(f * g)(t) = \int_{-\infty}^{\infty} f(\tau)\, g(t-\tau)\, d\tau \tag{2.2}$$

where t = time index.

2.4.6   Parameter Optimization

The best model classifier should not only be robust and efficient but its performance should be improved by careful selection and optimization of model parameters. The training and processing time majorly depends on the size of input given to the model. Therefore, it is crucial to test the model performance on different input resolutions to avoid the long processing time or underperformance of the model. Hence, we tested the CNN classifier model for different input sizes starting from 28 × 28 up to 256 × 256. For each resolution, we trained the model on the original dataset for 20 epochs. The model train and test accuracy did not vary much from input size of 28 × 28 to 256 × 256. However, the training time increases exponentially with increasing image size. This behavior of the model is depicted in Figure 2.5. From the table, it can be observed that there is a slight trade-off between training time and testing accuracy. Table 2.2 depicts performance comparison of the model for different input size, and Figure 2.6 shows a graphical representation of varying process time for each input resolution.

However, for input resolution 64 × 64 the testing accuracy is the highest. Additionally, its processing time is second lowest as shown in Figure 2.6. In the case of other input sizes, the model is converging well with a training accuracy

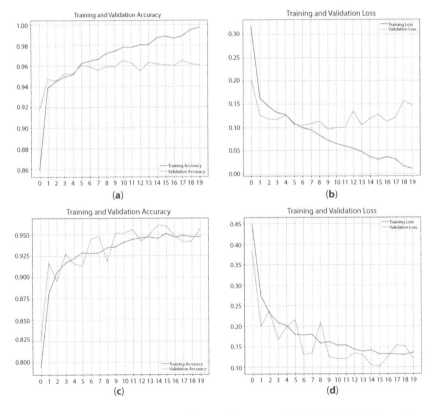

Figure 2.5 Graphical representation of the performance of CNN classifier for 20 epochs. (a) Training and testing accuracy of the model on original data. (b) Training and testing loss of model on original data. (c) Training and testing accuracy of model epochs on augmented data. (d) Training and testing loss for 20 epochs on augmented data.

Table 2.2 Performance comparison of the model for different input size.

Input resolution	Training accuracy (%)	Testing accuracy (%)
256 × 256	100	96.16
128 × 128	99.91	95.13
64 × 64	**99.90**	**96.**58
32 × 32	98.67	95.82
28 × 28	98.54	95.13

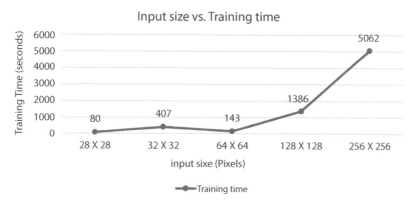

Figure 2.6 The performance CNN classifier with different input sizes and the processing time in each case.

of up to 100%. Therefore, 64 × 64 can be chosen as the optimal size of input for the model. However, the processing time increases sharply. Figure 2.7 illustrates the behavior of the CNN classifier for each case of input resolution. Figure 2.7 represents CNN classifier performance for different input sizes.

Salient Features
The CNN classifier is better than existing classifiers in terms of performance, generalization, and efficiency. The literature survey revealed a major limitation of existing classifier models, i.e., overfitting and poor generalization capabilities of the models. Using limited data for training can easily lead to overfitting of the model. To avoid this, we tried to train our classifier on a considerably large pool of data by appending the benchmark dataset with more samples using data augmentation techniques. Additionally, the literature also shed light on a limitation that the models were sensitive to the quality of input. Our classifier performs equally well on a variety of inputs such as different resolutions and orientation of

the image. Furthermore, the tedious and computationally intensive training process comes as a drawback in many existing models, making them inefficient. However, our classifier comparatively consumes less time and resources while training.

2.4.7 Performance Metrics

Often, it could be desirable to choose a model with a lower precision because it has a higher predictive power on the problem. The CNN classifier is proven to be a robust, optimized, and efficient model with a testing accuracy for detection of pneumonia disease on the benchmark dataset. However, only the accuracy is not enough. The confusion matrix, also called the contingency table, is the most simple and reliable way to evaluate the prediction result of the model. Figure 2.8 represents the confusion matrix of the CNN classifier.

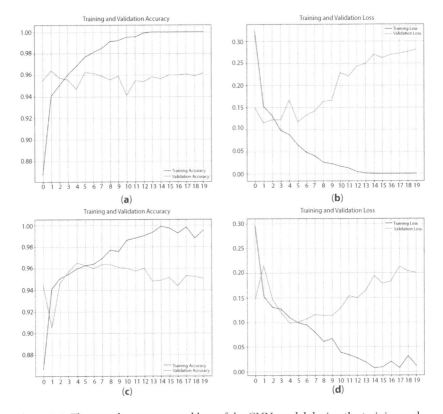

Figure 2.7 The growth, accuracy, and loss of the CNN model during the training and testing phase for various input resolutions. (a, b) CNN classifier with input 256 × 256. (c, d) CNN classifier with input 128 × 128.   (*Continued*)

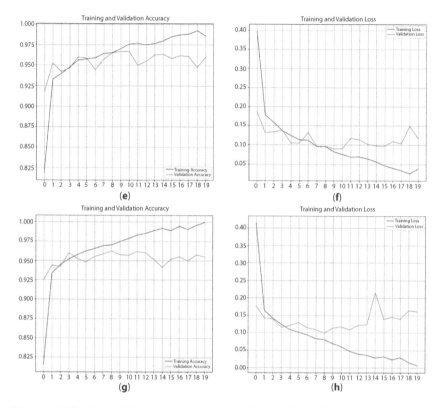

Figure 2.7 (Continued) The growth, accuracy, and loss of the CNN model during the training and testing phase for various input resolutions. (e, f) CNN classifier with input 32 × 32. (g, h) CNN classifier with input 28 × 28.

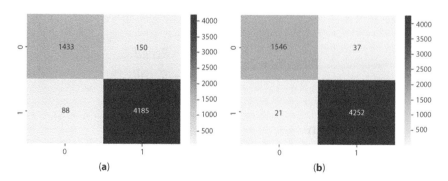

Figure 2.8 Graphical representation of confusion matrix for input size 64 × 64 (a) on augmented data (b) on original data.

In the confusion matrix for binary classification like our problem of detection of pneumonia, there are two rows and two columns. The columns are for actual class labels and rows are for predicted class labels. From this accuracy matrix, we can calculate different performance measuring scores like precision, recall, and F1 score. Precision is nothing but the exactness of the classifier. The number of true positive labels is divided by total positive labels. The CNN classifier has a precision of 94%. The formula for precision is given as follows:

$$Precision = \frac{n(True\ Positive\ labels)}{n(True\ Positive\ labels) + n(False\ Positive\ labels)}$$

The recall is another measure of performance, which is also called sensitivity or true positive rate is the measure of classifiers completeness. It can be calculated by dividing the number of true positive labels by the sum of true positive and false negative labels. The recall for the CNN classifier model is 95%. The formula for recall can be given as follows:

$$Recall = \frac{n(True\ Positive\ labels)}{n(True\ Positive\ labels) + n(False\ Negative\ labels)}$$

F1 score or F score also called the harmonic mean of precision and recall is a way to combine precision and recall. F1 score is often reliable when an uneven class distribution seeks a balance between precision and recall especially when there are more labels of true negatives. The measure for the F1 score for our CNN model is 94%. The formula for the f1 score is as follows:

$$F1\ score = 2x \frac{Precision * Recall}{Precision + Recall}$$

2.5   Conclusion

In this analytical study, we tested different approaches for the problem of pneumonia detection using AI. We identified three different approaches, namely, ML, DL, and transfer learning. All the algorithms were tested on a benchmark dataset and yielded good accuracy. Although the training accuracies yielded by all the algorithms were high, they did not learn the image features quite well which made them overfit the data. However, the CNN classifier among all the models gave the highest testing accuracy of 94.79%. This is because the model is fine-tuned, and it was able to generalize well. Additionally, we augmented the original dataset using random rotation and zoom on which the classifier gave an accuracy of 94%. Further, we fed different input resolutions to the classifier to select the optimum size as per the accuracy and processing time. Lastly, we evaluated the CNN model using different performance measures like precision, recall, and F1 score.

References

1. Varshni, D., Thakral, K., Agarwal, L., Nijhawan, R., Mittal, A., Pneumonia detection using CNN based feature extraction. *2019 IEEE International Conference on Electrical, Computer and Communication Technologies (ICECCT)*, pp. 1–7, 2019.
2. Toğaçar, M., Ergen, B., Cömert, Z., Özyurt, F., A deep feature learning model for Pneumonia detection applying a combination of mRMR feature selection and machine learning models. *IRBM*, 41, 4, 212–222, 2020. https://doi.org/10.1016/j.irbm.2019.10.006.
3. Hashmi, M.F., Katiyar, S., Keskar, A.G., Bokde, N.D., Geem, Z.W., Efficient Pneumonia detection in chest X-RAY images using deep transfer learning. *Diagnostics (Basel)*, 10, 6, 417, 2020Published 2020 Jun 19.
4. Militante, S.V., Dionisio, N.V., Sibbaluca, B.G., Pneumonia detection through adaptive deep learning models of convolutional neural networks. *2020 11th IEEE Control and System Graduate Research Colloquium (ICSGRC)*, pp. 88–93, 2020.
5. Zhao, D. *et al.*, Synthetic medical images using F&BGAN for improved lung nodules classification by multi-scale VGG16. *Symmetry*, 10, 5195, 2018.
6. Onishi, Y. *et al.*, Automated pulmonary nodule classification in computed tomography images using a deep convolutional neural network trained by generative adversarial networks. *BioMed. Res. Int.*, 6051939, 1–9, 2019.
7. Albahli, S., Efficient GAN-based Chest Radiographs (CXR) augmentation to diagnose coronavirus disease pneumonia. *Int. J. Med. Sci.*, 17, 10, 1439–1448, 2020Published 2020 Jun 6.
8. Ahsan, Mostofa & Gomes, Rahul & Denton, Anne, Application of a convolutional neural network using transfer learning for tuberculosis detection. 427–433.
9. Qjidaa, M. *et al.*, Development of a clinical decision support system for the early detection of COVID-19 using deep learning based on chest

radiographic images. *2020 International Conference on Intelligent Systems and Computer Vision (ISCV)*, Fez, Morocco, pp. 1–6, 2020.

10. Naik, R., Wani, T., Bajj, S., Ahir, S., Joshi, A., detection of lung diseases using deep learning, in: *Proceedings of the 3rd International Conference on Advances in Science & Technology (ICAST)*, 2020.

11. Chouhan, V., Singh, S.K., Khamparia, A., Gupta, D., Tiwari, P., Moreira, C. *et al.*, "A novel transfer learning-based approach for pneumonia detection in chest x-ray images,". *Appl. Sci.*, 10, 559, 2020.

12. Rajpurkar, P., JerIrvin, K.Z., Yang, B., Mehta, H., Duan, T., Ding, D., Bagul, A., Langlotz, C., Shpanskaya, K., Matthew, P.L., Ng, A.Y., CheXNet: Radiologist-level pneumonia detection on chest x-rays with deep learning. *ArXiv*, abs/1711.05225, arXiv:1711.05225 [cs, stat], November 2017. URL http://arxiv.org/abs/1711.05225. arXiv: 1711.05225.

13. Lin, C.-H., Lin, C.-J., Li, Y.-C., Wang, S.-H., "Using generative adversarial networks and parameter optimization of convolutional neural networks for lung tumor classification". *Appl. Sci.*, 11, 480, 2021.

14. Peng, L. *et al.*, Classification of Pulmonary Emphysema in CT images based on multi-scale deep convolutional neural networks. *2018 25th IEEE International Conference on Image Processing (ICIP)*, Athens, pp. 3119–3123, 2018.

15. Lessmann, N. *et al.*, Automated assessment of COVID-19 reporting and data system and chest CT severity scores in patients suspected of having COVID-19 Using Artificial Intelligence. *Radiology*, 298, 202439, May 2020.

16. Xu, X., Jiang, X., Ma, C., Du, P., Li, X., Lv, S., Yu, L., Ni, Q., Chen, Y., Su, J., Lang, G., Li, Y., Zhao, H., Liu, J., Xu, K., Ruan, L., Sheng, J., Qiu, Y., Wu, W., Liang, T., Li, L., A deep learning system to screen novel coronavirus disease 2019 pneumonia. *Engineering*, 6, 10, 1122–1129, 2020.

17. Brunese, L., Mercaldo, F., Reginelli, A., Santone, A., Explainable deep learning for pulmonary disease and coronavirus COVID-19 detection from x-rays. *Comput. Methods Programs Biomed.*, 196, 105608, 2020.

18. Ansari, N., Faizabadi, A.R., Motakabber, S.M.A., Ibrahimy, M., Ibn Effective pneumonia detection using ResNet based transfer learning. *Test Eng. Manage.*, 82, 15146–15153, Jan/Feb) (2020.

19. Antin, B. *et al.*, Detecting pneumonia in chest x-rays with supervised learning, 2017.

20. Abiyev, R.H. and Ma'aitah, M.K.S., Deep convolutional neural networks for chest diseases detection. *J. Healthc. Eng.*, 2018, 1–11, 2018.

21. Moujahid, H., Cherradi, B., El Gannour, O., Bahatti, L., Terrada, O., Hamida, S., Convolutional neural network based classification of patients with Pneumonia using x-ray lung images. 5, 167–175, 2020.

22. Tariq, Z., Shah, S.K., Lee, Y., Lung disease classification using deep convolutional neural network. *2019 IEEE International Conference on Bioinformatics and Biomedicine (BIBM)*, pp. 732–735, 2019.
23. Kermany, D., Zhang, K., Goldbaum, M., Labeled Optical Coherence Tomography (OCT) and chest x-ray images for classification. *Mendeley Data, V2*, 2018.

3

Contamination Monitoring System Using IOT and GIS

Kavita R. Singh[1]*, Ravi Wasalwar[2], Ajit Dharmik[3] and Deepshikha Tiwari[4]

[1]Department of Computer Technology, Yeshwantrao Chavan College of Engineering, Nagpur, Maharashtra, India
[2]T-Mobile, Herndon, Virginia, Washington, DC, Unites States
[3]6Simplex Software Solutions Pvt Ltd, Nagpur, Maharashtra, India
[4]T.I.E.T, Patiala, Punjab, India

Abstract

Contamination or pollution is one of the biggest challenges when environmental issues are considered. However, air pollution is one among all the key issues of our times and has become a primary issue, acknowledged by the international community. Owing to air pollution, medical problems have been emerging at a quicker rate, particularly in urban areas of the rising nations where industrial development and increasing vehicles lead to advent of a ton of gaseous contaminations. Therefore, pollution monitoring becomes a very important area of research to analyze the polluted and non-polluted area of a region based on which further decision can be taken by the authorities. In this context, we propose an analysis of particular areas that are more contaminated or polluted in Nagpur City, Maharashtra, India by calibrating the air quality index as an IOT-based air contamination monitoring framework and plotting the data using Geographical Information System. Additionally, the data analysis is done with the help of Tableau, and different parameters like air quality index, and temperature are provided to the end user through the Android application.

Keywords: IOT, air pollution, ArcGIS, monitoring system

*Corresponding author: ksingh@ycce.edu

R. Arokia Priya, Anupama V Patil, Manisha Bhende, Anuradha Thakare and Sanjeev Wagh (eds.)
Object Detection by Stereo Vision Images, (57–72) © 2022 Scrivener Publishing LLC

3.1   Introduction

Air contamination or pollution is one of the major problems for any nation, whether it is developed or emergent nation. Pollution is one with all the key issues of our times, and concrete air quality has become a primary issue, acknowledged by the international community. Medical issues have been developing at a quicker rate, particularly in metropolitan territories of the rising nations where industrialization and developing number of vehicles lead to arrival of a ton of vaporous contaminations. Hurtful impacts of contamination incorporate mellow unfavorably susceptible responses, for example, disturbance of the throat, eyes, and nose also as some major issues like bronchitis, heart ailments, pneumonia, lung, and exasperated asthma. According to a survey, among all the environmental parameters only due to air pollution, an estimated of millions of premature deaths annually occur across the worldwide [1]. Due to urbanization, urban air quality is considered one of the greatest threats to human health.

Consequently, a good number of researches are going on monitoring of air quality index (AQI). Based on the information provided by monitoring system, other related decision can be taken accordingly. With the advancement of technology such as Internet of Things (IOT) and Wireless Sensor Networks (WSN), it has become easier for the researchers to accomplish such monitoring framework. Leveraging the use of IOT sensors, in this paper, we present an IOT-based air contamination monitoring framework. The proposed IOT-based air contamination monitoring framework has been developed to identify which areas are more polluted in Nagpur City by calibrating the AQI through IOT-based monitoring system and plotting the captured data using Geographical Information System (GIS). Later, data analysis is presented with the help of Tableau and also provides an android application to the client. The air quality monitoring uses the weather station where IOT sensors will be installed and will be dependent upon the monitoring specific standards set by the World Health Organization (WHO) for the AQI.

This chapter is organized as follows. Section 3.2 talks about the literature review followed by the work proposed in Section 3.3. Furthermore, Section 3.4 discusses about the experimental setup, and Section 3.5 discusses the results, followed by conclusions and future scope in Section 3.6.

3.2   Literature Survey

This segment of the paper presents the ideas identified with the proposed work and the extensive writing study of the work done. At first, the AQI came into existence in 1968, when the National Air Pollution Control Administration embraced an activity to build up an air quality list and to apply the procedure to Metropolitan Statistical Areas. The driving force was to cause public to notice the issue of air contamination and in a round-about way push mindful neighborhood public authorities to make a move to control wellsprings of contamination and improve air quality inside their locales. On a similar line, in year 2013, authors in [2] introduced a contamination observing the framework utilizing a remote sensor of mechanization network for Visakhapatnam city.

The proposed work was capable of expanding the level of mechanization (limiting the labor) in practically all the divisions of the city. From the literature, it has been observed that WSNs are picking up the ground in all segments of life: from homes to processing plants, from traffic signal to ecological checking. Likewise, air pollution monitoring framework is additionally utilizing sensors to screen the necessary ecological parameters.

As of late, the work proposed in [3] has been vigorously affected by their duties to the general public. This duty has been coordinated toward the security of general well-being and government assistance. The venture introduced in [4] targets constructing a framework that can be utilized on all around at any scale to screen the parameters in every condition. The framework proposed in paper [5] is a serious answer for checking the climate conditions at a specific spot and make the data noticeable anyplace on the globe. The author in [6] presented a novel IIS that consolidates IOT, Cloud Computing, and Geoinformatics Remote Sensing (GRS). In [7], a credible real-time air quality monitoring framework was proposed, implemented, and tested in the open air. The proposed framework [7] detected and sent back various centralization parameters via the GPRS remote correspondence interface. Furthermore, in [8], an outdoor WSN predicated air quality checking framework (WSNAQMS) for modern and metropolitan zones was proposed. The device hub comprises of a lot of gas sensors, and a Zigbee remote correspondence connect predicated on the Libelium's gas detecting skilled bit. Information is transferred to the focal worker through the Zigbee correspondence interface. Endorsed air contamination data is accessible to the general population through email, short messages, and tweaked web-app. This framework professed to be straightforward and reusable in diverse applications.

The WSN air pollution monitoring system (WAPMS) was presented in [9] as a novel framework for monitoring air pollution in Mauritius using remote sensors distributed in massive numbers over the island. The suggested methodology makes use of an AQI of 5, which is currently unavailable in Mauritius. Researchers in [10] created an Environmental Air Pollution Monitoring System (EAPMS) to examine groupings of important air poison gases in accordance with IEEE 1451.2. Using semiconductor sensors, this framework calculates centralizations of various gases. The perceptive transducer interface module was realised using the ADuC812 miniature converter from simple creations.

Authors in [11] proposed a machine-driven air contamination examination system based on WSN innovation (WSNs). The system is integrated with the global structure for mobile communications (GSM), and the correspondence convention used is Zigbee. The system consists of device hubs, a control community, and a statistics base where detecting data can be saved for history and uncertain arrangements.

A mobile air quality monitoring network (MAQMN) was presented in [12], which used moving movements outfitted with sensor hubs to screen air quality in a massively large region. Every sensor hub is made up of a microcontroller, a locally available Ecumenical Situating System (ESS) unit, and a slew of sensors that detect ozone, carbon-monoxide, and nitrogen-dioxide convergences. Furthermore, authors in [13] proposed a productive and vigorous system for regulating the boundaries that cause contamination and limiting the impact of produced strictures without affecting the shrub or indigenous habitat. The proposed strategy was to demonstrate a framework for reading and screening contamination strictures, as well as to notify contamination regulate ascendant elements if some of these elements exceeded industry standards.

Besides, an ongoing distributed work [14] proposed an industrial contamination checking system based on lab-view and Zigbee to determine the nature of waste management and business workplaces, to identify the crucial signifiers to be measured in the contamination observing system, and to send the data to the pollution control board (PCB) and the general public. Regardless of the fact that there are significant constraints on mass and scope, a few frameworks could not quickly send the observing data back.

3.3   Proposed Work

This section of the paper describes the proposed work using GIS and Tableau. The complete process of proposed IOT-based air contamination monitoring framework is portrayed in Figure 3.1.

From Figure 3.1, it is obvious that, firstly, different IOT sensors are installed at different location under consideration. The data collected through IOT sensors are stored in internal storage, which is further utilized by GIS for projection on map using ArcGIS. Once the data is plotted, query can be fired from ArcGIS as discussed in result section in detail.

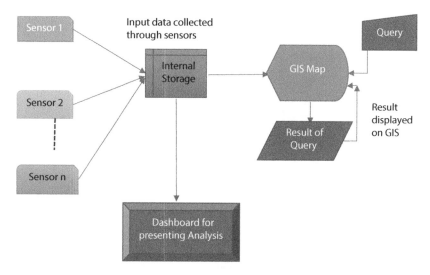

Figure 3.1 IOT-based air contamination monitoring framework.

Furthermore, information is used by Tableau to introduce a dashboard from where different perspective of data can be analyzed according to the necessity of the client. The detail of each step of the complete process is described in forthcoming experimental and result section of the paper.

3.4 Experimentation and Results

This section of the paper presents the detail depiction of experimental setup required for conducting the experiments followed by the output and results of the experimentation and how it can be beneficial for analyzing the contamination in an area using different parameters for further decision.

3.4.1 Experimental Setup

The proposed project uses novel sensors and hardware such as Arduino Uno, LM35, MQ135, and LDR. Arduino application board is used to collect environmental parameters to send them to the Apache server and MySQL database using the ESP-8266 Wi-Fi module. The system is given 5-V supply by connector cable (laptop to Arduino), and also the programs are uploaded using the cable.

Figure 3.2 depicts the Arduino Uno, a microcontroller board based on the ATmega-328 (datasheet). The ESP-8266 Wi-Fi module, as shown in

Figure 3.2 Arduino Uno.

Figure 3.3, is used for data transfer. It is a stand-alone SOC with a coordinated TCP/IP protocol stack that can grant access to the Wi-Fi organisation to any microcontroller. The ESP-8266 is ready to help an application or offload all Wi-Fi networking functions from another application processor. Each ESP-8266 module comes pre-programmed with an AT command set firmware, which means it can be connected to an Arduino device and provide roughly the same Wi-Fi capacity as a Wi-Fi Shield 11. The ESP-8266 module is a highly intelligent board. Temperature being one of the most commonly measured environmental quantities, we used the LM35 (temperature sensor) to measure it, as shown in Figure 3.4.

MQ135 (air quality sensor) as appeared in Figure 3.5 detects the gases like smelling salts nitrogen, oxygen, alcohols, fragrant mixes, sulfide, and smoke. The lift converter of the chip MQ-3 gas sensor is PT1301. The MQ-3 gas sensor has a lower conductivity to clean the air as a gas detecting material. In the air, we can discover contaminating gases; however,

Figure 3.3 ESP8266 Wi-Fi module.

Vcc
3-5.5 V

Analog Out
10 mV / °C

GND

Figure 3.4 LM35 (temperature sensor).

Figure 3.5 MQ135 (air quality sensor).

the conductivity of gas sensor increments as the grouping of dirtying gas increments. MQ-135 gas sensor can be castoff to recognize the smoke, benzene, and other hurtful gases. It can possibly distinguish diverse unsafe gases. The working voltage of this gas sensor is from 2.5V to 5.0V. Photo resistor also called as a light-dependent resistor (LDR) as shown in Figure 3.6 is a gadget whose resistivity is an element of the episode electromagnetic radiation. Next, a Geographic Information System (GIS) is designed to capture, manipulate, store, analyze, and display data. After the data are mapped, Tableau is used for analysis and finally Android for application development. Additionally, for the proposed project, we considered following maps, namely, Nagpur Base Map, Industrial areas/Industries base map, and Construction Sites. The collected base maps are integrated in ArcGIS in the form of layers as depicted in Figure 3.7. From Figure 3.7, it tends to be perceived how different layers such as city, industries, hospitals, roads, and railways are integrated over each other.

Figure 3.6 LDR (light-dependent resistors).

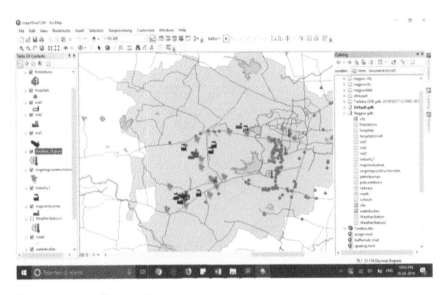

Figure 3.7 Map of Nagpur City.

Each layer is nothing but a feature class that stores information about similar data in that particular class. The data that are stored are called attributes, i.e., alike features and properties of that any particular feature class. The attributes are stored in the attribute table as portrayed in Figure 3.8.

3.5   Results

Once the IOT sensors are installed in different areas such as Wanadongri, Civil Lines, Laxmi Nagar, and IT park of Nagpur city, readings were

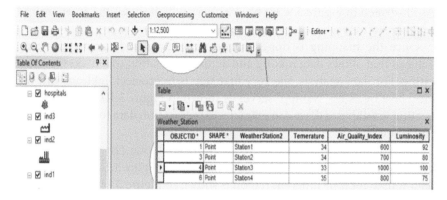

Figure 3.8 Attribute Table.

recorded from various industries, ongoing construction sites as well as weather stations and were plotted on the map. The weather station's attribute table contains information such as temperature, AQI, and luminosity values, as noticeable in Figure 3.9. Furthermore, using ArcGIS toolbox, buffers are created around the industries and ongoing construction sites. The buffer radius varies according to the hazard level. Then, we apply union operation over the overlapping buffer area so that we get the clubbed buffer areas where the pollution level is present. Based on this overlapping buffer, query can be fired on any parameter such as temperature and AQI and can be displayed on the map with the help of ArcGIS as shown in Figure 3.9.

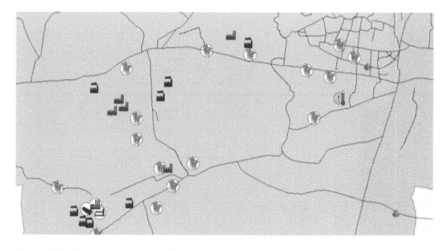

Figure 3.9 The weather station where temperature is less than 34.

As illustrated in Figure 3.9, we fired a query which shows the areas around weather stations whose temperature is less than 34.

Once the mapping is done, the next objective is data analysis using Tableau that allows data mixing and actual association that makes it interesting. For data analysis, the very first step is to connect Tableau with the local host by using "Xampp" server as shown in Figure 3.10. After the connection is established, we can extract weather station data for further usage and analysis.

Subsequently, when data source is connected, one can get all the data available in the Tableau environment as shown in Figure 3.10. The extracted data source for four different region is shown in Figure 3.11. Furthermore, one can classify them as dimensions and measures and create any hierarchy required.

For instance, a heat map of luminosity in the month of March, which shows information in solid square shapes, is shown in Figure 3.12. From the heat map shown in Figure 3.12, it is evident that dimensions define the structure of the tree map and measures characterize the size or shade of the individual square shape. Additionally, a side-by-side bar chart of temperature in the month of March of areas like Civil Lines, IT park, Laxmi Nagar, and Wanadongri is depicted in Figure 3.13. From the bar diagram appeared in Figure 3.13, it tends to be seen that the information spoke to with rectangular bars have length of the bar relative to the estimation of the variable.

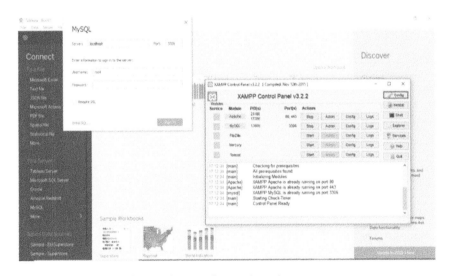

Figure 3.10 Tableau desktop and "Xampp" control panel.

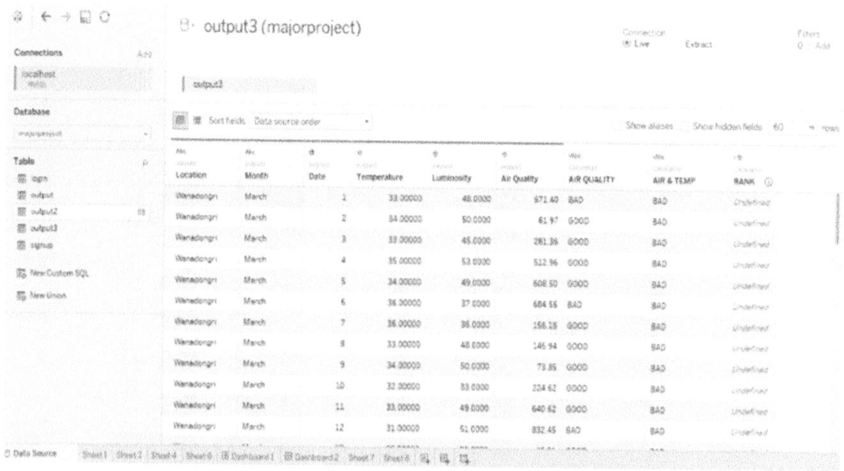

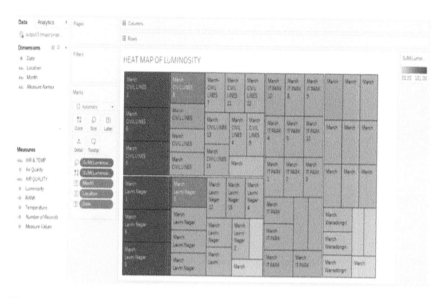

Figure 3.11 Data source of four areas.

Figure 3.12 Heat map of luminosity.

The next very important step is analysis based on various parameters such as temperature and air quality, shown as measures in Figure 3.14. Any of these listed parameters can be utilized in a singleton or pair for analysis. For example, an analysis of air quality, where on the off chance that the air quality is more noteworthy than 650, at that point "BAD" else "GOOD", is

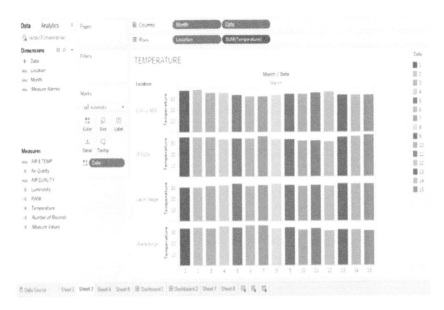

Figure 3.13 Bar graph.

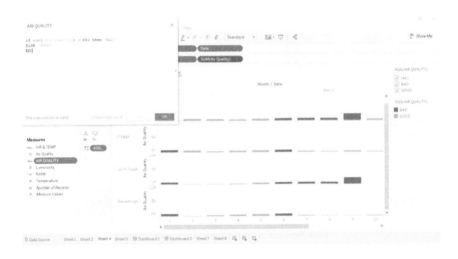

Figure 3.14 Analysis of air quality.

depicted in Figure 3.14. Similarly, Figure 3.15 speaks to the analysis based on temperature and air quality together. The stacked bars are used to visualize temperature and air quality. A complete dashboard as shown in Figure 3.16 is a merged presentation of numerous worksheets and related data in a solitary spot that will help the end client to comprehend the analysis initially.

Figure 3.15 Analysis of temperature and air quality.

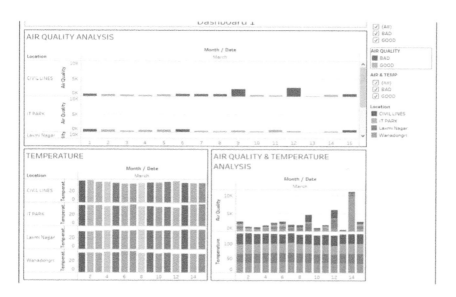

Figure 3.16 Dashboard.

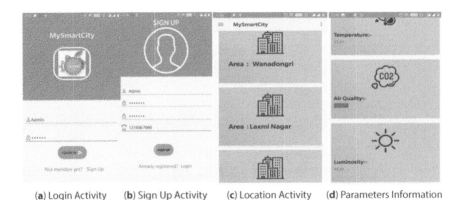

(a) Login Activity   (b) Sign Up Activity   (c) Location Activity   (d) Parameters Information

Figure 3.17 Android application "app".

Finally, to assist the end user or client with information about environmental parameters of different location on mobile, we have developed Android application as shown in Figure 3.17 named as "MySmartCity". In Figure 3.17 parameters information activity will show the different parameter's information, such as, temperature, air quality, and luminosity. In this page, the user gets the values of mentioned parameters if the values are more than the harmful limit and gets highlighted in red color as shown in Figure 3.17, then it can be easily identified to the user that the air quality is harmful in this area.

3.6   Conclusion

The primary objective of the proposed work was to distinguish the contaminated or polluted areas and give recommendation on the basis of the information gathered by the IOT sensors. The collected data were presented through the spatial analysis on ArcGIS followed by analysis using Tableau and, finally, providing the AQI to the user through the Android application. For data collection, the weather stations were installed at four locations in different parts of Nagpur city, namely, Civil Lines, Laxmi Nagar, IT park, and Wanadongri. The outcome of the analysis can be utilized by workshop proprietors, employees, and governing agencies to ascertain compliancy with the standard natural principles. This project provides thorough and consistent data on significant air pollutant strictures such as particulate matter, sulfur oxides, nitrogen dioxides, and carbon monoxide. The proposed project has opened up incipient opportunity to plan smart devices for better environmental conditions analysis. This analysis thus will assist with diminishing human well-being impacts of modern air toxins and expected harm to different parts of nature. In future, IOT sensors can be placed strategically all over the Nagpur city (one module in every proposed area, e.g., Laxmi Nagar and Civil Lines) for conducting analysis of the entire city. In addition, the Android application can be made available on Google Play Store and its database can be hosted on the suitable central server.

Acknowledgement

The authors would like to extend our sincere thanks to Mr. Shreyash Wyawahare, Mr. Sujay Gijre, Mr. Niraj Bhoyar, Mr. Pranay Girde and Mr. Akhilesh Jalamkar for the implementation of the project.

References

1. Tudose, D. Ş., Pătraşcu, N., Voinescu, A., Tataroiu, R., Ţăpuş, N., Mobile Sensors in Air Pollution Measurement, in: *IEEE Positioning Navigation and Communication (WPNC)*, pp. 166–170, 7 Apr 2011.
2. Vjnattha, P., Arvind, R., Sangeetkumar, B., Pollution monitoring system using wireless sensor network in Visakhapatnam. *IJETT*, 4, 591–595, April 2013.
3. Sumitra, A., Sujay Gijre Kartika, J., Gavaskar, S., A smart environmental monitoring system using IOT. *IJSEAS*, 2, 3, 261–265, March 2016.
4. Rao, A., Karishma, J., Pawar, K.P., Malvi, K., Sahoo, G., Environmental Monitoring Using Wireless Sensor Networks (WSN) based on IOT. *IRJET*, 4, 1372–1378, January 2017.
5. Rao, B.S., Srinivasa Rao, Prof.K., Ome, Mr. N., Internet of Things (IOT) Based Weather Monitoring system. *IJARCCE*, 5, 312–319, September 2016.
6. Fang, S., Xu, L.D., Zhu, Y., Ahati, J., Pei, H., Yan, J., Liu, Z., An Integrated System for Regional Environmental Monitoring and Management Based on IOT. *IEEE*, 4, 1596–1605, May 2014.
7. Kadri, A., Yaacoub, E., Mushtaha, M., Abu-Dayya, A., Wireless sensor network for real-time air pollution monitoring, in: *IEEE 1st International Conference Communications, Signal Processing, and their Applications*, pp. 1–5, February 2013.
8. Yi, W.Y., Lo, K.M., Mak, T., Leung, K.S., Leung, Y., Meng, M.L., A survey of wireless sensor network based air pollution monitoring systems. *Sensors*, 15, 12, 31392–31427, 2015.

9. Khedo, K.K., Perseedoss, R., Mungur, A., A wireless sensor network air pollution monitoring system. *International Journal of Wireless and Mobile Networks.*, 2, 2, 31–45, 1005–1737, 2010. arXiv preprint arXiv.
10. Kularatna, N. and Sudantha, B.H., An environmental air pollution monitoring system based on the IEEE 1451 standard for low cost requirements. *IEEE Sensors J.*, 8, 4, 415–422, 2008.
11. Swagarya, G., Kaijage, S., Sinde, R.S., A Survey on Wireless Sensor Networks Application for Air Pollution Monitoring. *Int. J. Eng. Comput. Sci.*, 3, 5, 5975–5979, 2014.
12. Völgyesi, P., Nádas, A., Koutsoukos, X., Lédeczi, Á., Air quality monitoring with sensormap, in: *IEEE International Conference on Information Processing in Sensor Networks*, pp. 529–530, 2008 April.
13. Pravin, J., Deepak Sankar, A., Angeline Vijula, D., Industrial pollution monitoring system using LabVIEW and GSM. *Int. J. Adv. Res. Electr. Electron. Instrum. Eng.*, 2, 6, 2685–2693, 2013.
14. Rambabu, K., Vasu, B., Raju, M., Vinod, T., Chinaaiah, M.C., Industrial Pollution Monitoring System Using LabVIEW. *International Journal of Scientific Research in Science, Engineering and Technology (IJSRSET)*, 2, 2, 1281–1284, 2016.

4

Video Error Concealment Using Particle Swarm Optimization

Rajani P. K.[1]* and Arti Khaparde[2]

[1]*Department of E & TC, Pimpri Chinchwad College of Engineering, Pune, Maharashtra, India*
[2]*Department of E & TC, Maharashtra Institute of Technology, Pune, Maharashtra, India*

Abstract

Video transmitting over wired or wireless channels such as internet is the area of research because of its fast growth. There are more chances of loss of packets in wireless medium. In existing video recovering methods, either there is a delay as packets are sending it again or redundancy of data, Video Error Concealment (VEC) is the method used for minimizing the errors in the video due to any transmission errors or addition of noise. There are different domains that are used for error concealment such as temporal, spatial, and spatio-temporal. To achieve error concealment techniques, there are different algorithms such as Boundary Matching Algorithm, Frequency Selective Extrapolation, and Patch Matching. The proposed method is a novel method in the spatio-temporal domain. It can significantly improve the subjective and objective video quality. Hence, spatio-temporal algorithm is adopted over other domains. There are many algorithms for VEC. The optimized algorithms should be used for obtaining better quality of videos. Particle Swarm Optimization (PSO) is one of the best optimized bio-inspired algorithms. This PSO technique can be used to conceal the errors in different formats of videos. Correlation is used for detection of errors in the videos, and each error frame is concealed using PSO algorithm in MATLAB. This was tested for different standard videos and different types and variety of errors for single, multiple, and sequential errors. In comparison to error videos, parameters including PSNR, SSIM, and Entropy improved for concealed videos, while MSE decreased. The results clearly indicate improvement in quality of videos. The errors in the video should be recovered as it is used in many applications such as in internet

---

Corresponding author: rajani.pk@pccoepune.org

R. Arokia Priya, Anupama V Patil, Manisha Bhende, Anuradha Thakare and Sanjeev Wagh (eds.)
Object Detection by Stereo Vision Images, (73–98) © 2022 Scrivener Publishing LLC

video streaming, mobile phone, TV, and video conference and in medical areas such as MRI and satellite transmissions.

Keywords: Video Error Concealment (VEC), Particle Swarm Optimization (PSO), spatio-temporal, optimized algorithm, error detection, PSNR, SSIM, entropy

4.1   Introduction

During the past few years, there has been an explosive growth in the number of videos that are transmitted. Besides the traditional way of watching videos on TV, significant number of internet users has seen several online video hosting services like YouTube and Skype growing in popularity. Besides that, live streaming such as for sports or any other events is another important aspect of internet videos that are expected to grow tremendously in the coming years. However, there are chances of data loss or noise addition during the transmission [1–3]. This paper investigates the application of Particle Swarm Optimization (PSO) [1, 2], which is an efficient optimization algorithm for Video Error Concealment (VEC). VEC is the technique used at the decoder side to hide the transmission errors.

Error can be block errors or random errors, as shown in Figure 4.1. This figure shows a frame with 36 blocks of errors of size 32 × 32. This figure also indicates random errors. Random errors can be of any shape or size. Both errors can be occurred during transmission, which needed to be corrected [2–5].

Traditional error correcting techniques for video signal such as Automatic Repeat Request (ARQ) result in retransmission of data and a

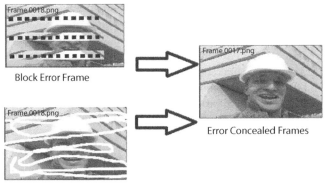

Block Error Frame

Error Concealed Frames

Random Error Frame

Figure 4.1 Error concealment for block and random errors.

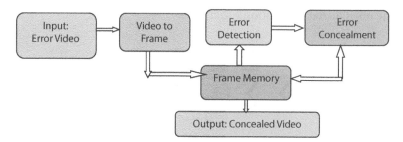

Figure 4.2 Overview of video error detection and concealment.

lot of delay as well as redundant data in the reception of video signal at the decoder side of the system. Hence, there is a need of reducing the delay as well as redundant data at the decoder side. VEC is the technique used at the decoder side to hide the transmission errors. VEC can be implemented by many techniques simple as well as complex algorithms [2–11].

4.2   Proposed Research Work Overview

The overview of video error detection and concealment is as shown in Figure 4.2. The input error video is converted into frames. The frames are checked one by one and, if the error is not detected, then the frames are stored into frame memory. If any error is detected, then the error frame is concealed using any of the error concealment algorithms [12–14].

The error frame is concealed using spatial, temporal, or spatio-temporal method with the help of current and or previous frames that are stored in frame memory. The error frame is replaced by concealed frame in the frame memory. Thus, all the frames in the frame memory are converted back into concealed video.

4.3   Error Detection

Correlation is similarity between the two images or frames. Correlation function gives statistical correlation between random variables that exist between spatial temporal distances between two variables. Correlation value of error frame and error free frame are different. Hence, correlation detects the error frame [12–14]. Correlation is used to determine 2D correlation coefficient between A and B matrices or vectors of the same size image or frame m X n.

The normalized correlation function is

$$\text{Correlation}, r = \frac{\sum_{m}\sum_{n}\left(A_{mn} - \overline{A}\right)\left(B_{mn} - \overline{B}\right)}{\sqrt{\sum_{m}\sum_{n}\left(A_{mn} - \overline{A}\right)^{2}\sum_{m}\sum_{n}\left(B_{mn} - \overline{B}\right)^{2}}}$$

where

    r = 2D correlation coefficient between A and B matrices or vectors of the same size image or frame m × n.

    $\overline{A}$ = is the mean of frame matrix A and $\overline{B}$ = is the mean of B frame matrix B.

The error detection using the correlation is done as shown in Figure 4.3. The correlation with threshold is found by trial and experimentations of different videos and different type of errors as follows.

The error frame is detected using correlation between the frames. The threshold value for different errors such as black block errors and random errors are found by trial and experimentation method for single frame errors, multiple frame errors, and sequential frame errors with different sizes and shapes. The results are analyzed. Hence, it can be concluded generally, that the threshold value can be set empirically as, less than or equal to 0.9 for detecting the error in videos. If more sequential errors are occurring in video, then the threshold value be set as less than or equal to 0.8.

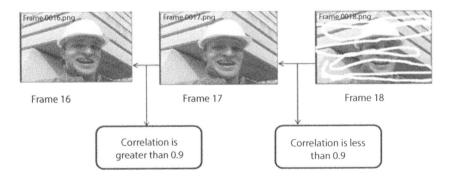

Frame 16   Frame 17   Frame 18

Correlation is greater than 0.9

Correlation is less than 0.9

Figure 4.3 Error detection using correlation.

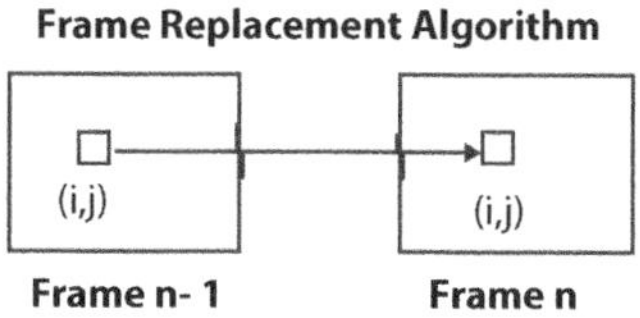

Frame Replacement Algorithm

Figure 4.4 Illustration of frame replacement algorithm.

4.4   Frame Replacement Video Error Concealment Algorithm

This is the basic and simplest method of Temporal Error Concealment algorithm in which the lost or damaged block or frame is replaced exactly by the same place block or frame of previous frame. It is easier to conceal linear movements in one direction because pictures can be predicted from previous frames if the scene is almost the same. It is a temporal VEC algorithm. Even though there are few VEC algorithms are available, it is the only algorithm which can conceal the random errors.

Frame Replacement Algorithm (FRA) replaces the missing image part with the spatially corresponding part inside a previously decoded frame, which has maximum correlation with the affected frame as shown in Figure 4.4.

The formula used in the FRA is as follows:

$$F_n\left(i,j\right)=F_{n-1}\left(i,j\right) \tag{4.2}$$

If there are movements in many directions or scene cuts, then find a part of previous frame that is similar is more difficult. Then, FRA will replace the current frame by previous frame. Then, the error is removed but at the cost of one or more entire frames missing. This will give a feel of no change in the scene. However, if there are many frames having errors, then these types of method will not solve the purpose of concealment in videos. It also degrades the quality of videos in that case.

4.5   Research Methodology

PSO is discussed first. Then, it discusses about the spatio-temporal VEC in which domain the proposed modified PSO algorithm has implemented.

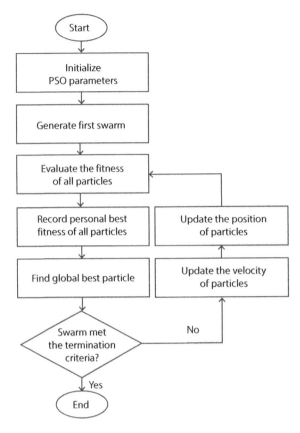

Figure 4.5 Flow chart of PSO.

4.5.1   Particle Swarm Optimization

One of the most well-known bio-inspired metaheuristic optimization algorithms is PSO. This algorithm is developed by James Kennedy and Russell Eberhart in 1995 [1, 19]. Nowadays, a lot of research work is going on in the field of science and engineering using this algorithm. PSO is population-based stochastic optimization algorithm. The concept that is used in PSO is the social behavior of bird flocks [13]. The flow chart of PSO is indicated in Figure 4.5.

4.5.2   Spatio-Temporal Video Error Concealment Method

The error frame and its previous two frames are taken from the frame memory. All these three RGB frames are separated into red, blue, and green channels. After this, PSO is applied to each channel separately. The absolute difference between the error frames along with other two frames is found. Ideally, the threshold should be zero. However, by analyzing, the threshold has kept as ±5. If it is ±5, then no need to replace the pixel otherwise replace the RGB component of the frame that is temporal error concealment. Finally, the RGB is merged back as a temporal error conceal frame. Finally, the frame intensity values or colormaps are adjusted as spatial concealment. This spatio-temporal error concealed frame is stored in the frame memory. Once all frames are concealed and transferred to frame memory, the concealed video can be prepared.

4.5.3 Proposed Modified Particle Swarm Optimization Algorithm

Once the error frame is detected from the video, the proposed PSO algorithm needs to be applied to conceal the frame.

The steps of the proposed modified PSO-based VEC in spatio-temporal implementation are as follows:

1. Set parameters: Initialize the PSO Parameters
    - P = swarm size = total number of frames = 30 = initial population (swarm)
    - Learning factor, $c1 = c2 = 2$; Also $c1 + c2 \geq 4$ and inertia term, $w = 1$.
2. Initialize the population of the particles having positions X and velocities V.
3. Set the iteration $k = 10$. Too many iterations increase the delay.
4. Apply the spatio-temporal error concealment for the error frame for $k = 10$ iteration by considering all the frames. Pixel replacement by considering the two previous frames and frame intensity or color map adjustment for spatial concealment.
    Spatio-temporal error concealment for the error frame is as follows:

    a) The temporal error concealment using current frame and previous two frames are to be done first. For that purpose, the error frame and its two previous frames are taken from the memory.

Example: $i = 18^{th}$ frame is the error frame, then $j = i - 1 = 17^{th}$ frame and $k = i - 2 = 16^{th}$ frame, are its two previous frames.

$$\left. \begin{array}{l} i = F\left(x,y,t\right) \\ j = F\left(x,y,t-1\right) \\ k = F\left(x,y,t-2\right) \end{array} \right\} \tag{4.3}$$

b) For all these, three frames RGB is separated into red, blue, green channels as follows:

$$\left. \begin{array}{l} F_r(x,y,t),\ F_g(x,y,t),\ F_b(x,y,t) \\ F_r(x,y,t-1),\ F_g(x,y,t-1),\ F_b(x,y,t-1) \\ F_r(x,y,t-2),\ F_g(x,y,t-2),\ F_b(x,y,t-2) \end{array} \right\} \tag{4.4}$$

c) The absolute difference between the two channels is taken. The absolute difference is preferred because it is in video frame which has a third dimension, time. In order to compensate the motion in different frames absolute difference is used.

Example: This can be considered as absolute difference between the two channels for 16 and 17 frames.

$$\left. \begin{array}{l} C_r = F_r(x,y,t-2) - F_r(x,y,t-1) \\ C_g = F_g(x,y,t-2) - F_g(x,y,t-1) \\ C_b = F_b(x,y,t-2) - F_b(x,y,t-1) \end{array} \right\} \tag{4.5}$$

Example: This can be considered as absolute difference between the two channels for 17 and 18 (error) frames.

$$\left. \begin{array}{l} E_r = F_r(x,y,t-1) - F_r(x,y,t) \\ E_g = F_g(x,y,t-1) - F_g(x,y,t) \\ E_b = F_b(x,y,t-1) - F_b(x,y,t) \end{array} \right\} \tag{4.6}$$

d) Threshold of +5 or −5 is used here by trial-and-error experimentation it, even though ideally it should be zero for each component.

For red component, the replacement of the error frame pixels is done as below:

$$\text{If } \left(E_r < (C_r - 5) \text{ or } E_r > (C_r + 5) \right)$$

then replace the pixel F_r (x, y, t) by C_r

Else replace the pixel F_r (x, y, t) by E_r

For green component, the replacement of the error frame pixels is done as below:

$$\text{If } \left(E_g < (C_g - 5) \text{ or } E_g > (C_g + 5) \right)$$

then replace the pixel F_g (x, y, t) by C_g

Else replace the pixel F_g (x, y, t) by E_g

For blue component, the replacement of the Error frame pixels is done as below:

$$\text{If } \left(E_b < (C_b - 5) \text{ or } E_b > (C_b + 5) \right)$$

then replace the pixel F_b (x, y, t) by C_b

Else replace the pixel F_b (x, y, t) by E_b

e) Once all the RGB component replacement is done, then merged/concatenated back as one frame.

$$F(x,y,t) = F_r(x,y,t) + F_g(x,y,t) + F_b(x,y,t) \qquad (4.7)$$

f) The intensity values or color maps are adjusted as spatial error.

Concealment, once the temporal error concealment is completed as follows:

$$Fsp(x,y,t)$$

5. Calculate the fitness of a particle,

$$F_i^k = f\left(X_i^k\right) \qquad \forall i \tag{4.8}$$

where X_i^k is the ith frame for kth iteration. Here, $k = 10$ iteration and $i = 30$ frames are taken and finding the index of the best particle b.

Evaluate the fitness of all particles using entropy. Entropy is a statistical measure of randomness that can be used to characterize the texture of the input frame.

$$\text{Entropy}, E = -\sum p\log_2 p \tag{4.9}$$

where p contains the histogram counts.

The histogram of the concealed frames is uniformly distributed that increase the entropy of the frame. Hence, entropy is used here as fitness function.

6. Select the personal best fitness of all particles.

$$\text{Pbest}_i^k = X_i^k \qquad \forall i \tag{4.10}$$

Where X_i^k is the ith frame for kth iteration.

If the fitness value (Entropy) is better than the best fitness, i.e., entropy of then spatio-temporal frame $\geq$ maximum of fitness value, then the best frame is obtained.

If entropy (Fsp (x,y,t)) $\geq$ maximum(fitness value), then Pbest=i, where i is the frame number having maximum entropy.

7. Find the global best particle.

$$\text{Gbest}^k = X_b^k \tag{4.11}$$

where k = iteration and b = index of the best particle.

Choose the particle with the best fitness value of all particles as the Gbest.

$$\text{Gbest=max(Pbest)} \tag{4.12}$$

8. If Swarm met the termination criteria, then stop
   If all frames and all iterations are completed, then it can be stopped.
9. Else update the velocity and position of particles

$$V_{i,j}^{k+1} = w \times V_{i,j}^{k} + c1 \times r1 \times \left(Pbest_{i,j}^{k} - X_{i,j}^{k} \right) + c2 \times r2 \times \left(Gbest_{j}^{k} - X_{i,j}^{k} \right)$$

(4.13)

$$X_{i}^{k+1} = X_{i}^{k} + V_{i}^{k+1}$$

(4.14)

Repeat the steps from 4, for all frames i = 1 to 30 and for all iteration, k = 10

10. Once all frames are concealed and transferred to frame memory, the concealed video can be prepared.
    This proposed method helps to flattens and stretches the histogram of the frames and balances different color components. It also preserves the brightness of the frame. This customized PSO is used to improve the contrast and details in the frame when compared to FRA. This method achieves better quality of video by maximizing the entropy of the frame. Thus, PSO is able to correct even the random errors.

4.6   Results and Analysis

MATLAB (MATrix LABoratory) Software is used for simulation due to its high-performance for technical computing, visualization, and programming environment. The input is the error video with a frame rate of 30 frames per second with a frame size of 454 × 232. Most of the video formats including avi, mp4, and wmv can be used. The frame can be of png or jpeg format. Analysis for 30fps avi video is included here, even though a greater number of frames and different fps videos are analyzed during this research work. The errors are introduced in the Macro-blocks of the random frames by using third-party software. The different types of pixel-based errors are introduced and the results are evaluated for different size of block and random errors. The input video is converted into frames and stored in frame memory. The error is detected in this research work is using correlation between two frames. The error frames are detected by setting the threshold of 90% for correlation by trial and experimentation method. The detected error frame is concealed using PSO concealment techniques. The error frames are replaced with concealed frames which is saved the frame memory. Once all the frame are considered, then the frames are converted back to the video from the frame memory as concealed video. It is illustrated in Figure 4.6.

Objective quality analysis is done here based on the parameters such as MSE, PSNR (dB), entropy, SSIM, and time in seconds for error frame and concealed frame. Double Stimulus Continuous Quality Scale (DSCQS) method is used for Subjective Video Quality Analysis.

The different standard videos in avi format such as Foreman, Human, Xylophone, Cat, Singleball, Road, VipMen, VipTrain, Air, and a combination of two videos named Mixed are used here for obtaining the results. In this research, Human, Xylophone, and VipMen color videos are discussed in detailed for all cases along with 10 videos average result.

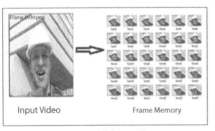

1. Input Video: Error Video to Frames

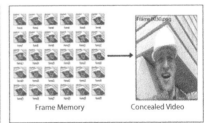

2. Error Detection

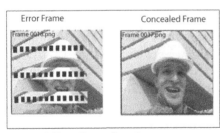

3. Error Concealment

4. Output Video

Figure 4.6 Proposed research results overview.

4.6.1   Single Frame With Block Error Analysis

First the single frame with more blocks of errors is introduced in all color videos. The results clearly indicate that the objective quality parameters such as PSNR, Entropy, and SSIM are improved in the proposed modified PSO-based VEC than FRA. Then, single frame with random errors is introduced in all color videos. Still, the proposed algorithm gives better results. Figure 4.7 shows the single frame Block errors for xylophone video for both frame replacement and modified PSO-based VEC algorithms (Tables 4.1 and 4.2).

Figure 4.7   Single frame block errors for xylophone video.

Table 4.1   Single frame block errors for xylophone video analysis [8, 13].

Parameters	Error frame (error blocks)	Concealed frame FRA	Concealed frame modified PSO
MSE	687.469	182.929	115.111
PSNR (dB)	19.758	25.507	27.519
Entropy	7.663	7.645	7.714
SSIM	0.886	0.939	0.943
Time (s)		3.951	6.414

Table 4.2   Single frame block errors average parameters analysis [8, 13].

Parameters (average)	Error frame	Concealed frame FRA	Concealed frame PSO
MSE	3202.007	524.414	256.848
PSNR (dB)	14.193	26.240	29.394
Entropy	6.961	7.212	7.440
SSIM	0.650	0.884	0.890
Time (s)		2.171	4.041

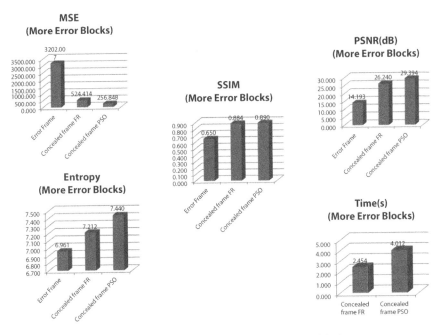

Figure 4.8 Average parameters graphical analysis of single frame block errors.

The different standard videos in avi format such as Foreman, Human, Xylophone, Cat, Singleball, Road, VipMen, VipTrain, Air, and a combination of two videos named Mixed are used here for obtaining the results.

The average parameter values such as PSNR, Entropy, and SSIM values are improved, and MSE is reduced in case of the proposed modified PSO-based VEC algorithm, even if time is increased a bit. Thus, better quality of concealed video is observed in the proposed modified PSO-based VEC algorithm. The graphical analysis of the same is shown in Figure 4.8.

4.6.2   Single Frame With Random Error Analysis

Figure 4.8 shows the human video with a single frame with random errors. The objective quality analysis using FRA and the proposed PSO is described in Table 4.3.

Table 4.4 is the average parameter analysis of single frame random errors. The average value of MSE is reduced in case of the proposed modified PSO-based VEC algorithm. The other average parameter values such as PSNR, Entropy, and SSIM values are improved. Thus, better

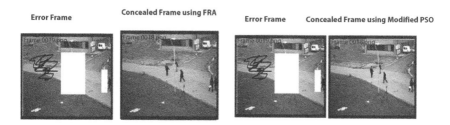

Figure 4.9 Single frame random errors for human video.

Table 4.3 Single frame random errors for human video analysis [8, 3].

Parameters	Error frame (random errors)	Concealed frame FRA	Concealed frame modified PSO
MSE	3108.179	399.454	46.528
PSNR (dB)	13.205	22.116	31.453
Entropy	7.232	7.790	7.851
SSIM	0.792	0.952	0.960
Time (s)		2.358	5.850

Table 4.4 Average parameter analysis of single frame random errors [8, 13].

Parameters (average)	Error frame	Concealed frame FRA	Concealed frame modified PSO
MSE	2973.541	211.493	100.969
PSNR (dB)	13.475	24.918	28.123
Entropy	7.227	7.635	7.700
SSIM	0.694	0.922	0.961
Time (s)		2.538	4.016

quality of concealed video is observed in the proposed modified PSO-based VEC algorithm.

The graphical analysis of the same is shown in Figure 4.10. The results indicate that proposed PSO-based algorithm gives a better result in terms of objective quality.

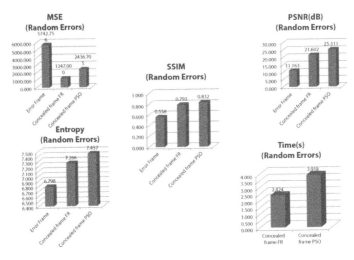

Figure 4.10 Average parameter graphical analysis of single frame random errors.

4.6.3   Multiple Frame Error Analysis

Figure 4.11 shows the human video with multiple frame random errors such as errors in frame number 5th, 18th, and 25th. These multiple frame errors are concealed using FRA and the proposed PSO-based VEC algorithms.

Objective quality analysis such as MSE, PSNR, Entropy, and SSIM are used for comparing the FRA and the proposed PSO-based VEC algorithms. Multiple frames with random errors are introduced in human color video. The proposed algorithm gives better objective quality results than FRA. Table 4.5 illustrates the objective quality analysis for the same.

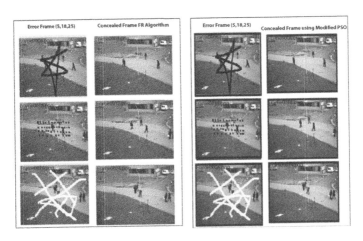

Figure 4.11 Multiple frame errors for human video.

Table 4.5 Multiple frame errors for human video quality analysis [8, 13].

Parameters	Frame 5			Frame 18			Frame 25		
	Error frame	Concealed FRA	Concealed PSO	Error frame	Concealed FRA	Concealed PSO	Error frame	Concealed FRA	Concealed PSO
MSE	2202.273	304.380	80.152	1224.941	226.939	72.125	3020.440	334.367	61.625
PSNR (dB)	14.702	23.297	29.092	17.250	24.572	29.550	13.330	22.889	30.233
Entropy	7.726	7.808	7.880	7.789	7.796	7.861	7.734	7.793	7.862
SSIM	0.850	0.958	0.931	0.886	0.963	0.946	0.770	0.955	0.951
Time (s)								7.189	8.642

After that, multiple frames with random errors are introduced in all color videos. Average parameter analysis is done as in Table 4.6. The proposed algorithm gives better objective quality results than FRA.

The objective parameters such as PSNR, Entropy, and SSIM values are improved and MSE is reduced in case of the proposed modified PSO-based VEC algorithm, even if time is increased. Thus, better quality of concealed video is observed in the proposed modified PSO-based VEC algorithm as in Figure 4.12.

Table 4.6 Average parameter analysis of multiple frame random errors [8, 13].

Parameters (average)	Error frame (random errors)	Concealed frame FRA	Concealed frame modified PSO
MSE	5139.433	660.864	307.487
PSNR (dB)	11.929	24.822	27.946
Entropy	6.910	7.161	7.393
SSIM	0.649	0.886	0.995
Time (s)		6.755	8.199

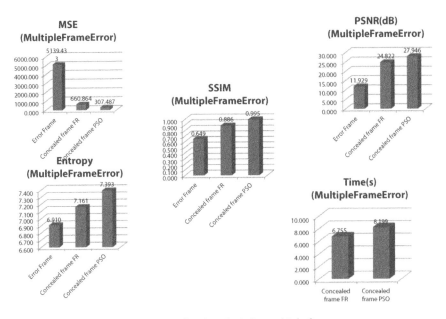

Figure 4.12 Average parameter graphical analysis for multiple frame errors.

4.6.4 Sequential Frame Error Analysis

Sequential frames with random errors are introduced in Xylophone color videos. That means, continuous frame errors such as error in frame number 17th, 18th, And 19th. These frame errors have to be concealed using FRA and the proposed PSO-based method as in Figure 4.13.

Sequential frames with random errors quality analysis for xylophone color videos is shown in Table 4.7.

Finally, sequential frames with random errors are introduced in all color videos. The objective quality such as Entropy is improved when average parameter values are considered. SSIM is increased in FRA. This is because, in sequential FRA VEC, the frames get repeated and show highest similarity.

The proposed PSO-based algorithm gives better objective quality than FR for sequential error frames such as 16, even though it takes a bit more time for execution. In FRA, frames 17 and 18 are improved because the same frame is repeated. The proposed modified PSO gives better objective quality in terms of more Entropy (3.23%). PSNR (3.21%) and SSIM (13.31%) are improved in FR concealment algorithm for sequential error frames because there is no difference between those frames. This indicates that subjective quality analysis should also be taken into account for final conclusion of the quality of video. The graphical analysis for the same is shown in Figure 4.14.

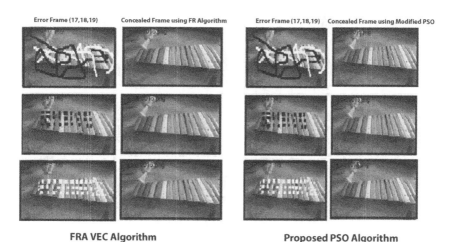

Figure 4.13 Sequential frame errors for xylophone video.

Table 4.7 Sequential frame errors for xylophone video [8, 13].

Parameters	Frame 17			Frame 18			Frame 19		
	Error frame	Concealed FRA	Concealed PSO	Error frame	Concealed FRA	Concealed PSO	Error frame	Concealed FRA	Concealed PSO
MSE	3674.968	102.959	102.016	4560.648	0.004	27.726	2019.260	0.004	8.206
PSNR (dB)	12.478	28.004	28.044	11.541	71.654	33.702	15.079	72.686	38.989
Entropy	7.614	7.646	7.715	7.675	7.646	7.688	7.652	7.646	7.699
SSIM	0.683	0.939	0.956	0.655	1.000	0.960	0.834	1.000	0.978
Time (s)								7.489	8.800

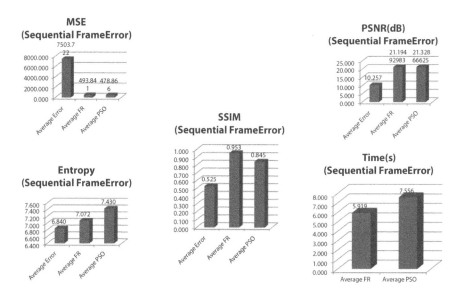

Figure 4.14 Graphical analysis of average parameters of sequential frame random errors.

Table 4.8 Average parameters analysis of sequential frame errors [8, 13].

Parameters	Average error	Average FRA	Average PSO
MSE	7,503.722	493.841	478.866
PSNR (dB)	10.257	21.19493	21.32867
Entropy	6.840	7.072	7.430
SSIM	0.525	0.953	0.845
Time (s)		5.919	7.556

The average parameters analysis of sequential frame errors are given in Table 4.8 [8, 13]. The proposed modified PSO gives improved objective quality analysis in-terms of PSNR (0.63%) and Entropy (5.06%). The SSIM is improved because in FR concealment algorithm, since there is no difference between those sequential frames. This clearly indicates that subjective quality analysis also should be taken into consideration for video quality analysis along with objective quality analysis.

4.6.5   Subjective Video Quality Analysis for Color Videos

DSCQS method is used for Subjective Video Quality Analysis. The error video, concealed video of FRA, and the proposed modified PSO for color are shown to 60 viewers, and rating is given in Table 4.9.

Table 4.9 Subjective video quality analysis [8, 13].

Rating	FRA	Modified PSO
Excellent	2	22
Good	26	35
Fair	28	3
Poor	4	0
Bad	0	0

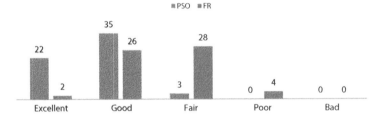

Figure 4.15 Subjective video quality analysis using DSCQS method [8, 13].

Figure 4.15 is the graphical analysis of the subjective quality analysis of Table 4.9 using DSCQS method.

4.6.6   Scene Change of Videos

Different videos in gray and color videos are used for comparing both FRA and the proposed modified PSO VEC algorithms in the above sections. The scene change indicates that scene is changed drastically from one frame to the other. Then, most of the VEC algorithm fails. However, the proposed PSO-based VEC algorithm still works and gives a better result than FR VEC algorithm.

Figure 4.16 shows the Single Frame Error Block Error video of VipMen Video with error frame and its previous frame, which are entirely different. This error frame is concealed using both FRA and the proposed PSO-based VEC algorithms. Table 4.10 shows its quality analysis. FRA cannot sustain for the scene change situations.

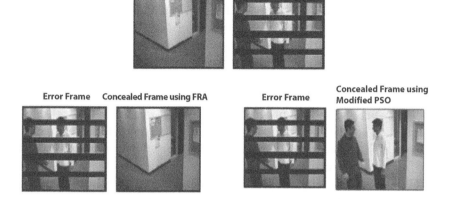

Figure 4.16 Single frame block error concealment for VipMen video.

Table 4.10 Single frame block error concealment for VipMen video.

Parameters	Error frame (error blocks)	Concealed frame FRA	Concealed frame modified PSO
MSE	5,928.730	2,112.718	83.274
PSNR (dB)	10.401	14.882	18.925
Entropy	7.288	7.721	7.788
SSIM	0.436	0.725	0.809
Time (s)		0.569	1.526

4.7   Conclusion

VEC is the technique used to hide errors in the video. This research paper investigated the Bio-inspired efficient optimization algorithm for VEC in spatio-temporal domain. PSO is one of the best bio-inspired algorithms. The proposed algorithm in this research works is modified PSO in spatio-temporal domain for concealing the video errors.

The major conclusions drawn from this research work are as follows. There are various standard videos such as Foreman, Human, Xylophone, Cat, Singleball, Road, VipMen, VipTrain, Air, and a combination of two videos named Mixed in which VEC was performed. There are various types of errors such as block errors and random errors in which the proposed modified PSO-based VEC algorithm was simulated using MATLAB.

The input is an error video, which is created using third-party software. The error frame is detected using correlation function which gives the similarity between two frames. Since the consecutive frames do not differ much, their similarity is found close to 0.9 (90%). Hence, this value is considered as threshold and the error frame is detected by comparing each of the frames with previous one.

Once the error frame is detected, then concealment algorithm is applied using PSO. Then, "video error concealment in spatio-temporal domain using bio-inspired algorithm PSO" is implemented and analyzed using different standard videos. The quality measuring parameters used here for videos are MSE, PSNR in dB, Entropy, SSIM, and time of execution of the algorithms in seconds.

Then, the proposed modified PSO is compared with FRA, as only both are able to correct random errors. PSO and FRA are compared for color videos. In both cases, block and random errors are introduced for single frame, multiple frames, and sequential frames. It can be concluded from the objective parameter analysis of PSO with FRA that MSE is reduced (55% to 14%) and PSNR (12% to 18%), Entropy (3% to 4%), and SSIM (2% to 8%) are improved even though it takes a bit more time (1 to 2 s more). The subjective quality parameter analysis also shows better video quality for PSO. Hence, the proposed modified PSO is a better algorithm in terms of video quality as compared to FRA for VEC in spatio-temporal domain.

The proposed modified PSO VEC is a better option for scene change videos than FRA. The quality analysis is based on the standards videos mentioned above. These videos are combination of still video, less motion videos, and scene change videos. If scene change videos or more movements in videos are only considered for quality analysis, then result will be much more improved.

The proposed modified PSO-based VEC algorithm first conceal the error frame using the spatio-temporal domain by considering the previous two frames of the error frame. After that, using the fitness function as Entropy, it finds the global best frame-based on PSO and replaces it in the frame memory. Hence, the proposed modified PSO-based VEC algorithm gives a better solution. Thus, from the result presented in this thesis, it can be concluded that the proposed modified PSO-based VEC algorithm in spatio-temporal domain is an efficient optimized algorithm for both block and random error concealment in both grayscale and color videos.

4.8   Future Scope

The direction for future research is briefly summarized below. VEC using PSO algorithm can also be implemented for real-time video streaming in TV receiver for correcting the transmission errors and thus improve the video quality. Presently, this algorithm is developed for database videos. The prototype for PSO-based VEC can be developed, and it can be directly used in various internet video streaming for concealing the error videos. Morphological (MP) operation is applied for VEC and able to implement the greyscale concealed videos. This can be further modified for color videos. VEC can also be implemented using Genetic Algorithm (GA) and Ant Colony Optimization (ACO) Algorithm, which may give a better optimized result. This can be implemented to correct errors in medical image processing such as MRI. In all the cases, the time complexity can be reduced by using GPUs.

References

1. Darwish, A., Bio-inspired computing: Algorithm's review, deep analysis, and the scope of applications. *Future Comput. Inf. J.*, 3, 2018Elsevier, 231–246, June 2018.
2. Rajani, P.K., Khaparde, A., Ghuge, A., Implementation and analysis of Video Error Concealment using Moment Invariants. *i-manager's J. Image Process.*, 4, 2, 1–9, April-June 2017 issue.
3. Chen, Y., Hu, Y., Au, O., Li, H., Chen, C.-W., Video error concealment using spatio-temporal boundary matching and partial differential equation. *IEEE Trans. Multimedia*, 10, 2–15, 02 2008.
4. Bovik, A., *The Essential Guide to Video Processing*, Academic Press an imprint of Elsevier, Austin, Texas, 2005.
5. Rajani, P.K., Khaparde, A., Ghuge, A., Implementation of Video Error Concealment Using Block Matching Algorithm, in: Published in *Springer SIST (Smart Innovation, Systems and Technologies) Series*, vol. 83, pp. 357–364, Springer, Cham, 2017.
6. Rajani, P.K. and Khaparde, A., Video Error Concealment Using Block Matching and Frequency Selective Extrapolation Algorithms. *2017 the Second International Workshop on Pattern Recognition (IWPR 2017)*, during May 1-3, 2017, held in Nayang Technological University, Singapore.

7. Rajani, P.K., Khaparde, A., Ghuge, A., Video Error Concealment using Moment Invariance. *2017 International Conference on Computing Communication Control and automation (ICCUBEA)*, Pune, India, held on 17th to 18th August 2017.

8. Rajani, P.K. and Khaparde, A., Comparison of Frequency Selective Extrapolation and Patch Matching Algorithm for Error Concealment in Spatial Domain, in: *the 8th International Conference on Signal Processing Systems (ICSPS 2016)*, from November 21-24, 2016, held at AUT University, Auckland, New Zealand.

9. Braik, M., Sheta, A., Ayesh, A., Image Enhancement Using Particle Swarm Optimization. *Proceedings of the World Congress on Engineering 2007*, July 2 - 4, 2007, vol. I, WCE 2007, London, U.K.

10. Chen, Y., Sun, X., Feng, W., Li, Z., Shipeng, L., Spatio-temporal Video Error Concealment using Priority-ranked Region-matching. *IEEE 0-7803-9134-9/05*, 2005.

11. Wang, Y. and Zhu, Q.-F., Error control and concealment for video communication: a review. *Proc. IEEE*, 86, 5, 974–997, May 1998.

12. P.K. Rajani and A. Khaparde, have filed a patent titled "Method and System for Video Error Concealment" with a patent application Number :TEMP/E-1/2887/1/2017-MUM on 11/08/2017, Published on 22/6/2018.

13. P.K. Rajani and A. Khaparde got registered a Copyright with Registration Number L-80232/2019, Diary No. 15923/2018-CO/L titled. Particle Swarm Optimization for Video Error Concealment, Literary/ Dramatic registered on 22/01/2019.

14. P.K. Rajani and A. Khaparde, got registered a Copyright with Registration Number L-76028/2018, Old Diary No. 4583/2018-co/L titled. Genetic algorithm for video error concealment using raspberry-pi, under Literary/ Dramatic registered on 28/04/2018.

5

Enhanced Image Fusion with Guided Filters

Nalini Jagtap[1*] and Sudeep D. Thepade[2]

[1]Dr. D. Y. Patil Institute of Engineering Management and Research,
Maharashtra, India
[2]Pimpri Chinchwad College of Engineering, Pune, India

Abstract

Elicitation of information from the data of several domains is called fusion. The process in which images are combined together from multiple sources is called image fusion. The image fusion method improves the fused image quality, making users easily detect, recognize, and identify targets. Image fusion is part of data fusion, where the input type is the image. The fusion process leads to an efficient way of utilizing a voluminous amount of image data. Fusion of multiple images combines several shots to get valuable information that was impossible through the single photo. It increases the interpretation of visual information from different sources of ideas. Further image fusion process leads to the accommodation of information from separate sensors to a single-image entity.

For our day-to-day real-life processes, high-quality information is achieved by process of image fusion, which gives all-in-one representation of the actual scenario. Multiple multi-focus fusion techniques are introduced for fusions. Still, in the end, some problems exist with those techniques such as poor visibility, extra ringing and blurring effects, and damage of focused regions information. Transform domain image fusion methods include admitted image decomposition, but they have drawbacks as computationally cumbersome. However, as discussed earlier, generation of artifact in the all in one fused image is a significant problem of these methods. Many researchers have proposed various ways to minimize these ringing and blurring effects but have not succeeded entirely yet. These ringing or blurring artifacts are noted in multiple transform domain multi-focus image fusion techniques in spite of excellent the fusion results. Transform domain methods have the inherent property of generating the blurring or ringing effects.

Corresponding author: nalinisjagtap@gmail.com

R. Arokia Priya, Anupama V Patil, Manisha Bhende, Anuradha Thakare and Sanjeev Wagh (eds.)
Object Detection by Stereo Vision Images, (99–110) © 2022 Scrivener Publishing LLC

The modified guided filtering approach called Novel Guided Filtering has overcome the blurring and ringing effects. The primary step in the modified guided filtering approach is to design the guidance image and generate the base and complex components based on the guidance image. The edge detection operator plays a significant role in deciding the guidance image. The focus map is generated using low-rank representation. This focus map is generated based on a detailed part of the original image. The built-in characteristic of removing ringing and blurring effects using LRR helps to develop artifact-free/noiseless detail images fusion. Guided filters were applied on a focus map. In the next step, the guided filter output is used to generate the resultant all in one fused image. In this case, ringing and blurring effects are removed using guided filters in resultant fused image.

Keywords: Medical image fusion, guided filters, low rank representation, image fusion

5.1   Introduction

For a medical imaging domain, modality serves a very high purpose. It has its aims, ambitions, goals, advantages, and disadvantages; one modality cannot superimpose another. Every modality has its purpose, and it is contained with high information too.

We have many advances in imaging techniques in the medical domain, leading to multi-modal medical images. Multiple medical modalities include MRI (magnetic resonance imaging), CT (computed tomography), and PET (positron emission tomography). These all modalities help to get more visual information about the bone and nervous system of human anatomy. Each of these modalities has its power and weakness, and a single modality may not serve its best to diagnose the disease.

Medical domain image fusion proposes the fusion for multi-modal images. Medical image fusion comprises multi-modal medical images to integrate the information to more depth of knowledge and helps in better decisions. The diversity of information from assorted modalities gives a better understanding of anatomy. It indeed turned to be the best information to doctors for diagnosis.

5.2   Related Works

High demands in medical image fusion have given researchers a new insight to work for the image fusion domain. Various techniques are proposed in medical domain image fusion for many years. In a broader sense, these multiple methods are categorised into spatial and transform domain techniques [1, 2].

Complete spatial information of an image is preserved in the spatial domain. Thus, it plays a significant role in retaining state-of-the-art information in multi-focus image fusion [3–5]. Spatial domain techniques are well used in multi-exposure [6, 7] image fusion. With many advantages of spatial domain techniques, it has limitations too. These methods suffer from merging the information from the exact location in source images.

In literature, it is observed that transform domain methods are frequently used for multi-modality medical domain image fusion [8, 9]. These transform domain methods mainly suffer from blurring effects.

Low-rank method with sparse dictionary learning techniques is proposed [10] for medical images consisting of noise. The method mainly focuses on sparse regularization and low rank for the dictionary learning method. It is used to elevate the detailed part of information. The sparse coefficients are coded with the Max-11 rule of fusion, making the fusion process more efficient. However, these sparse representation-based methods suffer from the computational cost, which is almost three times higher than other methods.

Among many other transform domain algorithms, the multiscale transform (MST) is the most popular algorithm. For the case of multi-modal medical domain image fusion, the methods, *viz.*, discrete wavelet transform (DWT) [11], curvelet-based transform (CVT) [12], shearlet based transform (ST) [13], non-subsampled with contourlet transform (NSCT) [14, 15], and non-subsampled with shearlet transform (NSST) [16, 17] are generally used methods. Non-subsampled with contourlet transform and non-subsampled with shearlet transform-based medical domain image fusion (multi-modal) techniques have gained popularity in many years. A common framework for multi-modal medical domain images is proposed by Liu *et al.* [15] for infrared-visible and multi-focus image fusion. The proposed methodology is based on the NSCT method obtained and outperforms in multi-modality medical domain image fusion.

Literature has proved that guided filter efficiently preserves the contents with less computational expense. The main advantage of guided filter is to delete the ringing and blurring effects which are commonly present with transform domain methods [18]. There are problems faced by guided filters as follows: (1) it fails to retain the local shape or edge data in input images, (2) poor visual information due to non-preservation of detailed information from the source image, and (3) versatile features are considered for extraction of information to avoid the damage of information; however, and lastly, these methods are time-taking techniques and hence not fruitful fusion solution.

All these limitations have risen for proposal of new methods in Guided Filters, namely, Novel Guided Filter (NGF). The main purpose of the NGF system is to retain the detail components information of input images and remove the blurring and ringing artefact effects from the resultant fused image efficiently. Even limitations like improper images texture and uneven illuminations can be removed using this proposed model.

5.3   Proposed Methodology

With the given limitation, the new proposed novel method for guided filters is used for medical image in multi-modality. Stepwise design is well used to experiment the novel method with aim of robustness and reliability.

5.3.1   System Model

The powerful and positive NGF method proposed in this paper uses the guided filtering technique with low rank representation (LRR) [19] to improvise the visual trait and objective measures by eliminating the ringing or blurring effects created by transform domain methods. The proposed NGF MIF technique system model is given in Figure 5.1. The symbols, with their meanings, are mentioned in Table 5.1.

Figure 5.1 depicts about the Novel Guided Filter (NGF) method. The input for the proposed method is two different modality images from medical domain, namely, I1 and I2. These input images are decomposed using Guided Filter. As demonstrated in the proposed model, initially, edge information is preserved using the edge detector operator, and then, these input images are fed to guided filter to get base components and detail components. The EDO helps in preserving information which may get loss due to

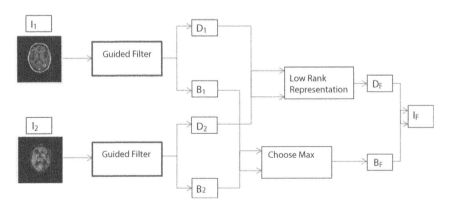

Figure 5.1 Proposed NGF MIF system model.

Table 5.1 Table of NGF system symbols and meanings.

Symbols	Significance
I_1	Focus image 1
I_2	Focus image 2
B_1	The base component of input image I_1
B_2	The base component of input image I_2
D_1	Detailed component of input image I_1
D_2	Detailed component of input image I_2
B_f	Fused base image
D_f	Fused detail image
I_f	Final fused image

blurring effect after fusion. Thus, here, we are using guided filters simply as decomposition filters. The detailed components are more important for fusion purpose, as they contain the large scale of information.

LRR method is applied on the detailed components. The main benefit of this LRR method is to resist the noise. The given LRR technique is sturdy to outliers. On the base components simple, computationally light choose max method is practiced to get the base resultant fused image.

The important goal in adopting the different methods on base and details components is to preserve the important information and discard the out of focus information from the input image.

The base components are specifically with large-scale intensity variations, so they are not prone to loss of information and ringing/blurring effects. Hence, just fusing with choose max method is sufficient for base components.

Minute details are present in the detail components of the source image, and thus, the fusion of these elements needs more care so that the condition of the resultant fused image is not compromised.

After using LRR method on detail components, noise is removed from the input image. This fused detail component and fused base components is again refined with the guidance image, which has been generated from the edge detector operator initially to prevent from the blurring and ringing effect. Finally, resultant fused image is created by combining the fused detail and base components.

5.3.2   Steps of the Proposed Methodology

The steps of NGF are summarized below:

1. If RGB image is an input, then it will be converted into grayscale.
2. On the given image the edge detector method is applied to generate guidance image.
3. On every medical input image the Guided Filter is applied.
4. The LRR method is applied on the detailed components of input images to get fused detail image.
5. Choose max strategy is applied for fusion of base components to get the fuse base component.
6. Using guidance image, the fused components are polished.
7. The fusion of fused detail and fused base components generates the final image.

5.4   Experimental Results

Performance measures are used to measure the Image fusion quality with standards. Table 5.2 depicts the decomposition of source images with guided filter. In our experiments objective evaluation metrics used are RMSE (Root Mean Square Error) (Table 5.3, Figure 5.2), EN (entropy) (Table 5.4, Figure 5.3), PSNR (Peak Signal-to-Noise Ratio) (Table 5.5, Figure 5.4), and QAB/F metric (Table 5.6, Figure 5.5), while comparing the proposed methodology (NGF) with three other states-of-the-art methods. The different techniques being evaluated for comparison are guided filtering with detection of focus region [20], DTCWTGF (Dual-Tree Complex Wavelet Transform with Guided Filter) [21], and MIFDWT (MIF using DWT) [22].

5.4.1   Entropy

Content of the information from the image is well expressed with Entropy (EN). Amount of intelligence in the fused image is given with EN. Hence, better quality of fused image is depicted with the higher the value of EN.

NGF consistently exceeds the other techniques in terms of the amount of information held by the fused image.

5.4.2   Peak Signal-to-Noise Ratio

One measure is based on the mean square error is a PSNR. The resultant image is closer to the original image if we have higher PSNR or SNR value in the fused image.

The NGF once again records the highest results with a large margin.

Table 5.2 Sample of guided filter decomposition of images.

	I_1	I_2
Generated guidance image		
Base component		
Detail component		

Table 5.3 RMSE analysis for medical image pairs.

Dataset	GFDF	DTCWTGF	MIFDWT	NGF
Set 1	0.1543	0.1455	0.1244	0.1155
Set 2	0.1454	0.1533	0.1354	0.1023
Set 3	0.1532	0.1455	0.1432	0.1133
Set 4	0.1443	0.1566	0.1354	0.1123

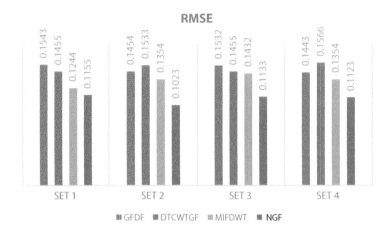

Figure 5.2 Comparison of RMSE values of different methodologies.

Table 5.4 Entropy analysis for medical image pairs.

Dataset	GFDF	DTCWTGF	MIFDWT	NGF
Set 1	0.5677	0.5978	0.5867	0.6055
Set 2	0.5732	0.5921	0.5789	0.6143
Set 3	0.5867	0.5832	0.5667	0.6123
Set 4	0.5489	0.5587	0.5786	0.6034

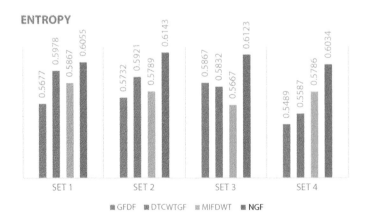

Figure 5.3 Comparison of entropy values of different methodologies.

Table 5.5 PSNR analysis for medical image pairs.

Dataset	GFDF	DTCWTGF	MIFDWT	NGF
Set 1	52.30	48.79	53.59	57.50
Set 2	53.95	49.04	54.67	56.55
Set 3	51.56	49.57	53.55	57.42
Set 4	50.39	47.36	53.46	56.37

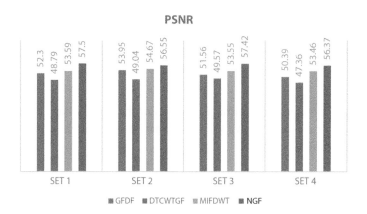

Figure 5.4 Comparison of PSNR values of different methodologies.

Table 5.6 QAB/F analysis for medical image pairs.

Dataset	GFDF	DTCWTGF	MIFDWT	NGF
Set 1	0.6642	0.5756	0.5827	0.7520
Set 2	0.7342	0.5645	0.4987	0.7199
Set 3	0.6656	0.5854	0.4262	0.7496
Set 4	0.7347	0.4876	0.4366	0.7299

5.4.3 Root Mean Square Error

Root Mean Square Error (RMSE) is an image quality metric technique that calculates the frequency of errors in the final resultant image. The trait of the image is inversely proportional to its RMSE value.

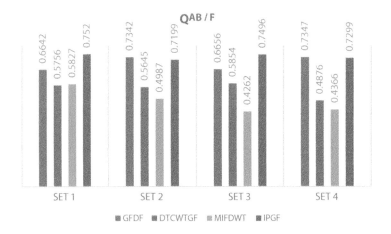

Figure 5.5 Comparison of QAB/F values of different methodologies.

The RMSE values of the images show that the fused image constructed using NGF consistently have the least amount of errors compared to the other methodologies.

5.4.3.1   QAB/F

Sobel edge detection operator is used to measure edge information from input image and resultant fused image in QAB/F metric. When we get the higher values of QAB/F metric, it says about complete conversion of information that is converted from the source image to resultant image, and the edge information is also excellently preserved.

The given methodology is successful for retaining a high quantity of edge information from the input images. The QAB/F values for NGF show that it performs at par with GFDF and tends to be more reliable when tested on different datasets.

It is noted that the given methodology (NGF) outperforms the current state-of-the-art techniques and provides more insight into the research trends for multi-modal medical domain image fusion.

5.5   Conclusion

The NGF approach has been given in the paper. The given methodology is based on guided filter technique that decomposed the input medical image into base and detail components. These components are further fused with different techniques to get the fused image with enhance quality. The burring and ringing effects are overcome with the guidance image, which is initially preserved using the edge detector operator. Comparing with state-of-the-art method, the proposed NGF method has outperformed in context with stated performance measures. In the future, we suggest to apply the method for VS and IR imaging.

References

1. Qi, G., Wang, J., Zhang, Q., Zeng, F., Zhu, Z., An integrated dictionary learning entropy-based medical image fusion framework. *Future Internet*, 9, 4, 61, 2017.
2. Wang, K., Qi, G., Zhu, Z., Chai, Y., A novel geometric dictionary construction approach for sparse representation based image fusion. *Entropy*, 19, 7, 306, 2017.
3. Li, H., Li, X., Yu, Z., Mao, C., Multifocus image fusion by combining with mixed-order structure tensors and multiscale neighbourhood. *Inf. Sci.*, 349_350, 25–49, Jul. 2016.
4. Li, H., Qiu, H., Yu, Z., Li, B., Multifocus image fusion via fixed window technique of multiscale images and non-local means filtering. *Signal Process.*, 138, 71–85, Sep. 2017.
5. Zhu, Z., Qi, G., Chai, Y., Chen, Y., A novel multi-focus image fusion method based on stochastic coordinate coding and local density peaks clustering. *Future Internet*, 8, 53, 2016.
6. Ma, K., Duanmu, Z., Yeganeh, H., Wang, Z., Multi-exposure image fusion by optimizing a structural similarity index. *IEEE Trans. Comput. Imag.*, 4, 1, 60–72, Mar. 2018.
7. Ma, K., Li, H., Yong, H., Wang, Z., Meng, D., Zhang, L., Robust multi-exposure image fusion: A structural patch decomposition approach. *IEEE Trans. Image Process.*, 26, 5, 2519–2532, May 2017.
8. Zhu, Z., Chai, Y., Yin, H., Li, Y., Liu, Z., A novel dictionary learning approach for multi-modality medical image fusion. *Neurocomputing*, 214, 471_482, Nov. 2016.
9. Zhu, Z., Yin, H., Chai, Y., Li, Y., Qi, G., A novel multi-modality image fusion method based on image decomposition and sparse representation. *Inf. Sci.*, 432, 516_529, Mar. 2018.
10. Li, H., He, X., Tao, D., Tang, Y., Wang, R., Joint medical image fusion, denoising and enhancement via discriminative low-rank sparse dictionaries learning. *Pattern Recognit.*, 79, 130_146, Jul. 2018.

11. Manchanda, M. and Sharma, R., An improved multimodal medical image fusion algorithm based on fuzzy transform. . *Vis. Commun. Image Represent.*, 51, 7694, Feb. 2018.

12. Baghaie, A., Schnell, S., Bakhshinejad, A., Fathi, M.F., D'Souza, R.M., Rayz, V.L., Curvelet transform-based volume fusion for correcting signal loss artifacts in time-of-flight magnetic resonance angiography data. *Comput. Biol. Med.*, 99, 142–153, Jun. 2018.

13. Liu, X., Zhou, Y., Wang, J., Image fusion based on shearlet transform and regional features. *AEUE-Int. J. Electron. Commun.*, 68, 6, 471_477, 2014.

14. Li, Y., Sun, Y., Huang, X., Qi, G., Zheng, M., Zhu, Z., An image fusion method based on sparse representation and sum modified Laplacian in NSCT domain. *Entropy*, 20, 7, 522, 2018.

15. Liu, Y., Liu, S., Wang, Z., A general framework for image fusion based on multi-scale transform and sparse representation. *Inf. Fusion*, 24, 147–164, Jul. 2015.

16. Qi, G., Zhang, Q., Zeng, F., Wang, J., Zhu, Z., Multi-focus image fusion via morphological similarity-based dictionary construction and sparse representation. *CAAI Trans. Intell. Technol.*, 3, 11, 83–94, Jun. 2018.

17. Yin, M., Liu, X., Liu, Y., Chen, X., *"Medical image fusion with parameter-adaptive pulse coupled neural network in nonsubsampled shearlet transform domain" IEEE Trans*, pp. 49–64, Instrum. Meas., vol. 68, no. 1, Jan. 2018.

18. Zhang, B.H., Lu, X.Q., Pei, H.Q., Liu, H., Zhao, Y., Zhou, W.T., multi-focus image fusion algorithm based on focused region extraction. *Neurocomputing.*, 174, 733–748, 2017.

19. Li, H., Wu, X.-J., Durrani, T., Multi-focus Noisy Image Fusion using Low-Rank Representation, *CoRR*, arXiv preprint arXiv: 1804.09325, 2018.

20. Qiu, X., Li, M., Zhang, L., Yuan, X., Guided filter-based multi-focus image fusion through focus region detection. *Signal Process.: Image Commun.*, 72, 35⁻46, March 2019.

21. Geng, P. and Liu, J., An effective multifocus image fusion method using guided filter. Industrial Robot. *Int. J. Robot. Res. Appl.*, 46, 3, 369⁻376, 2019.

22. Ch, M.M.I., Riaz, M.M., Iltaf, N. *et al.*, A multifocus image fusion using high-level DWT components and guided filter. *Multimed Tools Appl.*, 79, 12817–12828, 2020, https://doi.org/10.1007/s11042-020-08661-8.

6

Deepfake Detection Using LSTM-Based Neural Network

Tejaswini Yesugade¹, Shrikant Kokate², Sarjana Patil¹*, Ritik Varma¹ and Sejal Pawar¹

¹Computer Department, Pimpri Chinchwad College of Engineering, Pune, India
²Department of Computer Engineering, Pimpri Chinchwad College of Engineering, Pune, India

Abstract

In this rapid growth of social media, new developments in deep generative network have improve quality of creating more realistic fake videos; such videos are called as deepfake video. Such deepfake videos are used in politics to create political distress, for blackmail and for terrorism events. In order to reduce harm that can be done using such methods and prevent spread of such fake images or videos, we proposed a method that can detect such deepfake. In this paper, we proposed a new method to detect AI-generated fakeIvideos using algorithm such as CNN and LSTM. Our method will detect deepfake by using ResNext50 and LSTM algorithms, which gives accuracy around 88%.

Keywords: Deepfake detection, CNN, LSTM, ResNext50, data loader

6.1 Introduction

Because of the development in camera technology, easy availability of mobile phones, and increase in use of internet, social media, and video sharing apps, creating and editing a video become easier than ever [1]. Tampering videos and manipulating the information become convenient nowadays because of evaluation in technologies such as AI and deep learning.

Deepfake is a technique for human image synthes is based on artificial intelligence. Deepfakes are created by combining and superimposing

*Corresponding author: sarjanapatil2912@gmail.com

R. Arokia Priya, Anupama V Patil, Manisha Bhende, Anuradha Thakare and Sanjeev Wagh (eds.)
Object Detection by Stereo Vision Images, (111–120) © 2022 Scrivener Publishing LLC

existing images and videos on to source image or videos using deep learning techniques known as generative adversarial network. Such deepfake videos or images can be used intentionally to provide misinformation or damage an image of person, and such videos can also be used in politics to create political distress, for blackmailing someone and for terrorism events [2, 8, 9]. This makes it important to detect deepfake so that we avoid spreading of misinformation with the help of different technologies to prevent spread of such harmful information and to reduce harm that can be done by using such deepfake videos. To detect such deepfake, algorithms such as CNN and LSTM are used [2, 4]. To detect fake videos, we studied about creation of deepfake and the tools to generate fake videos such as FaceSawp and algorithms for deepfake generation such as GAN [1] and autoencoder [1, 3, 5]. For this model, we are using pretrained sequential model ResNext50 followed by LSTM to detect deepfake.

6.2   Related Work

6.2.1   Deepfake Generation

Tools used to generate deepfake are FaceSawp, FaceIt, DeepFacelab, Deepfake Capsule GAN, and Large resolution facemasked. These tools use generative adversarial network (GAN) and autoencoder algorithm to create deepfake. These tools use autoencoder-decoder technique; the autoencoder removes the hidden features of the face images and decoder used re-create facial images; it splits video into frame and passes it to autoencoder that replaces the target image on source image and the decoder generates the manipulated deepfake video; furthermore, quality is improved by removing left over traces, making the deepfake videos very realistic, but there are some leftover traces that are not visible to naked eye. Figure 6.1 shows how encoder and decoder are used to generate deepfake.

6.2.2   LSTM and CNN

It consists of iseveral blocks of iconv layers with an LSTM head. Each layer preceding an LSTM is time distributed, meaning that it was applied to every time step in an input example.

Input to the network was four-dimensional (4D), with the fourth dimension corresponding to time.

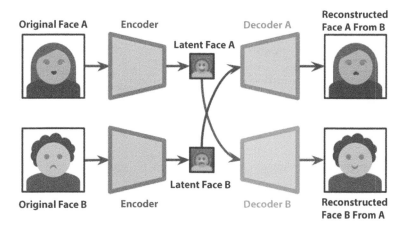

Figure 6.1 A deepfake creation model utilizing two encoder-decoder sets.

6.3   Existing System

6.3.1   AI-Generated Fake Face Videos by Detecting Eye Blinking

Here, the focus is on the detection of the lack of eye blinking. As it is a physiological sign that is not properly captured while generating deepfake videos, the inconsistence and time gaps are introduce [1]. Here, CNN is used for feature extraction and frequency counter is applied in state prediction. This technique is only dependent on eye region; it cannot be effective in case of less resolution videos. Method fully depends on eye landmarks, which is not reliable in many cases.

6.3.2   Detection Using Inconsistence in Head Pose

In this method of head pose, the central region of the face is extracted and estimation of real and fake based on the classification done by the SVM classifier [5]. The drawback of this method is that the training of SVM model requires the real set, which is also very difficult to provide; hence, the performance decreases. Only central region can be analyzed, and SVM classifier is restricted.

6.3.3   Exploiting Visual Artifacts

When deepfake videos are created using software like CelebA, ProGAN, and Glow [6], this technique compares the color of eyes of the person in

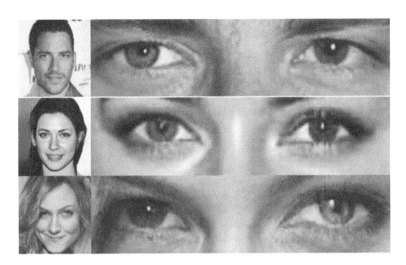

Figure 6.2 Mismatched eye color [7].

the target video. Hence, mismatched eye colors are detected (Figure 6.2), and video is labeled as deepfake [7]. Limitation to this technique is that the eyes of person in target should be open. In addition, in today's technology, the mismatched eye color can be corrected in post-processing using Photoshop. Hence, this technique is less effective.

6.4   Proposed System

6.4.1   Dataset

The total number of real and fake videos used is 23,186. The dataset is taken from Kaggle deepfake detection challenge; it consists of three files: test_videos, train_sample_videos, and sample_submission.csv. The dataset contains original videos of 50% and fake videos of 50%. We split dataset into 70% train data and 30% test data (https://www.kaggle.com/c/deepfake-detection-challenge)

6.4.2   Preprocessing

First, we split video into number of frames using frame extraction technique; then, we perform face recognition and crop the frame with detected face only the facial outline is considered. To maintain similarity in the number of frames, the mean of set video data is calculated, and face dataset

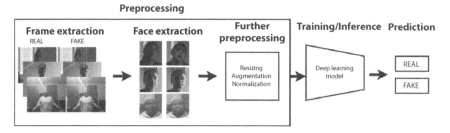

Figure 6.3 Preprocessing module.

is created containing frames that match the mean. A faceless frame in it is ignored during the preprocessing.

Here, the video of 10 s at 30 frames/s that is total of 300 frames is created. Three hundred frames cannot be processed due to heavy computing requirements, so 150 frames as threshold value is considered based on GPU system. We have saved first 150 frames in sequential manner for LSTM. The new video is having 30 FPS (Frames Per Second) with resolution of 112×112 (refer Figure 6.3).

6.4.3   Model

We use sequential model that consists of ResNext50 followed by LSTM.

The data loader loads the pre-processed face-cropped videos that are generated in preprocessing along with CSV and then splits the video into 70% train and 30% test.

For training deep neural network in optimized way, we used ResNext50-32 X 4D. It is a pretrained model for feature extraction. It has 50 layers with 32 nodes in each layer and is 4D model. It is capable of learning 25×10^6 parameters.

The output of ResNext model after the pooling layer is the feature vector, which goes to sequential layer. The sequential layer feeds input to LSTM layer. We use one LSTM layer with 2,048 latent dimensions and 2,048 hidden layer along with chance of dropout of 0.4.

The output of LSTM is processed by linear layer and adaptive average pooling layer. Then, the final output is given by SoftMax layer.

Figure 6.4 is flow chart of the model implemented. Step 1 is loading dataset consisting of fake and real videos. Then, preprocessing is applied on the dataset, and new dataset is created. The preprocessed dataset is then divided in two parts: train and test. Then, both datasets are loaded

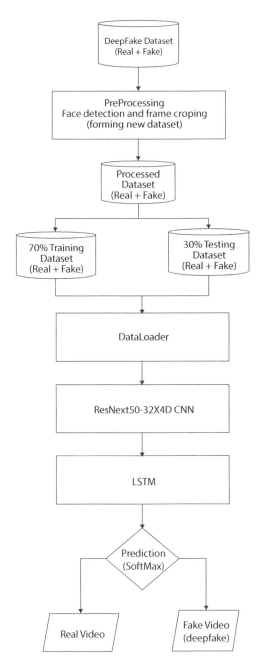

Figure 6.4 Flowchart of model.

into ResNext50-32x4D CNN model after that LSTM layer is applied, which then, after application of SoftMax layer, gives output if video is deepfake or not.

6.5 Results

The output of model is going to be whether the video is the fake or real video along with the accuracy of model (Figure 6.5).

Where:

Real: 1, Fake: 0.

The Calculated Accuracy of model is **88.54838709677419.**

Confusion matrix: [[127 29] [42 422]]

Figure 6.6 shows accuracy vs. epochs where the total number of epochs is 20. The training accuracy increases with each epoch and goes up to 88.54%.

Figure 6.7 shows loss vs. epochs where the loss decreases with each epoch and reaches min of 11.46%.

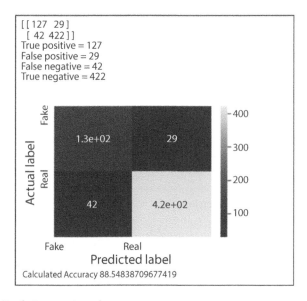

Figure 6.5 Confusion matrix and accuracy.

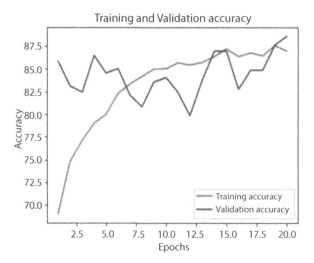

Figure 6.6 Training and validation accuracy.

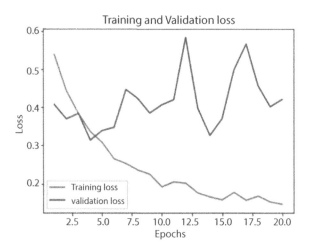

Figure 6.7 Training and validation loss.

Exposing AI-generated fake face videos by detecting eye blinking method gives accuracy of 79%, but the method is only dependent on eyes region, and temporal knowledge of previous state is not considered [1]. Deepfake video detection using recurrent neural networks method gives accuracy of 97%, but the method is limited to 2-s videos with 40 frames for videos sampled at 24 frames per second only, so the effective accuracy is 0.97 at rate of 24 fps [2].

6.6   Limitations

For our proposed model, we have taken dataset with limited videos, in which for prediction it will consider only first 150 frames. For prediction, the model will consider videos that will detect the face and other videos will be excluded. For our model, parallel processing is used for detection of deepfake so the proper GPU will be required. Because of these videos, high processing power computers will be required to detect whether the video is fake or not on large amount of dataset.

6.7   Application

YouTube: YouTube is most popular source of video-based information. Here, deepfake detection can be used for verification of video.

Military (Intelligence Bureau): Military has very classified information that can be manipulated and tampered; these techniques can be used to detect and refine information.

6.8   Conclusion

In this chapter, we present a method to detect deepfake videos. Our method will detect deepfake by detecting inconsistency in the facial area. In our model, we use sequential model that consists of ResNext50 followed by LSTM. We evaluated our model on dataset to detect whether the video is deepfake video or not; the result for this evaluation gives the highest accuracy.

As the technology keeps developing in AI, we will continue to improve our model accordingly. In the future, we would like to improve robustness of our proposed method with respect to the different dataset. We are currently using pretrained model for our proposed model, but, for more effective detection, we would like to study different dedicated network structure.

References

1. Li, Y., Chang, M.C., Lyu, S., In Ictu Oculi: Exposing AI Generated Fake Face Videos by Detecting Eye Blinking, in: *IEEE International Workshop on Information Forensics and Security (WIFS)*, 2018.

2. Deepfake Video Detection Using Recurrent Neural Networks. *2018 15th IEEE International Conference on Advanced Video and Signal Based Surveillance (AVSS)*, 2018.11.27-2018.11.30, IEEE, Auckland, New Zealand.

3. Li, Y. and Lyu, S., Exposing Deep Fake Videos by Detecting Face warping Artifact. *Computer Vision and Pattern Recognition*, 2018, arXiv preprint arXiv:1811.00656.

4. Fast Face-Swap Using Convolutional Neural Networks Networks. *2017 IEEE International Conference on Computer Vision (ICCV)*, 2017.10.22-2017.10.29, IEEE, Venice.

5. Exposing Deep Fakes Using Inconsistent Head Poses. *ICASSP 2019 IEEE International Conference on Acoustics, Speech and Signal Processing (ICASSP)*, 2019.5.122019.5.17, IEEE, Brighton, United Kingdom.

6. A Comparative Evaluation of Local Feature Descriptors for Deepfakes Detection. *2019 IEEE Symposium on Technologies for Homeland Security*, IEEE, USA.

7. Exploiting Visual Artifacts to Expose Deepfakes and Face Manipulations. *2019 IEEE Winter Applications of Computer Vision Workshops (WACVW)*, 2019.1.7-2019.1.11, IEEE, Waikoloa Village, HI, USA.

8. SWAPPED! Digital face presentation attack detection via weighted local magnitude pattern. *2017 IEEE International Joint Conference on Biometrics (IJCB)*, 2017.10.1-2017.10.4, IEEE, Denver, CO, USA.

9. Fake Information and News Detection using Deep Learning. *2018 15th IEEE International Conference on Advanced Video and Signal Based Surveillance (AVSS)*, 2018.11.27- 2018.11.30, IEEE, Auckland, New Zealand.

7

Classification of Fetal Brain Abnormalities with MRI Images: A Survey

Kavita Shinde* and Anuradha Thakare

Pimpri Chinchwad College of Engineering, Savitribai Phule Pune University, Pune, India

Abstract

Magnetic resonance imaging of fetuses allows doctors to observe brain abnormalities early on. Therefore, it is necessary to determine and categorize the fetal brain anomalies at an earlier, because nearly three in thousand mothers have fetuses with an abnormal brain. The literature survey finds less work for the classification of the abnormal fetal brain and is based on conventional methods of machine learning (ML), while more related work is done for the segmentation and feature extraction by using different techniques. In this article, we reviewed the different ML techniques used for complete MRI processing chain, starting with image acquisition to its classification. We provide an overview of current progress and challenges related with ML techniques used in image processing and analysis of brain MR image. In this review, we describe the different proposed methods for segmentation, as well as the MRI classification of the fetal brain and discuss their main contributions, while existing papers focused only on the evaluation of segmentation methods and do not include classification methods. We are concluding this review with a discussion of the limits of the ML techniques proposed to determine and classify the fetal brain diseases and their possible future.

Keywords: Machine learning classifier, segmentation, fetal brain, image processing, dimensionality reduction, deep learning, convolutional neural network

7.1 Introduction

Nowadays, the advancement in medical technologies provides researchers large amount of biological data such as medical images, protein structure, and genomic data. The magnetic resonance imaging (MRI) is widely used for

---

*Corresponding author: kavita.kolpe.kk@gmail.com

R. Arokia Priya, Anupama V Patil, Manisha Bhende, Anuradha Thakare and Sanjeev Wagh (eds.)
Object Detection by Stereo Vision Images, (121–146) © 2022 Scrivener Publishing LLC

the study and for the research of brain disease. Different machine learning (ML) models are used by researchers to improve quality of diagnosis and treatment planning for fetal brain abnormality using fetal brain MRI dataset [1]. In this article, the authors reviewed the different ML techniques used for complete fetal brain MRI processing chain, starting with image acquisition to its classification. This chapter gives an overview of current progress and challenges related with ML techniques used in image processing and analysis of fetal brain MR image. In recent years, it is observed that MRI has considerable attention for the assessment of fetal brain abnormality as its application gives detailed characterization of fetal brain development and any kind of abnormal growth or when in prenatal ultrasound (US) abnormality has been detected. This can be useful to manage high-risk pregnancies and to improve the treatment planning. Fetal brain MRI is clinically done to assess the fetal brain disorders where anomalies are find out in prenatal US; also, it evaluates the increased risk of neurodevelopmental disorder for fetuses who have normal brain. Early detection of fetal brain abnormality is very important since up to 0.3% of pregnant women have fetuses with an abnormal brain. Fetal MRI gives detailed structural information about the fetal brain, as it grants high contrast resolution for the brain tissues [2]. Radiologists examine the fetal brain abnormalities on the basis of visual explanation of the presence of a brain abnormality in the fetal brain MRI. However, in case of large volume of brain MRI, which is to be analyzed, there is the chance of misclassification. Another chance of some unacceptable analysis is a direct result of the affectability of the human vision decreases with the quantity of cases. Likewise, it is a tedious method [3]. Thus, there is a requirement for a proficient framework for investigation and categorization of fetal brain abnormalities. In the 20th century, many researchers and experts derived automated methods for fetal brain MRI segmentation and classification using fetal brain MRI. To overcome the limitations or drawbacks of conventional methods, ML algorithms have been improved recently. Segmentation of fetal brain MRI using ML methods is now penetrating complete field of medical imaging. The mail goal of this research study is to give a complete review of different methods used for brain segmentation and to classify the fetal brain. Existing current review by Makropoulos [4] presented different techniques developed for segmentation of the fetal and prenatal brain. In this paper, the authors provided a comprehensive assessment for fetal segmentation and classification. This chapter examines the different ML techniques used for complete MRI processing chain, starting with image acquisition, feature extraction, image retrieval, segmentation and classification. We provide an overview of current progress and some challenges related with ML techniques used in image processing and analysis of brain MR image.

The chapter is structured as follows: comparative analysis and related work for fetal brain abnormality is detailed in Section 7.2. An evaluation of the related research works is explained in Section 7.3. The general framework for the classification of fetal brain abnormalities is discussed in Section 7.4. This framework has five stages: a) image preprocessing, b) brain extraction/ segmentation, c) feature extraction, d) feature reduction, and e) classification. After this, in Section 7.5 presented the different performance metrics used in research for analysis of Fetal Brain anomalies. The challenges of fetal brain MRI analysis are discussed in Section 7.6. In Section 7.7, we summarize the paper and discussed various promising future directions in this domain.

7.2   Related Work

Many researchers have been working on the problem of fetal brain disorder using different datasets of fetal brain MRI. According to the literature survey, more related work is done for fetal brain MRI segmentation and feature extraction by using different techniques. In this phase, the authors examine the various reported works on detection and classification of fetal brain disorders by using various ML techniques. In this paper [1], the proposed method automatically segments fetal brain by using center of gravity. This method first identifies location of fetal in from two-dimensional (2D) MRI by the center of gravity method and finds the Region of Interest (ROI) by drawing circle around an input image. Then, image thresholding and image morphology operations are performed for the brain image extraction from ROI. The results obtained by this segmentation method for fetal brain from MRI agree well with the gold standard. In literature [2], the pipeline process is proposed to detect the brain abnormality at an early stage. This process consists of five phases: brain extraction/segmentation from whole image, image enrichment, extraction of important features, and classification of image into classes using ML classifiers. This method detects and classifies various abnormalities with the large range of GA (gestational ages) from 16 weeks to 39 weeks. This pipeline method is predicting different type of abnormalities and not only one. In this method, four ML classifiers like support vector machine (SVM), K-nearest neighbor (KNN), linear discriminant analysis (LDA), and ESD are used for fetal brain MRI classification. In literature [5], automatic segmentation method is proposed to segment brain structure from fetal brain MRI. The proposed system uses the T2 fetal brain MRI. The proposed segmentation pipeline method consists of image enhancement, region growing, and hole-filling methods. This method successfully segments the brain part which ROI from fetal brain image and gives good results. In literature [6], a computer-automated system for the segmentation of brain part from rest of the image is proposed in which 2D U-net and a voxelwise convolutional neural network (CNN) framework is used to segment the sections of the fetal brain in 2D brain MRI slices in real time. The results obtained for automatic segmentation method give high accuracy than that of semi-automatic segmentation methods. In case of fetal brain MRI, there are various promising methods proposed for detection and classification of brain abnormality. The literature [7] proposed a system which consists of active contour and deep learning (DL) methods for the detection of fetal brain abnormality. The experimental results of proposed methods for segmentation and classification of fetal brain abnormalities by using CNN algorithm provides less number of errors in abnormality prediction. In literature [8], the authors reviews existing artificial intelligence–based computer-automated diagnosis (CAD) system is explored for the diagnosis of different neuro-developmental disorders. These CAD systems assist doctors to analyze and interpret medical images and physiological signals effectively. In paper [9], an automated classification method is explored, which gives more robust and efficient results. This system automatically classifies the abnormal brain tissues into any one kind of specified abnormal class, and also this system auto-classify the abnormal slices into tumorous and non-tumorous one. In literature [10], the novel classification model is used to deal with intensity variance artifacts by using data augmentation method for the training data with synthesized intensity variance antiquity that found helpful for the result improvement in the segmentation process. However, the system does not give desired results with the limited dataset. The literature [11] proposed a system which consists of active contour and DL techniques for the identification of fetal brain abnormality. The experimental results of proposed methods for segmentation and classification of fetal brain abnormalities by using CNN algorithm provide less number of errors in abnormality prediction. This proposed system automatically segments the fetal brain by using an emerging spatio-temporal group-wise segmentation method. Manual segmentation of developing brain is very challenging task. In paper [12], DCCN algorithm based on 2D U-net and auto context, an automated segmentation technique is proposed segments the brain part in real time. CNN algorithm is used for automatic segmentation of fetal brain MRI, which segments the brain image into seven brain tissue classes.

We classify the survey of each literature according to the different techniques used, strengths, limitations, or future work and these are presented in the table. Table 7.1 summarizes comparative analysis of literature that we have examined.

Table 7.1 Comparative analysis of different techniques used for classification of fetal brain abnormalities.

Sr. no.	Title and authors	Publication and year	Techniques/ algorithms used	Strength	Limitations/future work
1	Somasundaram et al. [1]	IEEE, 2016	Center of gravity, image processing	The proposed method automatically localizes the fetal head and segments fetal brain from 2D slices of magnetic resonance imaging	
2	Somasundaram et al. [5]	The Imaging Science Journal, 2017	Automatic image segmentation, contrast enhancement, region growing, hole filling	The results obtained by automatic segmentation method is to segment brain structure from fetal brain MRI agree well with the gold standard	The further work can be done to classify abnormality of human fetus MRI by using fully automatic segmentation method
3	Salehi et al. [6]	IEEE, 2018	U-net, Image segmentation, brain extraction, convolutional neural network	A computer-automated system for the segmentation of brain part from rest of the image is proposed in which 2D U-net and a voxelwise CNN framework is used which gives the results with high accuracy	The future work can be done to improve the accuracy of the methods in segmenting the intracranial region of fetal MRI future work

(Continued)

Table 7.1 Comparative analysis of different techniques used for classification of fetal brain abnormalities. (*Continued*)

Sr. no.	Title and authors	Publication and year	Techniques/ algorithms used	Strength	Limitations/future work
4	Attallah *et al.* [2]	IEEE, 2018	ML classifiers: LDA, SVM, KNN, and ESD; adaptive thresholding, morphological operations; feature selection: DWT, GLCM + statistical	Detects and classifies brain abnormalities from fetal magnetic resonance imaging at an early age of fetal without any surgery	Future activities are possible to improve the performance with increased data set
5	Sangeetha *et al.* [7]	IJIRCCE, 2019	CNN adaptive thresholding, morphological operations	The proposed segmentation and classification algorithm can be provide less number of errors in abnormal tissue prediction.	Future work will be done to investigate integrating other diagnostic features that will be extracted from other brain structure

(*Continued*)

Table 7.1 Comparative analysis of different techniques used for classification of fetal brain abnormalities. (*Continued*)

Sr. no.	Title and authors	Publication and year	Techniques/ algorithms used	Strength	Limitations/future work
6	Raghavendra et al. [8]	European neurology, 2019	Machine learning: SVM and KNN; advanced signal processing techniques	Computer-automated system assist doctors to analyze and interpret medical images and physiological signals effectively	The further work should move to computer-automated systems for early diagnosis of the neurological diseases and for increased dataset
7	Gilanie et al. [9]	IJIST 2019	Machine learning: SVM classifier; non-linear feature extraction, image processing	The reported approach is able to auto-classify the abnormal slices whether the slice is tumorous or non-tumorous one	
8	Khalilia et al. [10]	Magnetic Resonance Imaging, 2019	Brain segmentation, intensity inhomogeneity augmentation (IIA)	The proposed method used data augmentation method for the training data with synthesized intensity variance antiquity that found helpful for the result improvement in the segmentation process.	Transfer learning and data augmentation would increase the training data size that may further improve segmentation performance

(*Continued*)

Table 7.1 Comparative analysis of different techniques used for classification of fetal brain abnormalities. (*Continued*)

Sr. no.	Title and authors	Publication and year	Techniques/algorithms used	Strength	Limitations/future work
9	Gayathri *et al.* [11]	IJITEE, 2020	Image processing and Segmentation: adaptive thresholding, morphological operations	Automatic segmentation method gives competitive results than that of existing to segment fetal brain by using fetal magnetic resonance imaging	This segmentation technique can be useful to study brain structure evolution.
10	Qu *et al.* [14]	IEEE, 2020	Image pre-processing, CNN, transfer learning	The image conversion method and domain transfer learning methods are used that overcomes the drawback of over-fitting occurred due to limited training data	Future work can be done to overcome the challenges of limited data by the application of CNN

7.3   Evaluation of Related Research

The Texture Analysis technique is applied to different MRIs of the fetal brain to detect brain differences in small for GA fetal and compared to those suitable for GA. This shows that there exist the microstructural changes in brain of SGA fetuses. MR images of the fetal brain of early GA are used to classify several fetal brain anomalies using different ML techniques such as SVM, LDA, and KNN. In addition, the embryonic neurodevelopmental disorders (ENDs) are detected at early stage from embryonic MRI of various GAs by using DL techniques. As far as we know, more work related to brain disorder focuses on automated fetal brain segmentation from rest of the image. The automatic segmentation process involves sequence of steps such as diffusion, opening and closing morphological operations, and maximum entropy thresholding for the extraction of the fetal brain. The DL technique includes a CNN algorithm to improve accuracy in predicting fetal brain abnormalities. It provides fewer errors in predicting abnormal tissue. The deep CNN-based method automatically recognizes standard fetal brain planes from 2D US images to detect different abnormalities accurately and to correct fetal brain standard planes. Similarly, a 2D U-net segmentation based fully deep CNN segmentation algorithm is developed for real-time extraction of brain sections from MR images. The automated brain extraction methods automatically segment brain tissues into seven tissue classes by using CNN. In addition, a CAD method is proposed to classify sections of abnormal images of the fetal brain into one of the defined abnormality groups. This method is also useful for automatically classifying these brain slices into tumorous and non-tumorous.

7.4   General Framework for Fetal Brain Abnormality Classification

As per the survey, it is found that most of the literatures [2, 5, 7] contain some common phases in their proposed method for classification of fetal brain images. The framework consists of five main phases: a) image preprocessing, b) brain extraction/segmentation, c) feature extraction, d) feature reduction, and e) classification. The general block diagram of typical framework from image acquisition to image classification into normal and abnormal brain is shown in Figure 7.1.

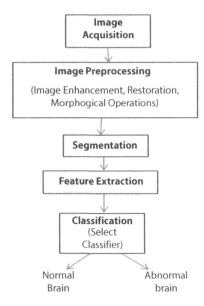

Figure 7.1 General framework for the classification of fetal brain abnormality.

7.4.1 Image Acquisition

This is the first basic step in which the data used is MRI of fetal brain. In general, the image acquisition phase involves pre-processing, such as the scaling [5]. Due to fetal movement and maternal breathing during the examination, each acquisition acts as an explorer for its successive acquisition [16]. MRI of the fetal brain is often obtained by using the very quick acquirement of 2D section that "freezes" movement within the brain section [3, 15].

7.4.2 Image Pre-Processing

The data which is used for this work contains raw images of fetal brain. The fetal head is surrounded by amniotic fluid, cerebrospinal fluid (CSF), as well as maternal tissues. Hence, for the enhancement of distinct features of the borders of lean layers in the MR image of the brain, pre-processing is necessary [1].

7.4.2.1 Image Thresholding

Image thresholding technique is used to take out the brain from MR image. This is very useful when images are having different intensity values. For this optimal intensity, threshold T is used to the divide the image pixels into two parts forefront and background. The binary image *Ibinary* is generated as follows:

$$\text{Ibinary}\,(i,j) = \begin{cases} 1, \text{if } I(i,j) \geq T \\ 0, \text{otherwise} \end{cases}$$

where *I* is image matrix.

7.4.2.2   Morphological Operations

Followed by thresholding, image restoration and morphological operations need to be performed. Opening and closing are two important mathematical operators used to perform morphological operations [7]. Using the opening operation in the morphology of the image, some weekly connected maternal tissues are removed from the fetal brain MR Images [2]. The morphological opening operation is applied to the Ibinary image to obtain "Io" by using the formula

$$\text{Io} = (\text{Ibinary} \ominus X) \oplus X$$

where $\oplus$ is an erosion operator and $\ominus$ is dilation operator, and X is a structuring element.

7.4.2.3   Hole Filling and Mask Generation

After Removal of weekly connected maternal tissues and the high-intensity CSF in ventricular, holes are generated inside the binary image *Io*. To fill these holes of binary image I_o, flood filling method is used [9]. After hole-filling method, the final brain mask is I_f is generated as

$$I_f = \begin{cases} 1 \text{ if } Io(x,y) = 0(\text{holes}) \\ 0, \text{otherwise} \end{cases}$$

where I_f is final extracted brain image which separated out from the rest of the part of the brain.

7.4.2.4   MRI Segmentation for Fetal Brain Extraction

This section presents various perspectives to evaluate the accuracy for brain MRI segmentation and criterion used for the quality of brain segmentation. Based on the techniques that have been used for segmentation, we classify them as ML-based segmentation and DL-based segmentation.

7.4.2.4.1   ML-Based Segmentation Methods

Manual segmentation of developing fetal brain is a challenging task. Therefore, automated brain extraction techniques have been proposed to extract the brain part from fetal MRI. By automatically localizing fetal head, fetal brain is segmented using 2D slices of brain MR images. This method uses intensity Thresholding technique and closing operation of morphology to extract fetal brain. This method automatically identifies ROI using the center of gravity operations [1]. The results obtained by using intensity-based segmentation method are nearly similar to the manually segmented gold standard results [11]. In literature [7], a fully automatic segmentation model is discovered in order to perform the brain segmentation of fetal from MR Images of human fetus. This segmentation method makes use of contrast image enhancement, seeded region growing and hole-filling methods.

7.4.2.4.2   DL-Based Segmentation Methods

The rapid progress and extensive reach of DL has leads to an upstanding series of advancement and investments in ML domain. The manual segmentation of fetal brain using ML techniques is a challenging task. To overcome the limitations or drawbacks of ML-based methods, DL algorithms have been improved recently. Segmentation of fetal brain MRI using DL techniques is now penetrating the complete field of medical imaging [13]. The novel method automatically segments the fetal brain into seven tissue classes by using CNN [14]. In addition, in paper [12], the proposed system automatically segments the fetal brain by using an emerging spatio-temporal group-wise segmentation method.

7.4.3   Feature Extraction

Texture analysis is the most common method to extract the features from MRI images. Different texture features are extracted on the basis of textural characteristics of MRI image. The texture feature extraction methods include the discrete wavelet transformation (DWT), the Gabor filter, and the gray-level co-occurrence matrix (GLCM) [17]. In most of the proposed systems, the DWT coefficients are used as feature vectors. Generally, to extract the appropriate features from MR images of fetal brain, wavelet mathematical tool is used. The wavelet coefficient provides the information of localized frequency, which is useful for classification [18]. For the extraction of features like contrast correlation, homogeneity, etc., in the images, GLCM algorithm is used [19]. In this section, the different feature extraction techniques are described.

7.4.3.1 Gray-Level Co-Occurrence Matrix

GLCM is very popular feature extraction technique to extract statistical texture features from an image. This approach is used in many applications to extract the second order features. However, GLCM computes only four second order features named correlation, energy, entropy, and inverse difference moment. Xilinx ISE 13.4 is used for calculation and implementation of these features [20].

7.4.3.2 Discrete Wavelet Transformation

DWT algorithm is mostly used in the applications for the analysis of medical images or signals. DWT algorithm uses the set of orthogonal basis function to decompose the image or signal and represent it in the form of time-frequency. One-dimensional (1D) DWT method is used for the decomposition of input signal S in the analysis of signal. In this process, the low-pass filter and high pass filter are used in loop. For the analysis of 2D image, a 2D DWT method is used. This can be done by applying 1D DWT for each dimension independently and result into four parts of coefficients [21]. The 2D DWT approach is applied to an image to execute the multiple levels of decomposition. There are different ways for implementing DWT algorithm. The most commonly used conventional algorithm is pyramidal algorithm. In this approach, smoothing and non-smoothing filters one are created by using the wavelet coefficients and those obtained two filters are repeatedly used to gain data for all the scales.

In the proposed system, the four stages of decomposition of 2D DWT are applied on pre-processed MR image for feature extraction. After four stages of decomposition process, the feature matrix is generated, which contain the vertical, horizontal, and diagonal coefficients [22]. As per the study, the DWT algorithm extracts the features in two ways. In the first one, it combines the estimation, vertical, horizontal, and feature coefficients and forms the feature vector of particular size. In another technique, it extracts the statistical features from the earlier produced features to create a new feature vector of different size.

7.4.3.3   Gabor Filters

Gabor filters is also most common method used to extract the textural features from an image by exploring the frequency domain. Gabor filters perform multi-level decomposition, to produce a various frequency and direction representation, same as the human vision. This method establishes so many variations between various textures after the analysis of an image and determines if it contains any specific frequency content with a particular direction situated in a minor place near the analysis region [23]. This feature extraction method can be observed to be sinusoidal signal of specific frequency and direction, modified by a Gaussian wave [22]. This feature extraction method is used in several applications to extract the feature in the analysis of image such as for document image processing, facial expression recognition, optical character recognition, and fingerprint recognition and similar.

7.4.3.4   Discrete Statistical Descriptive Features

Statistical descriptive feature extraction method is used to extract statistical features of an image or signal. These statistical features comprise of entropy, variance, mean, standard deviation1, smoothing, skewness, kutosis, root mean square, and inverse difference moments. These feature extraction is performed to get the small ROI of an image.

7.4.4   Feature Reduction

In feature reduction, the high-dimensional data is transformed into low-dimensional data with conserving the original meaning of data to the possible extent. This data transformation results into the new set of features with largest variation from original data [24]. In the proposed method, in the stage of feature reduction, two most common feature reduction methods, principal components analysis (PCA) and LDA, are compared and evaluated their impact on the classification accuracy of fetal brain MRI. Several linear and nonlinear feature reduction methods are explored in order to overcome the drawbacks of traditional methods [4]. In the process of dimensionality reduction, the high-dimensional data is transformed into low-dimensional data with conserving the original meaning of data to the possible extent. In addition, this low-dimensional data can help to defeat the issue of curse of dimensionality. "Curse of dimensionality" can be referred as the problems occurred during the training due to high-dimensional data. With the large increment in the use of high-dimensional data, the use of various types of feature reduction methods is common in many application areas. The use of feature reduction methods required less computational time and minimum storage space. The dimensionality reduction techniques extract the useful and more relevant features that are used for image analysis and remove the unwanted and unnecessary features [25]. Suppose, the dimensionality reduction techniques transforms the high-dimensional data X = [x1, x2, ⋯, xm] ∈ Rm×n having m observations and n dimensions into low-dimensional data Y = [y1, y2, ⋯, ym] ∈ Rm×j where j << m in ideal case. Dimensionality reduction techniques can have explicit, inverse mapping to recover a section from the low dimensions [4]. This section includes the detailed description of the linear and nonlinear dimensionality reduction methods. The Linear Dimensionality Reduction Techniques (LDRT) transform the high-dimensional data into lower dimensions by using simple linear functions. Let us see the two popular variants of LDRT such as PCA and LDA in brief.

7.4.4.1   Principal Component Analysis

PCA is statistical method used minimize the number of features extracted. PCA examines the relationship among the group of variables and result into developing new features which are independent of each other [26]. PCA is one of the unsupervised methods. This method is based on linear mapping search method and appropriate for Gaussian data. This Feature extraction method provides various methods to reduce the high-dimensional feature space and preserves as much as possible variance of the original data [25, 27]. The aim of PCA is to identify the principal components (PCs) where PC is the set of unrelated features. The first PC has the highest variation from the data, and then, the second PC has the second highest variation, and so on. Only initial "k" PCs have highest variation for original data [26].

The extensions of PCA have been introduced by the researchers for different data, structures, and types. The authors in [28] developed the variant named local PCA (LPCA) by applying the local linear approach. The experimental outcome shows that LPCA performs better as compared to PCA for image or speech data. The article [29] introduced the extension to PCA called robust PCA (RPCA) to improve the robustness of traditional methods. In literature [30], the new variant is introduced called generalized PCA (GPCA) that deals with high-dimensional data space having multiple subspaces. The PPCA was used for various data sets such as 3D motion segmentation, temporal video segmentation, and clustering faces.

Suppose the dataset has n-dimensions inputs. The PCA reduce the n-dimension data to k-dimensions (k<<n). The below steps describe PCA algorithm in detail:

Step 1: Standardize the raw data by subtracting mean "μ" and dividing by standard deviation "σ". The formula is given as follows:

$$Z = (x - μ) / σ$$

Step 2: Compute the covariance of "x" and "y" variables by using the given formula:

$$cov(X,Y) = \frac{1}{n-1} \sum_{i=1}^{n} (Xi - \vec{x})(Yi - \vec{y})$$

$$\Rightarrow \vec{v}(A - \lambda I) = 0$$

Step 3: From the given formula calculate the eigenvectors and corresponding eigenvalues of cov. Matrix "A"

$$A\vec{v} - \lambda\vec{v} = 0$$

$$\Rightarrow \vec{v}(A - \lambda I) = 0$$

where A is cov. Matrix, 'I' is the identity matrix and ' λ ' is eigenvalue.

Step 4: To find the largest eigenvalues sort the eigenvectors and choose k eigenvectors with largest eigenvalues that become the PC.

In this way, the n-dimensional data will be reduced to k-dimensional data using PCA.

7.4.4.2   Linear Discriminant Analysis

LDA is a linear feature reduction method for minimize number unwanted features in applications having large numbers of features. The goal of LDA is to convert the high-dimensional space into lesser dimensional subspace which results into reduced computational cost. Ronald Fisher developed the original concept of Linear Discriminant in 1936 [31]. LDA is supervised

LDRTs that give linearly combined features as linear classification model for dimensionality reduction [32]. LDA technique helps to determine the parameters that are used to show the relationship between a group and an object. In addition, it discovers the classification preceptor model that helps to separate the groups [33]. The performance of LDA is not good with small volume dataset. To overcome this problem, the variants of LDA such as SDA [34] and mixture SDA [35] have been proposed.

The following steps to project HD dimension into lesser subspace 'i' by using the LDA algorithm:

Step 1: First find the d-dimensional average vector for each class

Step 2: Then calculate the scatter matrices by using the mean vectors

Step 3: After this, compute the Eigenvectors and their respective eigenvalues

Step 4: To find the largest eigenvalues sort the eigenvectors and choose k eigenvectors with largest eigenvalues in order to form d*i matrix

Step 5: Transform the input data into a new low-dimensional subspace by using d*i eigenvector matrix.

7.4.4.3   Non-Linear Dimensionality Reduction Techniques

Recently, many non-linear feature reduction methods have been proposed in order to work with complex application data having non-linear structures [36]. Kernel method is used to build the relation present in data in non-linear structure. "Kernel trick" is another name of kernel method [37]. Non-linear DRTs are mainly classified into two categories: the methods that provide a mapping of high-dimensional space into low dimensions and vice versa and the methods that just give data visualization [25].

7.4.5   Classification by Using Machine Learning Classifiers

ML algorithms have the ability to train the computers without the help of explicit programs. ML techniques are very useful in the analysis of medical data to help out clinicians by making clear disease diagnosis and minimize the human made diagnostic mistakes. In addition, the ML technique shows reduced efforts and time complexity for an examination [7]. In recent times, ML techniques have been used for the classification of fetal brain disorders and its detection by using fetal brain MRI data [2]. Let us see each classification model briefly.

7.4.5.1　Support Vector Machine

SVM classifier works on the basic idea of classification in hyperplane. In SVM classifier from the input space, nonlinear training data is projected into the high-dimensional feature space by using kernel function [38]. As the data is nonlinear, quadratic kernel function produce the competitive results than the results generated by linear kernel function. The following equations show the difference between these kernel functions that convert the feature space into high-dimensional feature subspace [2].

$$K_{linear} = a \times b + c$$

$$K_{Quadratic.} = (a \times b + c)^2$$

In above equations, "a" and "b" represents the input for n-dimensional feature values, "K" is kernel function, and "c" is kernel parameter.

Figure 7.2 shows the difference between linear and quadratic kernel functions [4]. Many times, in the input space, the over-fitting problem can be caused by classification in n-dimensional feature spaces. SVM classifier used the structural risk minimization principle to control the problem of over-fitting [2]. For image classification, SVM has high accuracy.

7.4.5.2　K-Nearest Neighbors

This is one of the simplest classifier. This classifier is a standard nonparametric supervised method for optimal values of k [7]. Like other classifiers, KNN also includes a trained data and a test data. The trained data is has

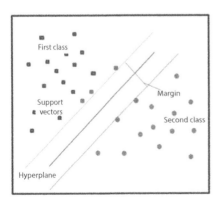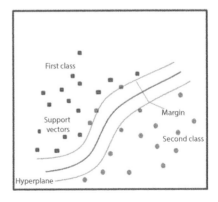

Figure 7.2 Variation in a linear kernel and a quadratic kernel.

labeled data points in the n-dimensional space, while the test data has unlabeled data points. The KNN classifier calculates the distances of data points that have to classify from the k nearest points in n-dimensional space [2].

7.4.5.3   Random Forest

Random forest (RF) classifier having good ability to identify the relations between data attributes. The RF classifier is the supervised ML classifier, which is used for regression and classification by using many number of uncorrelated decision trees (DTs). Hence, it is most popular classifier and widely used in the analysis of medical image data. Identifying these relations helps to understand the process of classification. The RF classifiers use Divide-and-Conquer (DAC) approach and build some trees from input data features to predict the class value [39]. The RF classifier has multiple DTs that are irrelevant of each other operating all together as a committee. These individual models give ensemble predictions more accurately as compared to existing predictions. RF is best ML classifier as it gives the best set of features that makes the model more predictable and result in good and accurate classification model. The RF algorithm works as follows.

Step 1: Select k random samples from the data
Step 2: Build the decision trees in association with the selected
    data samples
Step 3: Select n number of decision trees that to be built.
Step 4: Repeat step (1) and step (2)
Step 5: Select the new data samples from the ensemble predictions of each decision tree

7.4.5.4   Linear Discriminant Analysis

This technique is used as a classification model as well as used for dimensionality reduction operations. It is supervised classifier to find linear grouping of features that isolates different categories using hyperplanes. This algorithm is used to project the features from higher dimensional space to the lower dimensional space [32]. This algorithm protects most of the class biased knowledge without the any loss of data.

7.4.5.5   Naïve Bayes

Naïve Bayes (NB) is a most popular classification method used to classify the large data. It is supervised ML classification algorithm. In this algorithm, the occurrence of several features is independent of other features hence this algorithm is called as "Naïve". The NB classifier is simple to develop and predicts the results with good accuracy. The NB classification method is based on Bayesian theorem [40]. The NB algorithm gives good prediction results in case of categorical dataset. This algorithm typically used in real-time prediction applications, text classification methods, multi-class classification techniques, recommender system, etc. In the following equation, Bayes theorem is computed, where J belongs to the variable Kn:

$$P(J|Kn) = P(Kn|J)P(J) / P(Kn)$$

where $P(J|Kn)$ is the conditional probability of J given Kn
$P(Kn|J)$ is the conditional probability of Kn given J
$P(Kn)$ is the conditional probability of Kn
$P(J)$ is the conditional probability of J

7.4.5.6   Decision Tree (DT)

Decision Tree (DT) is supervised ML algorithm, unlike other ML algorithms this method also used to solve the regression and classification problems. The DT classifier is used to predict the target variables into their respective categories [40]. This classification method consists of two main types of trees such as classification trees and regression trees. Classification trees have categorical data types and regression trees have continuous data types. ID3 is the best algorithm to construct DT classification model [39]. The following are the steps to build DT model by using ID3 algorithm:

Step 1: Start from root node "S" (original set)
Step 2: On each iteration, calculate entropy (E) and information gain (IR) from attributes of set S
Step 3: After this, select the attribute with largest IR and smallest E
Step 4: Then, the set S is divided by chosen attribute to form the subset of the data
Step 5: Recursively follow the steps from step 1 to step 4 for each subset, by considering that the attributes not at all selected before.

7.4.5.7   Convolutional Neural Network

CNN is the most common neural network model for image classification. They are most commonly used to analyze visual images and often work behind the scenes in image classification [40]. CNN is formed by the stack of layers in which layers perform specific function. The first layer is connected to the input image dataset. The next layers convolve multiple filters that filter input image to extract main features. The next layer obtains the output of the previous layer such as pooling and loss calculation, as its input [11].

7.5 Performance Metrics for Research in Fetal Brain Analysis

Finally, the performances of the different classifiers for classification of MRI data are examined by various performance evaluation methods. Many researchers have evaluated the performance of classifiers in terms of confusion matrix, specificity, sensitivity, and accuracy.

Confusion matrix: It is the summary of predicted outcomes on a classification problem. It counts the number of correctly and incorrectly classified results. The confusion matrix is represented in tabular form in which every row presents the real labels, whereas every column presents the predicted labels. It depends on following three terms:

Sensitivity (TP_I fraction): sensitivity is also known as recall. It can be defined as the probability of diagnosis as positive test, given that the fetal brain is abnormal.

$$Sensitivity = TP_I / (TP_I + FN_I)$$

Specificity (TN_I fraction) is the probability of diagnosis as negative test, given that fetal brain is normal.

$$Specificity = TN_I / (TN_I + FP_I)$$

Accuracy is the simplest performance metric that can be defined as the probability of diagnosis that test is correctly performed,

$$Accuracy = (TP_I + TN_I) / (TP_I + TN_I + FP_I + FN_I)$$

where TP_I (True Positives) is positive cases classified correctly, TN_I (True Negative) is negative cases classified correctly, FP_I (False Positives) is negative cases classified incorrectly, and FN_I (False Negative) is positive cases classified incorrectly.

7.6   Challenges

It is clear that ML is very useful for medical image analysis as it provides exact results based on complex image data. However, still, these techniques have some challenges and drawbacks that many researchers trying to overcome. Automated segmentation of the fetal brain is significantly more stimulating than adult brain, because the fetal brain is small in size and varies considerably in terms of the shape of the brain and its appearance due to the rapid growth of the brain during early GA [16]. Image acquisition is also a difficult task due to significant fetal movement artifacts during image acquisition. Many researchers have faced the problem of over-fitting caused due to limited and variant datasets, which affects the learning accuracy of the system.

As per the progress of research in the study and design of different ML systems for segmentation and classification of fetal brain disorder, some research gaps are discussed here. a) The use of different types of the dataset for ML-based image features extraction and segmentation with less computational requirements. b) The use of appropriate feature extraction and feature reduction methods may help to number the number of features which may result in less computational time and improved accuracy. c) The recent research works do not considered severity analysis which is important part of appropriate treatment for brain disorder.

7.7   Conclusion and Future Works

In this survey, we studied and analyze existing techniques for segmentation and classification of fetal brain abnormalities. There are various techniques are developed The survey shows that KNN and SVM classifiers are the most commonly used classifier for the diagnosis of brain abnormalities, but CNN classifier gives more accurate and fast results for the classification of fetal brain MRI. With the promising results obtained from CNN for brain image segmentation and image classification, many researchers have explored CNN algorithm for brain image segmentation. In addition, it is found that different DL techniques like auto context methods give more robust results by automatically segmenting fetal MRI in real time.

We also present the challenges in the segmentation and classification of fetal brain. The survey reveals that there still some future work can be done for the obstacles in developing the techniques mainly because of the limited data. In addition, further work should move to computer-automated systems for early diagnosis of the neurological diseases and for increased dataset. However, with growing convenience of resources for the fetal brain, it is expected that these limitations will be accomplish in the near future.

References

1. Somasundaram, K., Gayathri, S.P., Shankar, R.S., Rajeswaran, R., Fetal head localization and fetal brain segmentation from MRI using the center of gravity. *ICSEC*, Thailand, 14–17 Dec 2016.
2. Attallah, O., Gadelkarim, H., Sharkas, M.A., Detecting and Classifying Fetal Brain Abnormalities Using Machine Learning Techniques. *ICMLA*, Orlando, FL, USA, 17–20 December 2018, pp. 1371–1376.
3. Lundervold, A.S. *et al.*, An overview of deep learning in medical imaging focusing on MRI. *Z. Med. Phys.*, 29, 2, 102–127, 2019.
4. Makropoulos, A., Counsell, S.J., Rueckert, D., A review on automatic fetal and neonatal brain MRI segmentation. *NeuroImage*, 2017.
5. Somasundaram, K., Gayathri, S.P., Rajeswaran, R., Dighe, M., Fetal brain extraction from magnetic resonance image (MRI) of human fetus. *Imaging Sci. J.*, 66, 3, 133–138, 2017.
6. Salehi, S.S.M. *et al.*, Real-time automatic fetal brain extraction in fetal MRI by deep learning. *2018 IEEE 15th ISBI 2018*, Washington, DC, pp. 720–724, 2018.
7. Sangeetha, K. and Venipriya, T., Abnormalities of Fetal Brain Classification Using Deep Learning Techniques. Copyright to *IJIRCCE*, 7, 10, October 2019.
8. Raghavendra, U., Acharya, U.R., Adeli, H., Artificial Intelligence Techniques for Automated Diagnosis of Neurological Disorders. *Eur. Neurol.*, 82, 41–64, 2019.
9. Gilanie, G., Bajwa, U.I., Waraich, M.M., Habib, Z., Computer aided diagnosis of brain abnormalities using texture analysis of MRI images. *Int. J. Imaging Syst. Technol.*, 29, 3, 260–27, 1–12, 2019.
10. Khalilia, N., Lessmanna, N., E. *et al.*, Automatic brain tissue segmentation in fetal MRI using convolutional neural networks. *Magn. Reson. Imaging*, 64, 77–89, Dec 2019.
11. Gayathri, S.P., Siva Shankar, R., Somasundaram, K., Fetal Brain Segmentation using Improved Maximum Entropy Threshold. *IJITEE*, 9, 3, January 2020.
12. Hesamian, M., Jia, W., Xiangjian, H., Kennedy, P., Deep Learning Techniques for Medical Image Segmentation: Achievements and Challenges. *J. Digit. Imaging*, 32, 582–596, 2019.
13. Dolza, J., Desrosiersa, C., Wangc, L., Yuanb, J., Shenc, D., Ayed, I.B., Deep CNN ensembles and suggestive annotations for infant brain MRI segmentation. *Comput. Med. Imaging Graphics*, 79, 2020.

14. Qu, R., Xu, G., Ding, C., Jia, W., Sun, M., Deep Learning-Based Methodology for Recognition of Fetal Brain Standard Scan Planes in 2D Ultrasound Images. *IEEE Access*, 8, 44443–44451, 2020.
15. Gratacós, E., Opportunities and challenges of biomedical imaging in fetal and neonatal brain disease. *ISBI*, Barcelona, pp. 493–494, 2012.
16. Nailon, W.H., Texture Analysis Methods for Medical Image Characterisation, in Biomedical Imaging. London, United Kingdom, IntechOpen, 2010 [Online]. Available: https://www.intechopen.com/chapters/10175 doi: 10.5772/8912
17. Haralick, R.M., Shanmugam, K., Dinstein, I., Textural Features for Image Classification. *IEEE Trans. Syst. Man Cybern.*, SMC-3. 610–621.
18. Romeo, V. and Maurea, S., The new era of advanced placental tissue characterization using MRI texture analysis: Clinical implications. *EBioMedicine*, 51, 102588, 2020.
19. Mohanaiah, P., Sathyanarayana, P., GuruKumar, L., Image Texture Feature Extraction Using GLCM Approach. *Int. J. Sci. Res. Publ.*, 3, 5, May 2013.
20. Lahmiri, S. and Boukadoum, M., Hybrid Discrete Wavelet Transform and Gabor Filter Banks Processing for Features Extraction from Biomedical Images. *J. Med. Eng.*, 2013, 104684, 2013.
21. Srivastava, V. and Purwar, R.K.A., Five-Level Wavelet Decomposition and Dimensional Reduction Approach for Feature Extraction and Classification of MR and CT Scan Images. *Appl. Comput. Intell. Soft Comput.*, Article ID 9571262, 9, 2017. https://doi.org/10.1155/2017/9571262.
22. Jain, K. and Farrokhnia, F., Unsupervised Texture Segmentation Using Gabor Filters. *Pattern Recognit.*, 24, 1167–1186, 1991.
23. Erichson, N.B., Zheng, P., Manohar, K., Brunton, S.L., Kutz, J.N., Aravkin, A.Y., Sparse principal component analysis via variable projection. *SIAM J. Appl. Math.*, 80, 2, 977–1002, 2020, arXiv:1804.00341.
24. Deegalla, S., Boström, H., Walgama, K., Choice of Dimensionality Reduction Methods for Feature and Classifier Fusion with Nearest Neighbor Classifiers, in: *15th International Conference on Information Fusion (FUSION)*, IEEE, pp. 875–881, 2012.
25. Abdi, H. and Williams, L.J., Principal component analysis. *Wiley Interdiscip. Rev. Comput. Stat.*, 2, 4, 433–459, 2010.
26. Ahmadkhani, S. and Adibi, P., Face recognition using supervised probabilistic principal component analysis mixture model in dimensionality reduction without loss framework. *IET Comput. Vis.*, 10, 3, 193–201, 2016.
27. Kambhatla, N. and Leen, T.K., Dimension reduction by local principal component analysis. *Neural Comput.*, 9, 7, 1493–1516, 1997.
28. Locantore, N., Marron, J., Simpson, D., Tripoli, N., Zhang, J., Cohen, K., Boente, G., Fraiman, R., Brumback, B., Croux, C. *et al.*, Robust principal component analysis for functional data. *Test*, 8, 1, 1–73, 1999.
29. Vidal, R., Ma, Y., Sastry, S., Generalized principal component analysis (gpca). *IEEE Trans. Pattern Anal. Mach. Intell.*, 27, 12, 1945–1959, 2005.

30. Ye, J., Janardan, R., Li, Q., Two-dimensional linear discriminant analysis, in: *Proc. Adv. Neural Inf. Process. Syst.*, pp. 1569–1576, 2005.

31. Tharwat, A., Gaber, T., Ibrahim, A., Hassanien, A.E., Linear discriminant analysis: adetailed tutorial. *AI Commun.*, 30, 2, 169–190, 2017.

32. Press, S.J. and Wilson, S., Choosing between logistic regression and discriminant analysis. *J. Am. Stat. Assoc.*, 73, 364, 699–705, 1978.

33. Zhu, M. and Martinez, A.M., Subclass discriminant analysis. *IEEE Trans. Pattern Anal. Mach. Intell.*, 28, 8, 1274–1286, 2006.

34. Gkalelis, N., Mezaris, V., Kompatsiaris, I., Mixture subclass discriminant analysis. *IEEE Signal Process. Lett.*, 18, 5, 319–322, 2011.

35. Vlachos, M., Domeniconi, C., Gunopulos, D., Kollios, G., Koudas, N., Non-linear Dimensionality Reduction Techniques for Classification and Visualization, in: *Proceedings of the Eighth ACM SIGKDD International Conference on Knowledge Discovery and Data Mining*, ACM, pp. 645–651, 2002.

36. Weinberger, K.Q., Sha, F., Saul, L.K., Learning a Kernel Matrix for Nonlinear Dimensionality Reduction, in: *Proceedings of the Twenty-First International Conference on Machine Learning*, ACM, p. 106, 2004.

37. Anthony, G., Greg, H., Tshilidzi, M., *Classification of images using support vector machines*, Cornell University, Library, 2007. https://arxiv.org/abs/0709.3967v1

38. Caruana, R. and Niculescu-Mizil, A., An Empirical Comparison of Supervised Learning Algorithms, in: *Proceedings of the 23rd International Conference on Machine Learning*, Pittsburgh, PA, USA, 25–29 June 2006, pp. 161–168.

39. Park, D.-C., Image Classification Using Naïve Bayes Classifier. *Int. J. Comput. Sci. Electron. Eng.*, 4, 135–139, 2016.

40. Lundervold, A.S. *et al.*, An overview of deep learning in medical imaging focusing on MRI. *Z. Med. Phys.*, 29, 2, 102–127, 2019, ISSN 0939-3889.

8

Analysis of COVID-19 Data Using Machine Learning Algorithm

Chinnaiah Kotadi[1], Mithun Chakravarthi K.[2], Srihari Chintha[3] and Kapil Gupta[4]*

[1]Computer Science and Engineering, G H Raisoni College of Engineering, Nagpur, India
[2]Computer Science and Engineering, Donbosco Institute of Technology, Kumbalgodu, India
[3]Computer Science and Engineering, Siddhartha Institute of Technology & Sciences, Hyderabad, India
[4]St. Vincent Pallotti College of Engineering and Technology, Nagpur, India

Abstract

The COVID-19 second wave created very terrible and outrageous situation in India. As a result, many families are living in abject poverty and living a miserable life, and it has also created an impact not only in the Indian economy but also in the worldwide economy. Experts say that the third wave is coming, and the variant name is Delta variant, which is the most terrible bitter truth, and there may be more terrible and critical situations soon. In this chapter, we are analyzing past COVID-19 data in order to create awareness to the people for COVID-19 second wave conditions and precautions to Delta variant. In this chapter, we are analyzing COVID-19 cases such as confirmed cases, cured patients cases, and death rate in India, as well as which states have top highest cases occurred and death rate occurred in India by using machine learning algorithm.

Keywords: COVID-19, death rate, delta variant, machine learning

8.1 Introduction

There is no one in the world who has not heard the word COVID-19; this disease is caused by another virus that is the genes of COVID-19 virus, called SARS-CoV-2; it is declared by WHO on December 31, 2019 [1], and it is a

---

*Corresponding author: kaps04gupta@gmail.com

R. Arokia Priya, Anupama V Patil, Manisha Bhende, Anuradha Thakare and Sanjeev Wagh (eds.)
Object Detection by Stereo Vision Images, (147–158) © 2022 Scrivener Publishing LLC

global pandemic on March 11, 2020 [2]. WHO declared that coronavirus disease (COVID-19) as a global pandemic on March 11, 2020 [4]. It belongs to one family of COVID-19 coronavirus (CoV) that causes severe illness ranging from common cold to serious diseases, and, sometimes, even death also occurs. A novel CoV (nCoV) is a new strain virus that has not been earlier identified in humans. The new terrible virus was subsequently named the "coronavirus" only, middle east respiratory syndrome (MERS-CoV), attacked in Saudi Arabia [3], and Influenza (H1N2) attacked in brazil country. The Danish authorities have reported to WHO that an extensive spread of SARS-CoV-2 virus caused by COVID-19 and influenza A(H3N2) has attacked on United States of America, and black fungus and yellow fungus also rounded in India. When the newly formed CoV produce mutation of virus itself, these changes are called "mutation". A virus produces one or more mutations is called "variant" of the virus [4], and these are named as alpha variants, beta variants, and delta variants; it roars around the world and causes serious illness. In United States, the Centers for Disease Control and Prevention (CDC) defines mutations of virus as "changes in the genetic code of virus that naturally occur over time when an animal or person is infected" [5]. These mutations of virus impacts on public may fast evolve and may be very serious health effects; sometimes, it can even be life threatening. According to WHO, the delta variant virus is very fast spread and it causes serious illness. Moreover, this pandemic brought vulnerable lives throughout world; the small industries and medium companies handed over; because of this pandemic, companies terminated their workers, and then, its aftermath has created many terrible conditions worldwide consequence of this result, private job seekers turned into beggars, workers lived a life of starvation without food to eat, and it could disrupt international and national trading and travel. These terrible conditions aside this pandemic time brought good news for the weather that is positive impact on ozone layer [6]; in this pandemic time, the ozone hole detected as closed.

In India, corona disease has brought difficult conditions; some of the existing jobs have been blown away, unemployed people are crying to find jobs, and farmers are struggling to sell their crops; moreover, India has more population, so analyzing spread of virus state-wise [7] helps for getting awareness to government and public also; so in this paper, coronavirus state-wise spread is analyzed.

8.2   Pre-Processing

Selecting datasets steps is concerned with all available data models, which always has strong desire critical features for data classification [8], which should address respective questions or problems to predict. After selecting desired dataset, unsuitable features should be eliminated and accuracy performance of classification should be improved. In this paper, datasets acquire from kaggle.com that is covid-19_india; the parameterized dataset has relevant features such as date, time, state/union territory, confirmed Indian national, confirmed foreign national, cured, and deaths, along with the number of cases on each day in India state-wise.

The data frame can be used to analyze the COVID-19 cases from January 30, 2020, to June 6, 2021, by using machine learning algorithm that is linear regression to predict second wave COVID-19 death rate, cured cases, and confirmed cases with respect to all states of India and predicting Maharashtra state daily COVID-19 cases. The reason to use linear regression analysis is that the COVID-19 data frame has dependent variable and has a continuous impact of changes with respect to one or more independent variable changes; here, dependent variable is either death rate or cured case or confirmed cases, and independent variable is states of India.

Linear regression is a dependent variable where values get continues impact of changes by change in one or more independent variables. The coefficient values along with independent variables add bias value of regression given in equation.

The equation of linear regression is

$$y = mx + c$$

Here, "y" is a dependent variable, and it is plotted along the y-axis; "x" is an independent variable, and it is plotted along the x-axis; "m" is a coefficient value or slope value; and c is bias value or intercept at the y-axis.

8.3   Selecting Features

Data frames have different types of features and data types; unwanted features should be eliminated and unrelated data types should be changed to convenient data type of data frame. The COVID-19 data frame has SNO, date, time, state/union territory, confirmed Indian national, confirmed foreign national, cured, death, and confirmed COVID-19 cases; this data model has the following features; it is displayed in Table 8.1. If data frame is df, then python code displays first the five rows of COVID-19 data model.

Table 8.1 shows the first five rows of COVID-19 data frame; this data frame has not suitable features and data types; hence, the incompatible columns were deleted from COVID-19 data model to make a solid data

Table 8.1 First five rows of COVID-19 data frame.

SNO	Date	Time	State/Union Territory	Confirmed Indian National	Confirmed Foreign National	Cured	Death	Confirmed
1	2020-01-30	6:00PM	Kerala	1	0	0	0	1
2	2020-01-31	6:00PM	Kerala	1	0	0	0	1
3	2020-01-02	6:00PM	Kerala	2	0	0	0	2
4	2020-02-02	6:00PM	Kerala	3	0	0	0	3
5	2020-03-02	6:00PM	6:00PM	3	0	0	0	3

frame. Convenient columns should be selected in the process of building a solid data frame to optimize prediction of dependent variable.

df.head (5) shows first five rows of data frame df.

> covid = covid[['Date', 'State/UnionTerritory', 'Cured', 'Deaths',
>   'Confirmed']]
> covid.columns = ['date', 'state', 'cured', 'deaths', 'confirmed']
> covid.head(5)
> covid.tail(5)

Tables 8.2 and 8.3 show a complete data frame with a nice and convenient column, which are used to optimize prediction of dependent feature, where columns of data model are date, state/union territory, cured, deaths, and confirmed cases; these features are used to predict cured cases, death rates, and confirmed cases in India with respect to states and daily

Table 8.2 First five rows of COVID-19 data model.

SNO	Date	State/Union Territory	Cured	Deaths	Confirmed
0	2020-01-30	Kerala	0	0	1
1	2020-01-31	Kerala	0	0	1
2	2020-01-02	Kerala	0	0	2
3	2020-02-02	Kerala	0	0	3
4	2020-03-02	Kerala	0	0	3

Table 8.3 Last five rows of modified data frame.

SNO	Date	State/Union Territory	Cured	Deaths	Confirmed
15801	2021-08-06	Telangana	504,303	3,394	593,103
15802	2021-08-06	Tripura	49,579	572	56,169
15803	2021-08-06	Uttarakhand	313,566	6,731	334,419
15804	2021-08-06	Uttar Pradesh	1,662,069	21,333	1,699,083
15805	2021-08-06	West Bengal	1,388,771	16,362	1,432,019

COVID-19 cases in India with respect to particular state. Table 8.1 shows the top five rows of data frame df, and Table 8.2 shows last rows of data frame.

8.4   Analysis of COVID-19–Confirmed Cases in India

COVID-19 second wave has made a huge impact in India, and the third wave will come soon, which will have a further impact. Hence, by using the confirmed analysis, this will create awareness in the public to avoid more impact in India for third wave. This analysis of COVID-19–confirmed cases can explain all confirmed cases in India with respect of all states. By using COVID-19 data model and python code, we predict confirmed cases of all states in India. In this paper, five states are selected as shown in Table 8.4, which are highest COVID-19–confirmed cases on August 6, 2021, where Maharashtra state has highest confirmed cases, Karnataka state has second highest confirmed cases, and Kerala state has third highest confirmed COVID-19 cases, followed by Tamil Nadu and Andhra Pradesh.

Python code for ascending order of confirmed cases with respect to states of India given as follows:

```
max_confirmed_cases=today.sort_values(by='confirmed',
    ascending=False)
max_confirmed_cases
```

Table 8.4 Highest COVID-19–confirmed cases states in India.

SNO	Date	State/Union Territory	Cured	Deaths	Confirmed
15790	2021-08-06	Maharashtra	5,564,348	100,470	5,342,000
15785	2021-08-06	Karnataka	2,436,716	31,920	2,707,481
15786	2021-08-06	Kerala	2,483,992	10,157	2,642,395
15800	2021-08-06	Tamil Nadu	1,,997,299	27,356	2,256,681
15771	2021-08-06	Andhra Pradesh	1,637,149	11,552	1,763,211

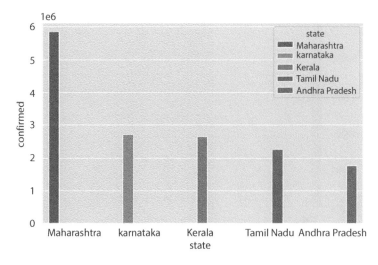

Figure 8.1 Bar plot for highest COVID-19–confirmed cases in five states of India.

8.4.1 Analysis to Highest COVID-19–Confirmed Case States in India

The graphical visualization of highest confirmed COVID-19 cases of five states of India is presented by using bar chats; we analyze these confirmed cases by using the graphical visualization. The following python code and Figure 8.1 show the top five states in India, which are highest confirmed cases.

```
top_states_confirmed=max_confirmed_cases[0:5]
sns.set(rc={'figure.figsize':(8,5)})
sns.barplot(x="state",y="confirmed",data=top_states_confirmed,
    hue="state")
<AxesSubplot:xlabel='state', ylabel='confirmed'>
```

8.4.2 Analysis to Highest COVID-19 Death Rate States in India

The graphical visualization of COVID-19 death rates in India is presented by using bar plot and the following python codes, and Figure 8.2 shows the highest death rate of five states of India. The following python code and graphical visualization are used for analysis of highest death rate states in India.

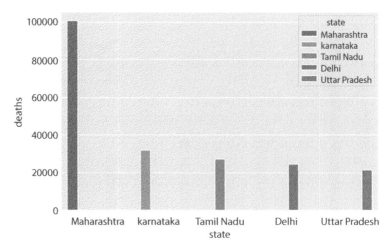

Figure 8.2 Bar plot for highest death rate in five states of India.

```
max_death_cases=today.sort_values(by="deaths",ascending=
    False)
top_states_death=max_death_cases[0:5]
sns.set(rc={'figure.figsize':(8,5)})
sns.barplot(x="state",y="deaths",data=top_states_death,
    hue="state")
<AxesSubplot:xlabel='state', ylabel='deaths'>
```

8.4.3   Analysis to Highest COVID-19 Cured Case States in India

The graphical visualization for cured cases in India which are of top five states. The following python code to get top five cured states in India, and Figure 8.3 shows that bar plot to visualization of cured cases in five states of India.

```
max_cured_cases=today.sort_values(by="cured",ascending=
    False)
top_sates_cured=max_cured_cases[0:5]
sns.set(rc={'figure.figsize':(8,5)})
sns.barplot(x="state",y="cured",data=top_sates_cured,hue="state")
<AxesSubplot:xlabel='state', ylabel='cured'>
```

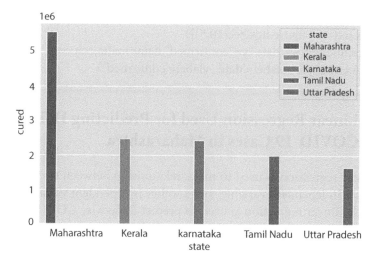

Figure 8.3 Bar plot to cured cases in top five states of India.

8.4.4   Analysis of Daily COVID-19 Cases in Maharashtra State

The COVID-19 second wave has made a more impact in Maharashtra state; here, highest confirmed cases and death rate cases are more than all states of India, which has huge impact on people and industries. The following python code used for selectin daily-wise cases in Maharashtra and Figure 8.4 shows prediction of daily-wise COVID-19 cases, and it is used to analyze cases.

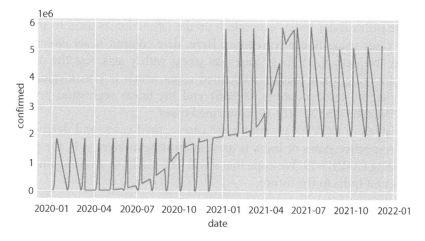

Figure 8.4 COVID-19 daily-wise cases in Maharashtra.

```
maha=covid[covid.state=='Maharashtra']
ns.set(rc={'figure.figsize':(10,5)})
sns.lineplot(x="date",y="confirmed",data=maha,color="g")
<AxesSubplot:xlabel='date', ylabel='confirmed'>
```

8.5   Linear Regression Used for Predicting Daily Wise COVID-19 Cases in Maharashtra

The linear regression is used to make relationship between two variables, which are independent variable, and another is dependent variable. In this paper, the linear regression is used to predict daily-wise COVID-19 cases in Maharashtra with the help of previous COVID-19 cases. The following code is used to predict daily-wise cases and analyze COVID-19 cases; here, LinearRegression package is imported from sklearn.linear module.

```
from sklearn.model_selection import train_test_split
x=maha['date']
y=maha['confirmed']
x_train,x_test,y_train,y_test=train_test_split(x,y,test_size=0.3)
from sklearn.linear_model import LinearRegression
lr=LinearRegression()
lr.fit(np.array(x_train).reshape(-1,1),np.array(y_train).reshape
    (-1,1))
LinearRegression()
```

The following code is used for testing COVID-19 daily-wise cases in Maharashtra state, India: example lr.predict()function is used to predict daily cases using linear regression. Here, date column is set along with x-axis and daily COVID-19 cases set along with y-axis, test the of date column value, then predict confirmed cases which is y-axis value. For example, the testing date is 7378861 and the linear regression predicts 2739559.4285725 COVID-19–confirmed cases.

Analysis of COVID-19–confirmed cases, cured cases, and death cases with respective states of India is used in creating awareness in the public regarding COVID-19. We hope that it will help public to avoid, again, huge impact on India in the future.

```
lr.predict(np.array([[737886]]))
arrays([[2739559.42985725]])
```

8.6   Conclusion

In this chapter, we explain how to analyze COVID-19–confirmed cases, cured cases, and death rate in states of India and to create awareness in the public to avoid COVID-19 impact on the public using machine learning model. In the future, using machine learning algorithm, we can predict and analyze other diseases too.

References

1. *WHO, Coronavirus diseases (COVID-19)*, 2021, https://www.who.int/emergencies/diseases/novel-coronavirus-2019.
2. Shah, S.G.S. and Farrow, A., A commentary on "World Health Organization declares global emergency: A review of the 2019 novel Coronavirus (COVID-19), International journal of surgery, London, England, 76, 128, 2020, Available: https://www.ncbi.nlm.nih.gov/pubmed/?term=Shah%20SG%5BAuthor%5D&cauthor=true&cauthor_uid=32169574.
3. Cascella, M., Rajnik, M., Aleem, A., Dulebohn, S.C., Di Napoli, R. Features, Evaluation, and Treatment of Coronavirus (COVID-19), StatPearls, 2022, https://www.statpearls.com/ArticleLibrary/viewarticle/52171
4. Dawood, A.A., Mutated COVID-19 may foretell a great risk for mankind in the future. New microbes and new infections, 35, p.100673, 2020.
5. Darling, H.S., Parikh, P., Vaishnav, R., Verma, A., Gulia, A., Kapoor, A., Singh, R., Severe acute respiratory syndrome coronavirus 2: Mutations and variants of concern – the Indian scenario. *Int. J. Mol. Immun. Oncol.*, 6, 2, 66–71, 2021.
6. Khan, I., Shah, D., Shah, S.S., COVID-19 pandemic and its positive impacts on environment: an updated review. *Int. J. Environ. Sci. Technol.: IJEST*, 18, 2, 521–530, 2020.
7. Ghosh, P., Ghosh, R., Chakraborty., B., COVID-19 in India: State-wise Analysis and Prediction. *JMIR Public Health Surveill.*, 6, 3, e20341, 2020.
8. Chen, R.C., Dewi, C., Huang, S.W., Caraka, R.E., Selecting critical features for data classification based on machine learning methods. *J. Big Data*, 7, 52, 2020, https://doi.org/10.1186/s40537-020-00327-4.

9

Intelligent Recommendation System to Evaluate Teaching Faculty Performance Using Adaptive Collaborative Filtering

Manish Sharma* and Rutuja Deshmukh

Department of Electronics and Telecommunication, D. Y. Patil College of Engineering, Akurdi, Pune, India

Abstract

This work presents an intelligent recommender system using deep learning model for the performance evaluation and enhancement of teachers in the educational institution. This work utilizes various features like student's assessment, intake quality, innovative practices, and experiential learning methods to present a recommendation framework. The dataset is used to train the proposed recommender and evaluate its performance and derived through the ERP of an educational institute. The major contribution of this research work is the implementation of adaptive collaborative filtering–based recommender system for the teacher's recommendation. The impact of the outcome of this recommender has the potential to improve the academic framework and student's performance many folds. The proposed model presents a personalized and customized recommendation to specific stakeholder over a particular time period. The common patterns of the preferences of the stakeholders in the educational framework have been identified in this work to utilize them for the effective and impactful recommendation. Various challenges have also been examined here to incorporate the unobserved preferences of the participants, which evolve over time. These challenges are addressed and resolved by the proposed recommender system, which utilizes the adaptive emission component to derive the personalized recommendations using the global preference patterns. The performance of the proposed systems has been verified and compared with the conventional collaborative filtering–based recommender systems through the experimental study to present the superiority of the proposed system.

Corresponding author: manishsharma.mitm@gmail.com

R. Arokia Priya, Anupama V Patil, Manisha Bhende, Anuradha Thakare and Sanjeev Wagh (eds.)
Object Detection by Stereo Vision Images, (159–170) © 2022 Scrivener Publishing LLC

Keywords: Recommender systems, collaborative filtering, changing preference, dynamic models, latent class models

9.1   Introduction

Education sector has witnessed a revolutionary change over the last few decades due to the advancements in the field of information and communication technologies. The digital transformation of the teaching and learning process has brought very encouraging modifications. The augmentation of conventional teaching methods with the new communication technologies has improved the learning characteristics of the students in terms of imagination and design thinking. The expectations of the students have also switched to very high level, which has made the teachers to develop new skills like communication skills, soft skills, emotional quotient, and technology friendly, apart from knowledge.

It has also changed the perception of educational administrators and academicians toward the teaching fraternity. The under-resourced institutions emphasize on the utilization of the knowledge and skills of teachers in a best possible ways. This paradigm shift has made the teachers to update themselves with the state-of-the-art information, recent trends, and high end technologies. To keep up with these fast-paced changes in the education field, teachers need to have the tremendous will, ability, and preparation. The challenges are variable depending upon the level of teaching like primary school, secondary school, and higher secondary. The requirements will be very different for professional courses like engineering, medical, pharmacy, and management. The theoretical and practical aspects that have to be covered in a subject while teaching are also dependent on the subject's requirements. The diversity in the delivery of content makes the process very complex. The education process followed for multi-dimensional curriculum environment is of varying degree and the students taking the respective course are also of different level of intelligence quotient.

The results of students have been the only conventional method for evaluating the performance of teachers. The diversity in quality and intelligence quotient of students has made the conventional evaluation method incomplete. Therefore, the performance evaluation of teachers through the results of students is quite unjustified in most of the cases. Hence, to complete the teaching learning process, there is requirement of a strategy to assess the performance of teachers through direct assessment parameters.

The last decade has seen a considerable increase in the attention to recommender systems because of its intuitive framework to present suggestions on the basis of available information. It also offers a more personalized experience to the user. The potential of recommender systems can be very well exploited in the education field for presenting suggestions and recommendations to the teachers. Right teacher for specific scenario can be utilized by identifying the area of expertise of each teacher and the areas, which need improvement to boost the teaching-learning process. However, the dependency of this process of evaluation of teaching process through a recommender system on various parameters makes it a very complex problem.

Recommender systems have completely changed the paradigm of digital marketing over the last decade. These systems have found a vast application in the areas of e-commerce, entertainment, digital publicity, healthcare, etc. The capability of recommender systems to estimate the interest area of consumers and suggest the suitable options has added a completely new dimension in this era of digital market. However, the application of recommender system in the education field has not been explored much. Teaching has always been a very important and demanding profession as it plays a very role in the nation building, character building, and humanity building. The growth in the information and communication technologies has changed the complete paradigm of education sector. The methods used for teaching has also been changed a lot as compared to the conventional education system. The educational framework followed conventionally in most of the countries is very much based on the quantitative assessment. The respective evaluation of the teachers' efforts in teaching has traditionally been performed indirectly through the marks that the students have received in the examinations throughout the academic year. However, due to the diversity in the student's quality and their intelligence quotient, the performance evaluation of teachers through the results of students is quite unjustified in most of the cases. Therefore, the requirement of a strategy to assess the performance of teachers through direct assessment parameters is the need of the complete teaching learning process.

A self-adaptive Hidden Markov Model (HMM) is used to present an intelligent recommender system for the performance evaluation of the teachers in the educational institution is presented in this work. It also provides the recommendations on the basis of the evaluation and assessment. Various features like student's assessment, intake quality, innovative practices, and experiential learning methods to present a recommendation framework have been used in this work to derive the model for recommender system. The dataset used to train the proposed recommender and evaluate its performance and derived through the ERP of an educational institute. The major contribution of this research work is the implementation of self-adaptive HMM-based recommender system for the teacher's recommendation. The parameters of the HMM framework have been optimized through PSO so as to reduce the time complexity.

This work is organized as follows: Section 9.2 deals with the review of the existing techniques in the field of recommendation systems and teachers performance evaluation methods. The mathematical framework for the collaborative filtering used in the recommender system is given in Section 9.3. The proposed self-adaptive HMM-based recommender system optimized with PSO is discussed in Section 9.4. Section 9.5 discusses the effectiveness of the proposed strategy through the analysis of the performance parameters, while Section 9.6 concludes the paper.

9.2   Related Work

The complex problem of teacher assessment in the field of education is addressed by many researchers. A variety of techniques like statistical, stochastic, and intelligent frameworks have been proposed over the last few years on the basis of different parameters, which can directly or indirectly affect the performance. In order to identify the advantages and drawbacks of the various strategies presented, several research papers are discussed in this section. The collective analysis of the drawbacks has resulted into the research gap and the rationale henceforth. The research work addressing the problem of teacher evaluation and various state-of-the-art decision-making algorithms are discussed in the following.

Through variety of activities, Fletcher *et al.* [1] have proposed a competence evaluation framework on the basis of reward-based model. These activities reflect the potential of teachers in their work. The different activities that are conducted by authors to evaluate the competence are performance appraisal, performance evaluation and review, performance assessment through measurement, employee evaluation, personnel review, staff assessment, service rating, etc.

The evaluation framework was extended by Grote *et al.* [2] to the performance analysis of employees on the basis of a different set of parameters. The analytical process has evaluated various aspects of career advancements of an employee like pay hikes, promotion, layoff, training, and development. The encouraging results of these assessment models have motivated Hamsa *et al.* [3] to implement it to the performance evaluation of employees of educational organizations also. The scenario of some developing countries was taken to show the orientation of education of these nations. They have collected the academic and non-academic performance of the students through information technological tools to create a large dataset. These datasets have been used to derive the statistical decision model, which reflected the performance of students and teachers.

Iam-On and Boongoen [4] proposed a statistical analysis to evaluate the performance through learning management system (LMS), Student Information Systems (SIS), Course Management System (CMS), and local institute database. To keep a continuous track of the progress of the teaching learning process, the derived model has created a formal strategy. Migueis *et al.* [5] have applied data mining techniques to extract the hidden knowledge from the data that are of qualitative importance. Various aspects of education systems like identifying the slow learners and fast learners and deriving strategies for these learners can also be micro-managed to improve the education system.

Altujjar *et al.* [6] and Zhang *et al.* [7] merged data mining and education system to proposed a novel term Education Data Mining(EDM). The huge amount of data generated in the educational institutes through the results of students, feedback and reviews of the stakeholders, etc., have provided the motivation to implement EDM. The outcomes of these models have also encouraged the developing countries to frame their educational policies.

Pandey and Taruna [8] presented the adaptive technique for the teachers to change their strategies on the basis of the performance evaluation. The depth of data intelligence is explored by the authors to identify the hidden information in the data. Important aspects of EDM from the point of view of students by Thai-Nghe *et al.* [9]. They presented the benefits of EDM for the students for self-evaluation and performance improvement through the analysis of their academic and non-academic history to predict the future behavior. The recommendation for the courses for any students could also be done using this approach.

Helal *et al.* [10] have used the set of features like scores of high school courses, assignments, and grades and compared them with the evaluation sheet of instructors to verify the correctness of the model. To explore the other dimensions of the features analysis, the participation of students on social media and their psychological characteristics are also considered. The detailed collection of features has presented a more accurate estimation of academic performance of students. This, in turn, could be of use for the teacher's appraisal analysis also.

9.3   Recommender Systems and Collaborative Filtering

The recommender system is an intelligent model to drive the user experience and assist for decision-making through the suggestions about the product. These recommendations are derived through the available information about various parameters, which have been considered by other users while doing the business in the same domain. The problem of recommendation may be formulated as $f{:}U \times I \rightarrow R$ where f represents the utility function, and U and I represent the user space and item space, respectively, which comprise of the features or attributes of the users and items. R is the set of predicted ratings represented as non-negative numbers. It is generated through the projection of f over the combinations of users and items. The most optimal value of u represented by $u_j^* = \arg Max_{j \in I} f(u,i)$ will be the recommended item for a specific user u [11, 12].

The recommender systems use collaborative filtering for recommendation framework due to its capability to utilize the ratings of other users for the predictions and recommendations. These ratings and reviews are aggregated and analyzed systematically to present a reasonable recommendation to the active user. It works on the principle of similarity of liking among the clusters of users. Collaborative filtering is classified into two categories: user-user CF and item-item CF. Concept of classification in user-user CF is the similarity of the ratings of various users. It relies upon the behavior of user and their orientation toward different items. It can be represented through the similarity function defined by $s : U \times U \rightarrow R$. However, the time complexity of user-user CF suffers the problem of scalability in case of large number of users. On the other hand, item-item CF utilizes the rating patterns of items and the respective similarities to predict the user's orientation toward the items. It is also found to be robust to the scaling issue and independent of the number of users. The similarity function derived in item-item CF is derived as $s : I \times I \rightarrow R$. Although both the methods of collaborative filtering are easy to implement and find applications in various fields with reasonable accuracies, they are subject to some implementation constraints. User-based method is found to be more suitable in the situation where the number of items is more than the number of users. However, item-based methods provide better performance in case where the number of users is more than the number of items. Item-item CF is used in this research work for the teacher recommendation because the number of parameters used to evaluate the performance of the teachers is less than the number of teachers [13–15].

9.4   Proposed Methodology

The proposed work comprises of a recommender for teachers of an educational institution depending upon various attributes. These attributes are qualitative and quantitative. The nature of these attributes is random because of the behavioral dependency of the stakeholders in the process. Therefore, a probabilistic framework using hidden Markov model is proposed in this paper. The HMM model is modified to make it adaptive in nature. The framework is continuously observed and parameters are modified on the basis of the error values. This way the model is made adaptive so as to deal with the operational dynamic uncertainties. A stochastic model is presented to resemble the time varying user preferences in terms of joint probability as

$$p(U,I) = \sum_{Y} p(Y)p(U|Y)p(I|Y) = \sum_{Y} p(U)p(Y|U)p(I|U) \quad (9.1)$$

It can be deduced from (9.1) that the occurrence of user and item within an observation space is independent event if the distribution of latent class (Y) is known for the observation space. This allows us to encode the entire preference of the user over the various items using the latent classes. The varying user preferences are mapped over the dynamic latent class model to derive the HMM. The overall HMM model is defined using various parameters like the initial state probability distribution for each user (π), transition probability table (A), and respective observation model. The initial state distribution model considered in this paper is derived as

$$\sum_{u}\sum_{n} p\left(Y_u^1 = n \,\middle|\, X; \Gamma^{n-1}\right)\log \pi_n \quad (9.2)$$

where Γ^{n-1} is the parameter estimation of previous iteration, Y_u^1 represents the latent estimate of uth user at first iteration, and π_n is the probability distribution for nth iteration. $p\left(Y_u^1 = n|X\right)$ represents the summary statistics of the posterior distribution. Similarly, the transition model derived in this work is given by

$$\sum_{u}\sum_{t=2}^{T}\sum_{i}\sum_{j} p\left(Y_u^{t-1} = i, Y_u^t = n \,\middle|\, X; \Gamma^{n-1}\right)\log A_{ij} \quad (9.3)$$

where t resembles to the transition instance. The respective observation model is given by

$$\sum_u \sum_{t=1}^{T} \sum_j p\left(Y_u^t = n \middle| X ; \Gamma^{n-1}\right) \log p\left(N_u^t\right) \qquad (9.4)$$

The three models may now be independently tuned to derive the maximum likelihood estimation. The overall HMM model is derived by adding (9.2), (9.3), and (9.4), which transforms the problem into an estimation of maximum a posteriori (MAP) estimates. Bayes' theorem can be used further to deduce the maximum posterior distribution. It also resolves the issue of over-fitting of the model with the outliers of the small training samples. The final prediction can be performed using the fine-tuned observation model as given in (9.4). The parameters of the derived HMM model are then optimized using the particle swarm optimization. PSO is an evolutionary algorithm based on stochastic method where each particle is representing the possible solution for the HMM parameter optimization. The parameters are moved in the space after each iteration and the process continues until the best possible solution is not attained. The final solution is considered as the optimal weights of the HMM framework.

The optimal solution in PSO is derived through the following folmulation:

$$v[] = W \times v[] + c_1 \times r \times (pbest[] - present[]) \\ + c_2 \times R \times (gbest[] - present[]) \qquad (9.5)$$

and

$$present[] = present[] + v[] \qquad (9.6)$$

Here, $v[]$ represent the weight vector, W is the inertia weight, and c_1 and c_2 are the acceleration constants. P_{best} and g_{best} represent the individual extremes and global extremes of the algorithms respectively. Variables r and R are the random numbers ranging from 0 to 1. The weights calculation is done iteratively on the basis of present solutions.

The overall algorithm used in the proposed HMM-based teacher recommender system is shown in Algorithm 9.1.

Algorithm 9.1 HMM-based recommender system algorithm.

---

1. *Collect the user data and Item data for the complete time T.*
2. *Initialize the model parameters π, A, Γ.*
3. *Compute the values of initial state distribution using the model given in (9.2).*
4. *Evaluate the transition model using (9.3).*
5. *Tune the observation model given in (9.4) through MAP estimates and modify the weights.*
6. *Derive the final estimates through the PCO model.*

9.5   Experiment Analysis

The performance of the proposed recommender system was evaluated using the real time data of the teachers and other stakeholders from an educational institute. Various attributes of the teachers are collected as primary parameters like Job_skills (Qualification_ID, Exp_ID, Level_ID), User_skills (User_qualification, User_Exp), and research publications. Some secondary parameters like feedback, ratings, and student's marks are also considered. The evaluation is performed for four teachers over these 10 parameters. The data is collected from over 1,000 students and is converted into a large dataset. The qualitative features like the soft skills, communication skills, sensitivity, and extracurricular aptitude are also considered while creating the dataset. The dataset is the used to train the proposed HMM-based recommender system. The outcome of the proposed model consists of four classes: primary teaching, secondary teaching, and higher secondary teaching and college teaching. The recommender system is expected to generate the outcome on the basis of these training attributes and should be able to classify that the respective teacher should be recommended for which level of teaching. For example, a teacher with doctoral degree, rich experience, and good publication should be recommended for college teaching, but a teacher with graduate degree should be classified as a secondary or higher secondary teacher. The classes and the respective decision-making, however, are not a straightforward simple problem. It is indeed a very complex problem in nature due to the time changing behavioral attributes. The performance of the proposed model is evaluated in terms of various metrics like accuracy, precision, and recall. It is also compared with the performance of some conventional recommendation frameworks like content-based filtering, cost-sensitive collaborative filtering, and hybrid recommender. Table 9.1 shows the comparative analysis of various techniques and shows that the proposed recommender provides a better performance.

Table 9.1 Performance comparison.

Technique/Metrics	Accuracy	Precision	Recall
Content-based filtering	0.473	0.060	0.679
Cost-sensitive collaborative filtering	0.921	0.143	0.132
Hybrid recommender	0.509	0.089	1
Proposed recommender	0.965	0.150	0.135

9.6   Conclusion

A recommender system for teachers is proposed in this chapter using the HMM framework to deal with the probabilistic distribution of the attributes. The recommendation is proposed on the basis of various primary and secondary parameters, which directly and indirectly governs the characteristics of the teacher entity. The parameters like job skills required, user skills attained, research publications, feedbacks, ratings, soft skill, communication skills, and students' assessment have been considered in this work to evaluate the class of the teacher. The classification is made under the decision base including the primary level, secondary level, and higher secondary level of college level teaching. The parameters of the HM model are optimized using the PSO algorithm to attain the best recommendation solutions. The HMM framework is made adaptive by tuning the weights with reference to the error. The performance of the proposed technique is evaluated in terms of parameters like accuracy, precision, and recall. It is also compared with the other conventional techniques and found to be performing better than those techniques.

References

1. Fletcher, C., Performance appraisal and management: The developing research agenda. *J. Occup. Organ. Psychol.*, 74, 4, 473, 2001.
2. Grote, R.C., *The performance appraisal question and answer book: A survival guide for managers*, American Management Association, New York, 2002.
3. Hamsa, H., Indiradevi, S., Kizhak, J.J., Student academic performance prediction model using decision tree and fuzzy genetic algorithm. *Proc. Technol.*, 25, 326–332, 2016.

4. Iam-On, N. and Boongoen, T., Improved student dropout prediction in Thai University using ensemble of mixed-type data clusterings. *Int. J. Mach. Learn. Cybern.*, 8, 497–510, 2017.

5. Migueis, V., Freitas, A., Garciab, P.J., Silva, A., Early segmentation of students according to their academic performance: A predictive modelling approach. *Decis. Support Syst.*, 115, 36–51, 2018.

6. Altujjar, Y., Altamimi, W., Al-Turaiki, I., Predicting critical courses affecting students performance: A case study. *Proc. Comput. Sci.*, 82, 65–71, 2016.

7. Zhang, X., Sun, G., Pan, Y., Sun, H., He, Y., Students performance modelling based on behavior pattern. *J. Ambient Intell. Hum. Comput.*, 9, 1659–1670, 2018.

8. Pandey, M. and Taruna, S., Towards the integration of multiple classifier pertaining to the Student's performance prediction. *Perspect. Sci.*, 8, 364–366, 2016.

9. Thai-Nghe, N., Drumond, L., Krohn-Grimberghe, A., Schmidt-Thieme, L., Recommender system for predicting student performance. *Proc. Comput. Sci.*, 1, 2811–2819, 2010.

10. Khasanah, A.U. and Harwati, A comparative study to predict student's performance using educational data mining techniques. *IOP Conf. Ser.: Mater. Sci. Eng.*, 215, 1–7, 2017.

11. Mohamed Ahmeda, A., Rizanerc, A., Ulusoy, A.H., Using data mining to predict instructor performance. *Proc. Comput. Sci.*, 102, 137–142, 2016.

12. Naser, S.A., Zaqout, I., Atallah, R., Alajrami, E., Abu Ghosh, M., Predicting student performance using artificial neural network: In the faculty of engineering and information technology. *Int. J. Hybrid Inf. Technol.*, 8, 2, 221–228, 2015.

13. Romero, C. and Ventura, S., Educational data mining: A review of the state of the art. *IEEE Trans. Syst. Man Cybern. Part C: Appl. Rev.*, 40, 6, 601–618, 2010.

14. Helal, S., Li, J., Liu, L., Ebrahimiea, E., Dawsonb, S., Murrayc, D.J., Predicting academic performance by considering student heterogeneity. *Knowledge-Based Syst.*, 161, 134–146, 2018.

15. Mohamed Ahmeda, A., Rizanerc, A., Ulusoy, A.H., Using data mining to predict instructor performance. *Proc. Comput. Sci.*, 102, 137–142, 2016.

10

Virtual Moratorium System

**Manisha Bhende[1]*, Muzasarali Badger[2], Pranish Kumbhar[2], Vedanti Bhatkar[2]
and Payal Chavan[2]**

*[1]Marathwada Mitra Mandals Institute of Technology, Pune, India
[2]Department of Computer Engineering, Dr. D.Y. Patil Institute of Engineering,
Management and Research, Akurdi, Pune, India*

Abstract

This chapter entitled "Virtual Moratorium System" gathers data about why the customers have opted for the moratorium. This is a web and android application. We have developed a chatbot for easy communication. In today's time, it is difficult to use physical banking services to resolve the issue. By using a proposed system, the banker will get all the information regarding a customer who has opted for the moratorium. The user will interact with the chatbot and submit the moratorium request. The chatbot will ask questions based on customers' responses. Rasa Natural language Processing (NLP) and Rasa Natural Language Understanding algorithm will classify the intents from user response. Intents will be compared with predefined patterns to extract the specific data. These responses will be stored in the NoSQL (MongoDB) database. These data will be shared with the banker, who will further analyze them. The main purpose of this chapter is to help the banker to know whether the customer who has applied for the moratorium is genuine. With this system, both the customer and the banker will be able to save their time and efforts. The proposed system will allow the customers to register moratorium at anytime and anywhere using a dedicated web platform and android application as well as some social media platform. Complete chatbot moratorium system will be encrypted with secure encryption algorithms (AES-256, SSH). This system does not contain only moratorium functionalities but also has some extra features like news and updates that are crawled from various genuine news platforms and official banking sites. With all of these features, REST API services are also available for further enhancements and integration to multiple platforms.

Keywords: Chatbot, moratorium, Rasa, webhook

**Corresponding author*: manisha.bhende@gmail.com

R. Arokia Priya, Anupama V Patil, Manisha Bhende, Anuradha Thakare and Sanjeev Wagh (eds.)
Object Detection by Stereo Vision Images, (171–184) © 2022 Scrivener Publishing LLC

10.1   Introduction

We are developing an application for the bank that will help the customers to avail the moratorium facility without going to the bank.

In today's time, it is difficult to go to the bank and resolve the issue. Hence, we are designing an Android + Web application that will be beneficial to customers to know the information about moratorium from anywhere at any time. For more easy access, we are developing a chatbot. Customers will interact with the chatbot and will solve his/her queries. Customers can also get other details rather than a moratorium. We are also providing a moratorium calculator.

All the data of customers will be stored in a database, and this data will be forwarded to bank employees. They will then decide whether the moratorium request is genuine or not depending on all the criteria. Customers can check the status of his/her request. The customer will also be notified with an important update from time to time.

We are using Rasa for the chatbot for more efficiency. This will also save customers time. Customers can apply for a moratorium on any loan. We are going to create dummy bank data for the whole application. We are also going to use web scrapping so that we can get some information related to bank data [2].

This system will reduce the customer's time to go to the bank and apply for the facility. It will also provide easy access and more efficiency.

10.1.1   Objectives

- To gather the data about why the customers have opted for a moratorium.
- To identify the mindset of the customer by raising multiple queries.
- To store the responses of customers.
- To check whether the customer is genuine or not.
- Easy communication through chatbot.

10.2   Literature Survey

10.2.1   Virtual Assistant—BLU

BLU is a self-service chatbot, which is available at https://www.bajajfin-serv.in/. Using this, customers can interact with a digital assistant and get answers to any queries regarding our product and service, as well as about any existing relationships with the bank. This service is out there around the clock and provides instant resolution to customer queries.

Features:

- My Accounts
- EMI Card
- E-Statements
- Update Details
- Important Updates
- eMandate Registration

10.2.2 HDFC Ask EVA

EVA is your personal assistant on HDFC Bank's website, available 24/7 to help you with your banking queries. You can get answers that you are trying to find without the effort of waiting on a call or at a branch.

Features:

- Insta Account
- WhatsApp Banking
- UPI Payment
- Block Card
- Report Failed Transaction
- Loan Service Request

10.3 Methodologies of Problem Solving

EJS, CSS, Bootstrap, and JS are used for the frontend. Node.js is used for the backend. Rasa is used for chatbots. The chatbot will work in the following way:

- User sends a text message through a web application or an android app [4].
- Then, the message will be transferred to Rasa.
- This message is categorized and compared with a corresponding intent.
- The actions for each intent are defined in the webhook.
- When the intent is found by Rasa, the webhook will use APIs to find a response in the database.

- The database sends back the information to the webhook.
- Webhook then sends a response in the format of JSON data to the intent.
- Intent generates the data.
- The data go to the output web application and android device.
- The user gets a text response.

Before using the chatbot, the user first has to register to the website. After registering, the user needs to log in with the proper credentials, and then the chatbot interface will appear where the customer will interact with the chatbot. All the responses during the interaction with the chatbot will be stored in the database. We are using MongoDB as the database. MongoDB is a real-time database that helps to store and synchronize data.

The data stored in the database will then be forwarded to the banker. The banker then will decide whether to accept or reject the moratorium request. As we cannot access real-time bank data, we are creating dummy bank data. To create dummy bank data, we are going to use web scraping. We will extract information from bank websites and will use it for creating moratorium criteria. We are using Axios which is a web scraping library [5].

As we are dealing with bank applications, security is a must. We have used the AES algorithm for security. AES uses symmetric key encryption, which involves the utilization of just one secret key to cipher and deciphers information.

10.4 Modules

10.4.1 Chatbot

The chatbot module is the base module that performs the operations based on user inputs. Chatbot module uses artificial intelligence and natural language processing (NLP) to understand what a user wants and guide them to their desired outcome with as little work for the end user as possible [1] like a virtual assistant for your moratorium-related services.

This module consists of various features like applying moratorium, giving timely news related to the banking sector, registration and login to moratorium platform, and answers some general questions. When the chatbot does not recognize what the user wants to say, then it replies with

"Sorry, I cannot recognize that..." and takes a user request once again until the user stops the chatbot.

This module is the heart of this research paper. Because we are trying to replace the traditional form-filling system with a conversational system, which will ask questions related to the user's current situation.

10.4.2   Android Application

This module is the user interface module that organizes and represents all the backend functionalities in user understandable UI.

Android app features activities like news, history, and profile activity as base activities. Along with them, Chatbot activity is included to interact with users.

10.4.3   Web Application

This module is the user interface module for web users. This module is divided in sub-modules, which are follows:

- Registration: The customer needs to be registered on our system. He needs to register with an email-id and password. After registering, the credentials are encrypted and stored in MongoDB. The credentials are encrypted using AES-256.
- Login: After completing the registration, the user will log in to the system. The user needs to log in using an email id and password. While login email-id and password will be checked with the email-id and password stored in the database. While checking the encrypted password in the database, it will be decrypted first and then will be checked with the password entered by the user. If the credentials are right, then the login will be successful else fail.
- Moratorium Calculator: Used to calculate loan EMI and interest rate. Here, the user needs to give the principal loan amount, interest rate, and the no of months as input. This will be calculated, and then, the result will show the monthly payment and the interest rate on it.
- News and Notifications: News related to banking will be displayed. News is web scrapped so that the user will get the latest news related to banking. Axios is used for web scrapping. The web scrapped data will be stored in the database.

News will be retrieved from the database and then displayed to the user.

- Status: Users can check the status of their request in the Moratorium Request section. To check the status, user first needs to login into their account. The status can be pending, approved, or rejected. The status is changed by the Admin. Admin will decide whether to approve or reject. In addition, the mail of approval or rejection will be sent to the user.
- Profile: Information related to the user will be displayed in the profile section. User name, contact no., adhar no., account no., and more data will be displayed in the profile section. This data will be encrypted and stored in the database. Users can also edit this profile anytime.

10.5   Detailed Flow of Proposed Work

10.5.1   System Architecture

Figure 10.1 illustrates the architecture of our system. User and Admin will interact with the system. Users can interact through the web or android application. The system will take all the necessary input and then encrypt the data. The system will generate the API requests and send them to the server through the API gateway. Server operations will receive the data, decrypt the data, process the data, generate responses, encrypt responses, and send data to the user. All the data in the server then will be stored in the main database. The operational data will be stored in the proxy database. The proxy database will contain the sessional data. While retrieving

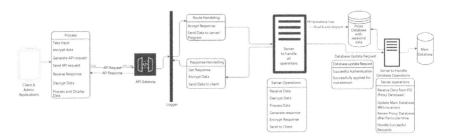

Figure 10.1 System architecture.

the data, data from the database will send to the server, and then, this data will be decrypted and send to the user through the API gateway. While requesting, the data will be stored in Logger as well.

10.5.2   DFD Level 1

In DFD 1, process is divided into more small processes, as shown in Figure 10.2. The database is also included. Customer and Admin will be the entities. customer_db, account_db, and details_db are the databases. Processes are Registration, Login, Edit Profile, Checking Account Details, Asking Query to Chatbot, Checking Status, Approval for Moratorium Request, and View Moratorium Request. Customers will interact with the Registration, Login, Edit Profile, Checking Account Details, Asking Query to Chatbot, and Checking Status processes. While registration, data will be stored in customer_db. While login, data will be verified from customer_db. While editing the profile, data will be stored and retrieved from customer_db. Account details will be checked from account_db. Queries of chatbot will be stored in details_db. The status will be retrieved from details_db. Admin will interact with Approval for Moratorium Request and View Moratorium Request processes. The status will be stored in details_db. The moratorium requests will be retrieved from the details_db.

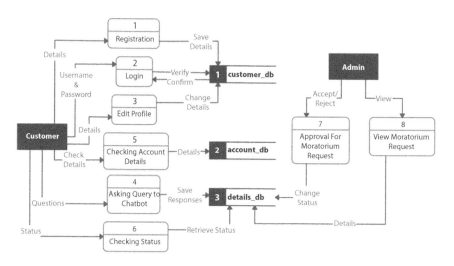

Figure 10.2 DFD level 1.

10.6   Architecture Design

10.6.1   Main Server

Main server is the backend server for the application which performs all the operations. All the requests from the web app, Android app, and Chatbot are processed by the main server. This server consists of various API routes to handle the requests asynchronously.

Technology Stack:

- Node.js: Node.js application provides the backend support to handle users requests asynchronously and provides a platform to develop the backend services.
- Express.js: Express.js is the lightweight Node.js framework to create and manage HTTP requests in the form of API. All the routes are designed by Express.js as per the requirement of the particular operation.
- Nodemailer: Nodemailer services are used to send application status via registered email.

Request and Response Format:

- Request: All the requests use either HTTP GET or HTTP POST methods.
  Example:
  Operation / Function: Login
  API route: http://localhost:8040/login/
  Method: POST
  Data / Body: Email, Password (Encrypted format)
- Response: Responses are generated in JSON format with all encrypted data.
  Example:
  Operation / Function: Login
  Data: login_status, user_profile_data, application_data
  Operation / Function: News
  Data: title, time, id

10.6.2   Chatbot

Chatbot performs all operations based on user input in a conversational format.

Technology Stack:

- Python: Generate responses, predict users' next question, and connect to the main server.
- YML: Conversational data, classifiers, conversational structure, and response.

NLP:

NLP is used everywhere in an application when it needs to take raw user text as input: whether it is a chatbot receiving input from speech-to-text software, or a user type question in the textbox. NLP is the essential step that transforms a string of words into a form that can be interpreted and acted upon by other systems in the application.

Action:

When a chatbot detects a custom action, the Rasa NLU server sends an HTTP POST request to the action server with a JSON payload including the name of the detected action, the user's conversation ID, the entities from the tracker, and the entities of the domain.

When the action server completes the tasks of a custom action, it returns a JSON payload of responses and events. The Rasa action server then returns the responses to the respective user and adds the events to the conversation tracker.

Webhook:

Webhooks typically are used to connect chatbot and client applications. When an event take effect on the trigger application, it serializes data about that event and sends it to a webhook URL from the action application..

Storage Structure:

Structure for request:

```
{
  "sender": "User",
  "message": "Apply Moratorium"
}
```

Structure for response:

```
[
  {"text": "Hello user! Please answer the following questions."},
  {"image": "http://example.com/image.jpg"}
]
```

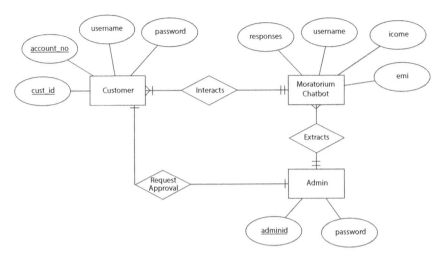

Figure 10.3 ER diagram.

10.6.3   Database Architecture

Technology Stack:

- MongoDB: MongoDB is a source-available cross-platform document-oriented database program. MongoDB is a NoSQL database program. It uses JSON formatted documents with optional schemas.
- Collections: ER diagrams in Figure 10.3 show the collections and their interconnections with other collections.

10.6.4   Web Scraper

Technology Stack:

- Axios and Cheerio: Axios and Cheerio are used to crawl the web for the latest news whenever a user sends a request to a server via applications or chatbot.

Sources:

- Banking sector: Latest News on Banking sector Top News, Photos, Videos at Business Standard (business-standard. com)

- Banking News | Latest Banking News | Banking and Finance News Updates (moneycontrol.com)

Storage Structure:
  Title: { type: String},
  Link: { type: String},
  Time : { type : Date, default: Date.now }

10.7   Algorithms Used

10.7.1   AES-256 Algorithm

The working of AES-256 algorithm is shown in Figure 10.4. First, the plain text, i.e., data to be encrypted will be given. This data will be encrypted using a secret key. Then, this cipher text, i.e., encrypted data will be stored in the MongoDB database. For decryption, data will be retrieved from the database and will be decrypted using the same secrete key we used for encryption [3].

For example, "11223344" is plain text; then, it will be encrypted using encrypt method of AES-256, and "secret_keyword" will be the key for encryption. After encryption, we will get the ciphertext as "AB@123d^7fhf"; this cipher text will be stored in the database. While for decryption, the decrypt method of AES-256 will be used. Parameters for this method will be "AB@123d^7fhf" cipher text and the key "secret_keyword". After decryption, we will get "11223344" as decrypted data.

10.7.2   Rasa NLU

Figure 10.4 describes about the working of AES-256.

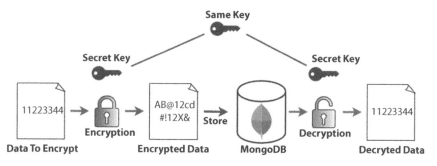

Figure 10.4 AES-256 working.

10.8   Results

Figure 10.5 shows the result.

Figure 10.5 Results.

10.9   Discussions

10.9.1   Applications

- Banking sector
- Conversational software platform

10.9.2   Future Work

- Multilingual chatbot
- Voice assistant
- Application for IOS platform
- Multi-bank Integration

10.9.3   Conclusion

This chapter mainly focuses on the low-cost implementation of the moratorium, which can help the needy people in the crucial period, due to pandemic, and the proposed system provides end-to-end security for all personal details using the advance technologies of Rasa along with EJS, CSS, Node.js, JavaScript, and MongoDB.

The overall system is to help the affected people to a particular period of time, since we use Rasa, direct interaction can be done with the chatbot and get all the responses from the Admin and the chatbot. The further version can be made for not only the people affected by pandemic even who are unable to make payments with a vital reason.

References

1. Kannadasan, R., Prabakaran, N., Krishnamoorthy, A., Krishna, N.T., Giri, S.V., Reddy, K.P.K., Chatbot Using Dialogflow and Web Services. *International Journal of Innovative Technology and Exploring Engineering (IJITEE)*, 9, 1S, 253–260, November 2019.
2. Oruganti, S.C., *Virtual bank assistance- an AI-based voice bot for better banking*, January 2020.
3. Mugdha, K.P. and Kulkarni, S., Artificial Intelligence in Financial Services-Customer Chatbot Advisor Adoption. 9, 1, November 2019.
4. Fatima, S., Avasthi, S., Nalawade, C., James, J., Mohammad, M., Ayisha, S., Ravi, G., Shrotri, P., A Mobile Application for Voice Enabled Virtual Bot. August 2018.
5. Uzun, E., A Novel Web Scraping Approach Using the Additional Information Obtained From Web Pages. March 2020, *IEEE Access*, 99, 1-1 April 13, 2020.

11

Efficient Land Cover Classification for Urban Planning

Vandana Tulshidas Chavan[1]* and Sanjeev J. Wagh[2]

[1]CSE Department, Sharad Institute of Technology, Ichalkaranji, India
[2]Information Technology, Government College of Engineering, Karad, India

Abstract

Understanding spatiotemporal urban dynamics is incredibly vital within the context of the speedy urban boom with severe social and environmental challenges, like urban impoverishment, numerous sorts of pollution, vulnerabilities to seasoning activities, climate alternate effects, modifications in native weather, and their probable impacts on water level and so on. Findings of the strategies is expected so that it will facilitate in making plans belonging urban improvement rules and complete framework for its designing and control. Knowledge of land cover, land use, and land change is very essential for understanding human activity and creating plans, policies, and solutions for urban planning. This paper proposes the development of a land cover classification system that can classify images efficiently based on the land cover in an efficient manner without any human intervention.

Keywords: Land cover, land use, urban planning, image classification, fuzzy logic, deep learning

11.1 Introduction

As larger than half of the world population abode in town regions, urbanization well modified our residing environments. Likewise, environmental changes are impacted by urban development. Urban planning has become crucial for future development. Knowledge of human activity is very essential for creating plans, policies, and solutions for cities. Many

---

*Corresponding author: vandana.t.chavan@gmail.com

R. Arokia Priya, Anupama V Patil, Manisha Bhende, Anuradha Thakare and Sanjeev Wagh (eds.)
Object Detection by Stereo Vision Images, (185–194) © 2022 Scrivener Publishing LLC

urban planning professions study people's behavior as they need to analyze data about places, routes, transportation, urban design, community and economic development, and many other social and economic factors [13].

The progress made in earth observation technologies has generated a huge amount of data that combines geolocation with spectral and spatial information. As new generations of satellites are being released with up-to-date and progressed sensors, Landsat pictures are continuously improving and offering richness in radiometric, spectral, spatial, and pixel resolution. This data is conceivably helpful to numerous crowds. For instance, metropolitan organizers could utilize it to more readily comprehend the employments of the city and to distinguish approaches to fit recognized examples, and land engineers could find out about how regions inside the city is recognized and how to work for explicit business sectors. As of late, these kinds of information have been utilized for metropolitan investigation of different components of urban areas like centralization of human movement, food trucks social occasions, and authentic examination of urban communities [12].

Land use/land cover (LULC) has been considered as one of the important factors of global environmental and urban development. Land cover exhibits the territory highlights in the world's floor, and land use mirrors the use of accessible land by the individuals for example residential area, farm utilization of landscapes, and so forth. Exact information on LULC gives basic data for urban planning [11].

For many environmental and socioeconomic applications, image classification is playing an important role, especially for LULC applications. Image classification results are very helpful, especially for medical imaging, forensic sciences, acoustic imaging, hyperspectral image processing, etc. It has long attracted the attention of the research community. Image classification process involves categorizing and labeling groups of pixels, objects found in images, or vectors within an image-based on specific rules. The categorization law can be derived from one or more spectral or textural characteristics.

The importance and necessity of digital image processing is due to two most important software regions: the primary being the improvement of pictorial records for human interpretation and the second one being the processing of scene statistics for an autonomous machine belief. Digital image processing has a vast variety of applications including faraway sensing, medical imaging, acoustic imaging, forensic sciences, and commercial automation [2]. Satellite images are useful in monitoring earth resources, geographical mapping, and prediction of agricultural vegetation, urban population, weather forecasting, flood, and fire management.

The earth's surface is greatly influenced due to certain impacts by society and natural reasons. Over the previous decades, the foremost liked topic within the sector of remote sensing and GIS (geographic information system) environments has evolved LULC analysis due to the enlargement of several urban modifications and developments [12]. Figure 11.1 shows forest cover change detection during 1991, 2002, and 2019 [15].

The critical environmental parts, like temperature, rainfall, and groundwater level, are influenced by the unsystematic, fast, and impromptu urbanization development process. To deal with this issue, there is a requirement for precise and extensive planning for reasonable improvement of the urban areas with a solid metropolitan environment and protection of natural resources. This requires an incorporated way to deal with urbanization to assure the conservation of water, the balance of climatic conditions at the miniature level, and so on. Moderate urban planning might help for provisions of natural resources [14].

In image classification, a category label is assigned to a picture. In object localization, it draws a bounding box around one or more objects in a picture. The object detection method combines these two tasks. It draws a bounding box around each observed object within the image. Category

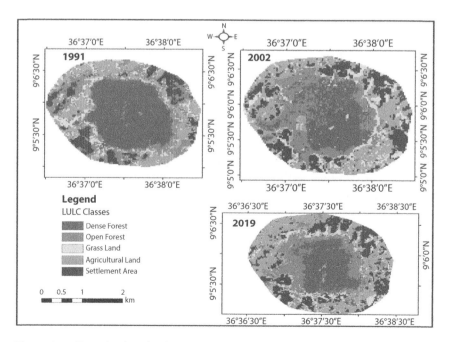

Figure 11.1 Forest land use land cover map of 1991, 2002, and 2019.

label is assigned to each object. These three terms together are called object recognition [1].

Researchers follow different image classification approaches based on the strategy such as supervised and unsupervised, or crisp and fuzzy, parametric and non-parametric classification. Image classification is a complex process that is suffering from many factors. It is a very challenging task, largely because of a great deal of variability, which arising from misalignment, different lighting conditions, non-rigid deformations, etc. [7].

Two well-known techniques of classification are "supervised" and "unsupervised". The unsupervised classification approach is a completely automatic process without the usage of education statistics. The desired traits of an image are detected systematically at some point of the image processing level by using an appropriate set of rules. Image clustering frequently used unsupervised classification.

The supervised classification method is the manner of visually deciding on samples (i.e., training data) within the image and assigning them to preselected categories (i.e., car, roads, homes, water frame, and plant) to create statistical measures to be implemented to the entire image. Methods "maximum probability" and "minimal distance" are categorization techniques [2].

Conventional image classification techniques limit the accuracy of the classification. Many factors affect accuracy like different alignment, different lighting conditions, and variations due to changes in device angels.

Many researchers proposed various methods for image classification using machine learning algorithms. To obtain high performance in visual feature learning from satellite images, large-scale labeled data is feed as input to train deep neural networks. Other major factors that limit accuracy is the feature uncertainties, small number of labeled data, and noise in the raw data for image classification tasks. The main objective of land cover classification is to associate labels to different parts of physical land type or land area. Various methods implemented for land cover classification are dependent on the accuracy of the initial label map. In addition, this technique needs to deal with the hidden or black portion of images like shadows [8].

In machine learning, representation learning is a set of techniques to find out a feature transformation of data input to a representation that will be effectively exploited in machine learning tasks like clustering and classification of big data. Deep learning (DL) has become an immensely active area of machine learning for several computer vision applications, and language processing tasks. Deep learning has come to be the buzzword these days due to the results acquired in the various domains like image classification, object detection, and natural language processing. Especially, for clinical image classification strategy, deep neural networks play a very crucial role [1]. The image category accepts the given biomedical images and produces the output class for identifying different diseases.

DL has become an important branch of machine learning for different applications. DL module performance is dependent on sufficient network training by large-scale data, which is a very expensive task. That is, they require large amounts of labeled data to supervise the network learning. Manual labeling of information is not easy as it is a complicated and time-consuming task [3]. Existing approaches for land cover classification scenarios categorized images to a single class, whereas a given scene can belong to more than one class. In multi-label classification, each image is associated with multiple labels.

Another technique that come to be a buzzword is fuzzy logic. It provides useful techniques to deal with imprecise information. Fuzzy logic partial membership function allows the knowledge about more complex situations, like cover mixture or intermediate conditions, and is often better represented using fuzzy logic, and imprecise information can be better utilized by it.

A fuzzy logic system is flexible and allows modification in the membership rules. Even distorted, inaccurate, and erroneous input data is additionally accepted by this system. The fuzzy logic theory covers uncertainty, particularly unclearness (i.e., fuzzy) within the dataset.

11.2 Literature Survey

This section reviews the image classification–related works using various techniques.

For image classification, there have been few early attempts that successfully blended fuzzy logic with the neural network.

Yue *et al.* [2] proposed a technique that consists of three modules: a reconstruction module, a feature learning module, and a fuzzy self-supervision module, termed as a self-supervised fuzzy clustering network (SFCN). The representation ability of the network is ensured by the first two modules. The fuzzy self-supervision module provides training direction for the whole network. SFCN adds the fuzzy clustering technique results to supervise the network. It displays the probability about the membership of each retinal image for a respective cluster.

To reduce and exposing hidden uncertainties within the dataset, Riaz *et al.* [3] proposed semi-supervised method to create a fusion of fuzzy-rough c-mean clustering with convolutional neural network (FRCNN). This method uses labeled and unlabeled data for obtaining information from fuzzy-rough c-mean clustering and CNN representations.

To highlight the benefits of the fusion of fuzzy logic techniques with DL, Price *et al.* [5] proposed a strategy to incorporate fuzzy-based fusion approaches. It introduced a fuzzy layer directly into the DL architecture. This semi-supervised fuzzy rough convolutional neural network (SSFR-CNN) technique approach combining supervised neural network and unsupervised fuzzy difficult C-mean clustering to train a proposed semi-supervised convolutional neural network.

DL is a rising and powerful method. It allows feature learning from a large datasets. However, it is a fully deterministic model, which cannot capture information hidden due to uncertainty in a given dataset. To overcome the limitations of fixed representation, Deng *et al.* [6] introduced hierarchical deep neural network, the concepts of fusion of fuzzy learning with DL. This derives information from both neural and fuzzy representations. Then, the knowledge extracted from this is utilized to form the final data representation which is used for further classification. This paradigm outperforms compared to other crisp learning approaches when applied to the practical tasks of image categorization for datasets having a high level of uncertainties in the raw data, e.g., brain MRI segmentation and financial data prediction.

Recently, DL has also been successfully used for hyperspectral image classification tasks like other image classification applications. For classification, training deep neural networks, like a convolutional neural network, needs a large number of the labeled dataset to train the neural networks. However, in remote sensing applications, usually, only a small amount of labeled data is available for training. These datasets are expensive to collect and may have unlabeled data. For hyperspectral image classification, Wu *et al.* [7] proposed a semi-supervised DL approach convolutional recurrent neural network (CRNN) that uses finite labeled and unlabeled data to train network. For hyperspectral image classification, a CRNN is used. The unlabeled data are utilized with pseudo labels (cluster labels). With the use of all the training data together with their pseudo labels to pre-train a deep CRNN. For hyperspectral classification, this method has given improved performance over supervised and semi-supervised learning methods [4].

Stivaktakis *et al.* [8] proposed multi-label land cover classification method that can increase the size of a smaller data set. Their experiments improve accuracy after being applied to the UC Merced Land Use data set.

Zou *et al.* [9] proposed an object-based image classification (OBIC) scheme integrated with object-level and pixel-level features for the PolSAR image classification.

Li *et al.* [10] proposed a model called multiaugmented, attention-based CNN (MAA-CNN) for high-spatial-resolution remote sensing (HRRS) image scene classification mechanism, which can capture the most judicial areas in HRRS images as much as possible.

Natural and organic landscapes like water lands, forests, grasslands, and urbanized and developed areas are considered as the land cover region. The developments that happen in the land address the current utilization of the properties like developed industries, malls, parks, and reservoirs are depicted as land use classifications. At the point when the land areas of a specific spot or territory have been changed or changed one kind to another, then it is considered as the problem of LU/LC change, for example, the difference in the woodland region to either fruitless land, desolate land, or rural land. At least two satellite pictures taken on various periods were compared for the execution of the LU/LC change investigation measure. Researcher must focus on the prediction problem of LU/LC change, considering the supply of the anticipated results to the land resource management and to urban planners to assist them in taking suitable decisions for the land cover environment [12].

11.3   Proposed Methodology

The proposed methodology for land cover classification is given in Figure 11.2. The LU/LC classification requires image datasets that can be collected from different resources like satellite data, arial photographs, and field or ground survey data. Image datasets feed input to the preprocessing phase.

Preprocessing is a fundamental interaction in upgrading the satellite pictures, and it helps in the additional preparation of satellite information.

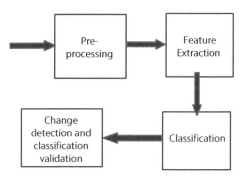

Figure 11.2 Proposed system for land cover classification.

Analysts had utilized various preprocessing methods for preparing the satellite information for eliminating cloud effects, clamor, blunders, etc. Different correction techniques like geometric, atmospheric, radiometric, and other spatial upgrades are preferred for the satellite picture preprocessing procedures. Numerous specialists utilize preprocessing techniques for the improvement of satellite pictures, which helps in accomplishing better precision results during the classification of LU/LC.

The various significant feature extraction techniques that can be utilized are feature selection, K-mean text clustering, enhanced krill herd algorithm, multi-verse optimizer algorithm, etc.

Traditionally, the neural network architecture consists of an input layer, an output layer, and some hidden layers. Fuzzy classifiers that deal with uncertainty issues in input data have the property to better represent real-world features as compared to the crisp method. The proposed method introduces the fusion of fuzzy layers with the DL architecture. It helps to exploit the aggregation properties expressed through fuzzy methodologies.

Researchers extract the data by characterizing the satellite information through the possibilities of diverse classification techniques. They are as follows: per pixel, sub-pixel, object-based, parametric, and non-parametric, hard, soft classifiers, supervised, unsupervised, and semi-supervised.

11.4　Conclusion

This chapter provides an evaluation of the land cover classification analysis for multispectral and hyperspectral images. It gives a special glide of LU/LC change evaluation and strategies related to every stage of the land cover classification process. The fundamental purpose of this land cover classification is to inspire future researchers to work accurately and to aid the land useful resource planners, urban development management, forest department, and authorities officers in taking crucial action, which helps to protect our precious earth's environment.

References

1. Jing, L. and Tian, Y., Self-supervised Visual Feature Learning with Deep Neural Networks: A Survey. *TPAMI*, 43, 11, 4037–4058, 2021.
2. Luo, Y., Pan, J., Fan, S., Du, Z., Zhang, G., Retinal Image Classification by Self-Supervised Fuzzy Clustering Network. *IEEE Access*, 8, 92352–92362, 2020.

3. Riaz, S., Arshad, A., Jiao, L., A semi-supervised CNN with fuzzy rough C-mean for image classification. *IEEE Access*, 7, 49641–49652, 2019.

4. Dasi, S., Peeka, D., Mohammed, R.B., Phaneendra Kumar, B.L.N., Hyperspectral Image Classification using Machine Learning Approaches. *Proceedings of the International Conference on Intelligent Computing and Control Systems (ICICCS 2020)*, IEEE Xplore Part Number:CFP20K74-ART.

5. Price, S.R., Price, S.R., Anderson, D.T., Introducing Fuzzy Layers for Deep Learning. *2019 IEEE International Conference on Fuzzy Systems (FUZZ-IEEE)*, New Orleans, LA, USA, pp. 1–6, 2019.

6. Deng, Y., Ren, Z., Kong, Y., Bao, F., Dai, Q., A Hierarchical Fused Fuzzy Deep Neural Network for Data Classification. *IEEE Trans. Fuzzy Syst.*, 25, 4, 1006–1012, Aug. 2017.

7. Wu, H. and Prasad, S., Semi-Supervised Deep Learning Using Pseudo Labels for Hyperspectral Image Classification. *IEEE Trans. Image Process.*, 27, 3, 1259–1270, March 2018.

8. Stivaktakis, R., Tsagkatakis, G., Tsakalides, P., Deep Learning for Multilabel Land Cover Scene Categorization Using Data Augmentation. *IEEE Geosci. Remote Sens. Lett.*, 16, 7, 1031–1035, July 2019.

9. Zou, B., Xu, X., Zhang, L., Object-Based Classification of PolSAR Images Based on Spatial and Semantic Features. *IEEE J. Sel. Top. Appl. Earth Obs. Remote Sens.*, 13, 609–619, 2020.

10. Li, F., Feng, R., Han, W., Wang, L., An Augmentation Attention Mechanism for High-Spatial-Resolution Remote Sensing Image Scene Classification. *IEEE J. Sel. Top. Appl. Earth Obs. Remote Sens.*, 13, 3862–3878, 2020.

11. Xu, Y., Advanced Multi-Sensor Optical Remote Sensing for Urban Land Use and Land Cover Classification: Outcome of the 2018 IEEE GRSS Data Fusion Contest. *IEEE J. Sel. Top. Appl. Earth Obs. Remote Sens.*, 12, 6, 1709–1724, 2019.

12. Mohan Rajan, S.N., Loganathan, A., Manoharan, P., Survey on Land Use/Land Cover (LU/LC) change analysis in remote sensing and GIS environment: Techniques and Challenges. *Environ. Sci. Pollut. Res.*, 27, 29900–29926, 2020, Springer-Verlag GmbH Germany, Part of Springer Nature, 2020. https://doi.org/10.1007/s11356-020-09091-7.

13. Hu, T., Huang, X., Li, J., Zhang, L., A novel co-training approach for urban land cover mapping with unclear Landsat time series imagery. *Remote Sens. Environ.*, 217, 144–157, 2018, https://doi.org/10.1016/j.rse.2018.08.017. (https://www.sciencedirect.com/science/article/pii/S0034425718303869).

14. Patra, S., Sahoo, S., Mishra, P., Mahapatra, S., Impacts of urbanization on land use /cover changes and its probable implications on local climate and groundwater level. *J. Urban Manage.*, 7, 70–84, 2018, 10.1016/j.jum.2018.04.006. (https://www.researchgate.net/publication/325198135_Impacts_of_urbanization_on_land_use_cover_changes_and_its_probable_implications_on_local_climate_and_groundwater_level).

15. Negassa, M.D., Mallie, D.T., Gemeda, D.O., Forest cover change detection using Geographic Information Systems and remote sensing techniques: a spatio-temporal study on Komto Protected forest priority area, East Wollega Zone, Ethiopia. *Environ. Syst. Res.*, 9, 1, 2020, https://doi.org/10.1186/s40068-020-0163-z.

12

Data-Driven Approches for Fake News Detection on Social Media Platforms: Review

Pradnya Patil[1]* and Sanjeev J. Wagh[2]

[1]Department of Computer Science & Engineering, T.K.I.E.T Warananagar, Maharashtra, India
[2]Department of Information Technology, Government College of Engineering, Karad, Maharashtra, India

Abstract

In recent years, evolution in social media platforms enabled peoples usage of social media applications extensively to connect with others and communities. Nowadays, it is very easy and quick to connect with anywhere in the world and share piece of information to individuals and group of people with ease of use. Thus, increase in sharing of information or news on social media becomes challenging for social media users to distinguish between what is real and fake information or news that reached them. Social media users certainly trusts that whatsoever news or information coming social media is true, but sometimes, its misinformation had spread with some intentions. Fake news is defined as spread of misinformation with some purpose to mislead people. Recently, such incidents of fake news have been rapidly increased across globe and that are causing tension in society and affecting millions of social media users. Nowadays, data-driven analysis approach is used progressively in numerous decision-making processes. Similarly, it can be also used for detection of fake news on social media platforms, so that fake news can be detected easily as earliest and its lateral movement can be controlled before reaching it to millions of users. Hence, it is important to have system that will be helpful for social media users and communities to identify fake news.

Keywords: Fake data, fake news detection, text classification, data-driven analysis, machine learning

**Corresponding author*: pkpatil19@gmail.com

R. Arokia Priya, Anupama V Patil, Manisha Bhende, Anuradha Thakare and Sanjeev Wagh (eds.)
Object Detection by Stereo Vision Images, (195–206) © 2022 Scrivener Publishing LLC

12.1   Introduction

Nowadays, with the rapid growth of the internet era, it promotes today's generation's use of social media as a unique platform for communication. As a result, social media acts a critical role in influencing feelings or emotions of people in favor of or against people, organizations, and government [13]. Positive aspect of social media is that it enables people to reach, nurture, and engage with their target audience anywhere in the world [14]. In today's world, with an incursion in rate of smartphone consumers and the growing acceptance of social media platforms, individuals have started the overwhelming usage of social media than the traditional form of media [1]. Social media platforms allow people to share their views, opinions, and disagreements on the same platform about shared content. Social media users surely trust that whatsoever news or updates reported on social media will be the fact but, actually, sometimes, it is fake news just to hide the truth or mislead readers and make a harmful impact on the real news [1]. Fake news causes many problems or tensions occurred in society.

Data-driven analysis has been gradually applied in numerous decision-making processes. Fake news detection as well different data-driven approaches can be efficiently used. By analyzing content, context data of news with stance detection classification of news into fake or real can be achieved. Different data-driven approaches that are based linguistic features and extracted from news body for news articles can be used in detection [23]. Similarly, using graph of social interaction between different users and processing with little dimensional embedding and nurtured to LSTM classifier used in the detection are content-based approaches [24]. Additionally, identification of fake news on the basis of who most liked or adored them on social media and context-based is with intelligence that they focus on information derived from social interactions between users.

12.2   Literature Survey

In recent years, the identification of fake news is a key and hot research area in the social networking field. The research conducted as of today described many automatic detection techniques of fake news and deception posts. Since there are multidimensional characteristics of fake news detection ranging from using chat-bots for the spread of misinformation to use of clickbait for the rumor spreading [2]. There are several clickbaits available in social media networks including Facebook, which enhances sharing and liking of posts, which, in turn, spreads falsified information quickly [4].

Data-driven approaches of fake news detection have shown good results in recent research using different approaches like content-based, context-based, and mix of both using machine learning techniques. In data-driven approach, it concentrates on a grouping of the features that are used in each study to characterize false information and on the datasets used for instructing classification methods. In addition, different false news diffusion models are discussed based on machine learning techniques [24].

Fake news detection models based on working samples are discussed, and examples are Expert fact checker, CrowdSourced, Machine Learning, Natural Language Processing technique, and hybrid techniques based on nature of news. Hybrid model uses data-driven approach where content-based model and social context–based technique utilize auxiliary data from various different perspectives [27].

Data-driven approach based on raw dataset collected for fake news detection is used; however, in collected news, it contains more noise such as missing different required attributes of news. This requires additional novel data preprocessing method where missing attributes of categorical and numerical handled properly. Method that combined traditional machine learning models that has ability of managing multi-class classification responsibilities with preprocessing techniques is discussed. In addition, TD-IDF vectorization is used for feature extraction to filter irrelevant features [26].

Fake news discovery from data streams implements detection as data stream classification task. Proposed innovative classification method uses feature extraction techniques to address detection of fake news at streaming data of social media. It uses Principal Components Analysis (PCA) analysis, Count Vectorizer, and Feature Selection method for grouping of each feature. For training of classifier on data stream, Streaming Ensemble Algorithm is used for training new base classifier on each detected data portion of stream [29].

In some cases, human intervention [6] is used to verify information accuracy. International Fact Checking Network (IFCN) allows social media users of Facebook in different countries to flag purposely created fake news. Some of the media organization also does fact-checking and accordingly mark news as fake news, but all of these are manual process and not efficient.

In [6], authors thoroughly characterized the website and reputations of publishers of fake and real news articles with registration patterns. It has also taken into account website age, ranking of a domain, and its popularity. In addition, they analyzed how to identify fake and real news based on TF-IDF and LDA topic modeling. In [4], fake news detection using machine learning approaches had described different forms of social media networking news items:

- Text: analyzed based on the genesis of text semantically and systematically
- Multimedia: analyzed based on audio, video, images, and graphics
- Hyperlinks: cross-references of different media or site source links

Some methods use visual information to differentiate between fake and real news. In [3], authors used a multi-domain visual neural network to recognize fake news with visual frequency and pixel domains. This model can automatically capture complex patterns in the fake image and compare its properties. According to exploration, fake news images have maliciously altered, but also, in some cases, real images are erroneously used to show unrelated events.

In [2], general approaches to identify fake news different algorithms are used. Different methods are used like an algorithm that is based on the nature of the content; some of them are based on the diffusion of dynamics of the messages, and hybrid algorithms that work based on a group of features.

Different methods used for accepting parameters and classification of category of news are also explained.

Observation is that the dataset is first preprocessed using preprocessing methods such as stopword removal, tokenization, and stemming. Different methods like TF-IDF and probabilistic context-free grammar that can be also used feature extraction are acknowledged. On the basis of the literature, it is observed that the correctness for forecasting fake news in social media is much better than any other online news media [21].

The term "fake news" was barely used prior to United States prudential election in 2016. It is observed that, during election campaign, there were hundreds of news with misinformation or biased news broadcasted on social media to gain capitalizing advertising social media and with political influence. These fake news affected citizen during election period with some misinformation. Similarly, fake news trend is observed in India during corona pandemic, and there were lots of message on home remedies, and misinformation about treatment was circulated through social media messages to gain with financial aspects. Articles on corona virus treatment were not fact checked with medical field experts and caused side effects to people.

Research Gap

Sr. no.	Paper	Research gap
1.	False News on Social Media: A Data-Driven Survey [24]	1. Methods analyzed are based on content- or context-based approaches 2. Analyzed methods has only linguistic aspect of news 3. Fact checking not considered while conclusion
2	A model of Fake Data in Data-Driven Analysis [25]	1. Mathematical model shown on static set of news data for conclusion 2. Data model is based on static aspects of news
3	Fake News Types and Detection Models on Social Media a State-of-the-Art Survey [27]	1. Models discussed are based on single aspects of the news like Expert fact checker 2. Hybrid model discussed not efficient and needed more manual fact checking
4	Fake News Detection Enhancement With Data Imputation [26]	1. Based on raw news dataset 2. Requires more preprocessing for missing attributes of news
5	Fake News Detection From Data Streams [28]	1. Fake news detection are based on social media data streams 2. Considers static characteristics of incoming message and that could change over time
6	A Framework to Identify and Secure the Issues of Fake News and Rumors in Social Networking [1]	1. Based on a static database of news 2. Analyzed a limited number of fake news 3. Unable to handle new news structure and strategies used

(Continued)

(Continued)

Sr. no.	Paper	Research gap
7	Exploiting Multi-Domain Visual Information for Fake News Detection [3]	1. Only work with the MVNN framework 2. Ability to analyze only visual data 3. Limited support for handling text data 4. Domain or site trust information not considered while analysis
8	Manually Classified Real and Fake News Articles [5]	1. Manually classified fake and real news articles 2. The news database is created and handled manually
9	Detecting Fake News Over Online Social Media via Domain Reputations and Content Understanding [6]	1. Based on domain reputation analysis 2. Unable to handle new content type characteristics 3. Unable to handle different media types 4. Based on PIIDF model 5. Since based on reputation hence false positive detections for new websites
10	Evaluating Machine Learning Algorithms For Fake News Detection [8]	1. The evaluated model is not reliable since it is using an absolute probability threshold and hence probability scoring not calibrated well
11	A Hybrid Model for text classification [9]	1. Does not work for images videos on social media on twitter but only for text. 2. A manual dataset of 25K used
12	Fake News Detection Using Naïve Bayes Classifier [11]	1. Does not leverage hybrid or complex models for classifier 2. Facebook news posts database used which is created manually and has a limited amount of variety of posts

(Continued)

(*Continued*)

Sr. no.	Paper	Research gap
13	Detection of Online Fake News: A Survey [21]	1. The input to the model is a URL parameter based 2. Static parameters are considered for computation of score like source, author, and headline

12.3   Problem Statement and Objectives

Based on a literature survey and rigorously analysis of papers, we have decided our research problem statement and objectives specified as follows.

12.3.1   Problem Statement

Social media has become a popular means for people to consume and share the news. At the same time, however, it has also facilitated the extensive broadcasting of fake news, that is, news with intentional misinformation, affecting substantial adverse effects on communities. Fake news is frequently written with a hidden purpose to gain financially, politically and religious tensions within communities, etc., with most of the time having a catchy headline that attracts users, and it affects people and communities. Hence, detection of fake news detection on social media is vital so that its spread and its negative impact on society can be avoided before it reaches to millions of users within a very short span of time

Using data-driven approaches detection of fake news on social media can be achieved as it help us to analyze different types of news formats along with its content and context using grouping of the features that are used in each study to characterize false information using machine learning techniques. Additionally, stance detection intelligence of news can be also utilized in accurate detection of fake news shared on social media.

12.3.2   Objectives

1. To develop an efficient data-driven fake news detection model that can serve more accurate detection by using a different aspect of news like text, stance, real factual data, and sentiments analysis

2. To develop reliable data-driven fake news detection model that can able to handle different format of news data, structures and content types
3. To use of advanced machine learning classification techniques to classify news type as fake, real, and unclear
4. To validate experiments of proposed methods and techniques with social media platforms

12.4   Proposed Methodology

To achieve our research goal, our proposed methodology has three different phases, and each step has its own significance to accomplish desired output. The details about each step and its details are as follows:

- Pre-processing
- Feature extraction
- Classification

12.4.1   Pre-Processing

The proposed methodology plans to use Natural Language Processing; hence, it is important to first pre-process all news contents. In this phase, any news targeted for analysis gets pre-processed. The aim of this proposed function is to compile all news contents and refine data. Refinement starts with removal of stopword, segmentation of sentences, and removal of punctuation. Additionally, non-essential contents of news like any additional hyperlinks, references, and any attachment that are contained in the news are refined. After removal of non-essential details of news, tokenization and keyword generation are performed on refined data. To remove noisy data and for speed with accuracy, Support Vector Machine (SVM) machine learning classifier can be used [13].

Since news under detection is from the social media, so comments and sentiments expressed by users on the news becomes extremely important while concluding that it is fake or real news. We have proposed this function as "Sentiment Extraction", and it processes all expressions used by users like sad, love, and angry and its count per expression. Additionally, this extracts all comments details and pre-processes it to get exact details as refined data.

12.4.2   Feature Extraction

Feature extraction is next phase in proposed methodology, and it aims to extract details on processed data from above mentioned phase. The main motive is on extraction of different features of texts and then combining those features into different classification models, e.g., decision tree, SVM, and logistic regression [7]. Additionally, different methods like Word count, Sentiments, Authenticity, Clout, Tone, and TF-IDF methods for the classification are used.

Stance detection is also important for conclusion of fake new, and it is a process that can determine readers of the news that are in favor of or against or has unbiased stance. There are two types of stance; we need to process it as explicit and implicit stance. Explicit stance gets processed based on sentiment extracted data like thump up, down or like, love, sad, and angry emoji's expressed by readers. Implicit stance detection is done based on comments data extracted by pre-processing steps.

12.4.3   Classification

Classification is final phase of proposed methodology where conclusion about fake news gets finalized (Figure 12.1). For training and understanding the classifier, it is proposed to first apply publicly available datasets for

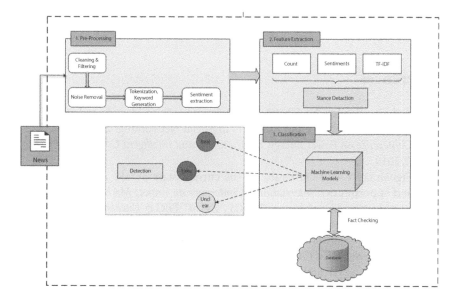

Figure 12.1 Proposed model of fake news detection using data driven approach.

classifier learning and that is based on thousands of news articles extracted from news organization and from social media. For final decision-making about news, Random Forest supervised learning algorithm can be used since it provides improved accuracy and good performance [13]. Fact-checking methods are primarily focus on to check facts of the news on the basis of recognized facts. There are fact-checking organizations that provide online fact-checking services like Snopes, Politificat, and Fiskkit. These organizations refer it to the domain experts, individuals, or organization on specific topic. Further, based on fact-checking results factual data and stance based data, the classifier will conclude on news as it is fake, real, or unclear type (Figure 12.1). Finally, the accuracy and performance of the model can be evaluated with a comparison of already present models. Our plan to use target standard datasets available like "NewsBag: A Benchmark Dataset for Fake News Detection" available from IIT Delhi [20].

12.5   Conclusion

Here, we defined our research objectives with the aim of designing a data-driven technique for the detection of fake news on social media platforms, because fake news and rumors will continue to grow in social media. This data-driven technique will help to increase the accuracy of fake news detection mechanism and perform classification, i.e., fake or real news. Through this research, we can be able to detect fake news with a well-efficient way and categorizing news into a fake, real, and unclear types (Figure 12.1).

References

1. Bedi, A., Pandey, N., Khatri, S.K., A Framework to Identify and secure the Issues of Fake News and Rumours in Social Networking. *2nd International Conference on Power Energy, Environment and Intelligent Control (PEEIC) G. L,* 2019.
2. Figueiraa, A. and Oliveirab, L., The current state of fake news: challenges and opportunities. *International Conference on Project MANagement / HCist - International Conference - CRACS / INESC TEC & University of Porto,* vol. 1021/1055, Rua do Campo Alegre, Porto, Portugal, pp. 4169–007.
3. Exploiting Multi-domain Visual Information for Fake News Detection. *2019 IEEE International Conference on Data Mining (ICDM).*
4. Manzoor, S., II and Dr Jimmy Singla, N., Fake News Detection Using Machine Learning approaches: A systematic Review. *Proceedings of the Third*

International Conference on Trends in Electronics and Informatics (ICOEI 2019) IEEE Xplore Part Number: CFP19J32-ART.

5. Snell, N., Fleck, W., Traylor, T., Straub, J., Manually Classified Real and Fake News Articles. *2019 International Conference on Computational Science and Computational Intelligence (CSCI),* .

6. Xu, K., Wang, F., Wang, H., Yang, B., Detecting Fake News Over Online Social Media via Domain Reputations and Content Understanding. *TSINGHUA Sci. Technol.*, 25, 1, 20–27, February 2020.

7. Ahmed2, S., Hinkelmann2, K., Corradini1, F., Combining Machine Learning with Knowledge Engineering to detect Fake News in Social Networks-a survey, Department of Computer Science, University of Camerino, Italy 2FHNW University of Applied Sciences and Arts Northwestern Switzerland Riggenbsachstrasse 16, 4600 Olten, Switzerland, in: *Proceedings of the AAAI 2019 Spring Symposium on Combining Machine Learning with Knowledge Engineering (AAAI-MAKE 2019),* Stanford University, Palo Alto, California, USA, March 25-27, 2019.

8. Gilda, S., Evaluating Machine Learning Algorithms For Fake News Detection. *IEEE Conference,* 2017.

9. Kamruzzaman, S.M. and Haider, F., A hybrid learning algorithm for text classification. *3rd International Conference on Electrical Computer Engineering (ICECE 2004),* p. 1009.4574, 2010.

10. Vivek Singh, D.S.K.R., Dasgupta, R., Ghosh, I., Automated fake news detection using linguistic analysis and machine learning. *International Conference on Social Computing, Behavioral-Cultural Modeling, & Prediction and Behavior Representation in Modeling and Simulation (SBPBRiMS),* pp. 1–3, 2017.

11. Granik, M. and Mesyura, V., Fake News Detection Using Naïve Bayes Classifier. *2017 IEEE First Ukraine Conference On Electrical And Computer Engineering, (UKRCON),* 2017.

12. Daily time spent on Social Networking per year graph. https://www.broadbandsearch.net/blog/average-daily-time-on-social-media#:~:text=On%20average%2C%20we%20spend%20144,others%2C%20they%20spend%20far%20less.

13. Vinit Bhoir, Ms. S., An Efficient FAKE NEWS DETECTOR. *2020 International Conference on Computer Communication and Informatics (ICCCI -2020),* Coimbatore, INDIA, Jan. 22-24, 2020.

14. The Importance of Social Media. https://www.maisonworkshop.org/aims-and-scope.

15. Fake news in India. https://en.wikipedia.org/wiki/Fake_news_in_India.

16. Communications blackout in Kashmir: A quick fix that can backfire. https://www.orfonline.org/expert-speak/communications-blackout-in-kashmir-a-quick-fix-that-can-backfire-54430/.

17. India Internet Clampdown Will Not Stop Misinformation. https://www.hrw.org/news/2019/04/24/india-internet-clampdown-will-not-stop-misinformation.

18. About Forwarding Limits. https://faq.whatsapp.com/general/coronavirus-product-changes/about-forwarding-limits/?lang=en.

19. Facebook's Approach to Misinformation: Partnering with Third-Party Fact-Checkers. https://www.facebook.com/journalismproject/programs/third-party-fact-checking/selecting-partners.

20. News Bag: A Benchmark Dataset for Fake News Detection Indraprastha Institute of Information Technology, New Delhi BTP report submitted in partial fulfillment of the requirements, IIIT-Delhi Institutional Repository, April 15, 2019. https://repository.iiitd.edu.in/jspui/handle/123456789/779?show=full

21. Gaonkar, S., Itagi, S., Chalippatt, R., Detection Of Online Fake News: A Survey. *2019 International Conference on Vision Towards Emerging Trends in Communication and Networking (ViTECoN)*.

22. Elhadad, M.K., Li, K.F., Gebali, F., Dept. of Elec. and Comp. Eng. University of Victoria Victoria, in: *Canada Fake News Detection on Social Media: A Systematic Survey*, IEEE, Pacific Rim Conference on Communications, Computers and Signal Processing (PACRIM), 2019.

23. Vaibhav, V. and Hirlekar, Dr., A.K., Computer Science & Engineering Department Sir Padmapat Singhania University,Udaipur, Rajasthan, India Natural Language Processing based Online Fake News Detection Challenges – A Detailed Review. *Proceedings of the Fifth International Conference on Communication and Electronics Systems (ICCES 2020) IEEE Conference Record # 48766; IEEE Xplore.*

24. Pierri, F. and Ceri, S., False News On Social Media: A Data-Driven Survey, *ACM SIGMOD Record*, 48, 2, 18–22, 28 Jan 2020. arXiv:1902.07539v3 [cs.SI].

25. Li, X. and Whinstone, A.B., A model of fake data in data-driven analysis. *J. Mach. Learn. Res.*, 21, 1–26, 2020.

26. Madhav, C.M., Kotteti, X.D., Li, N., Qian, L., Fake News Detection Enhancement with Data Imputation. *2018 IEEE 16th Int. Conf. on Dependable, Autonomic & Secure Comp., 16th Int. Conf. on Pervasive Intelligence & Comp., 4th Int. Conf. on Big Data Intelligence & Comp., and 3rd Cyber Sci. & Tech. Cong.*

27. Collins, B., Hoang, D.T., Nguyen, N.T., Hwang, D., Fake News Types and Detection Models on Social Media A State-of-the-Art Survey, Communications in Computer and Information Science. *12th Asian Conference, ACIIDS 2020 Phuket, Thailand, March 23–26, 2020 Proceedings*, .

28. Ksieniewicz, P., Zyblewski, P., Choras, M., Kozik, R., Giełczyk, A., Wozniak, M., *Fake News Detection from Data Streams, International Joint Conference on Neural Networks (IJCNN)*. Carleton University from IEEE Xplore, 2020.

29. Sanjeev, M., Dwivedi, S., Wankhade, B., Survey on Fake News Detection Techniques. *Adv. Intell. Syst. Comput.*, 1200, 342–348, 2021.

13

Distance Measurement for Object Detection for Automotive Applications Using 3D Density-Based Clustering

Anupama Patil[1], Manisha Bhende[2], Suvarna Patil[1*] and P. P. Shevatekar[1]

[1]DYPIEMR, Pune, Maharashtra, India
[2]Marathwada Mitra Mandals Institute of Technology, Pune, India

Abstract

In a continually changing urban setting, obstacle detection and categorization are tough to explore. In such a scenario, the challenge is to split objects in a complex and changing environment. A unique object segmentation strategy based on position-based principles is proposed to overcome this challenge. The proposed method performs object segmentation in two stages: in layered photos in XY planes and in the depth map in XZ planes. The stereovision concept is used for the reconstruction of image points and the production of a depth map for a given image. In the final depth chart, objects are discovered. The original edge image is then separated into several pieces. After this stage, the original edge picture is split. Basic Computer Vision techniques and Convolutional Neural Networks are just two examples of perception-based algorithms for recognizing and categorizing objects accessible today (CNN). The purpose of this research is to determine how effective a stereovision-based item detection system is. However, this method has a flaw in that it deletes parts of the image that are not needed for detection. The proposed method has been proved to give an accurate assessment of obstacle position and magnitude as well as reliable detection of prospective obstructions. After removing such regions with segmentation, this work presents a method for detecting artifacts using 3D density-based clustering.

Keywords: CNN, computer vision, obstructions, object segmentation

*Corresponding author: suvarnapat@gmail.com

R. Arokia Priya, Anupama V Patil, Manisha Bhende, Anuradha Thakare and Sanjeev Wagh (eds.)
Object Detection by Stereo Vision Images, (207–226) © 2022 Scrivener Publishing LLC

13.1   Introduction

Many methods for calculating the distance between objects or targets have been developed in recent years. For these approaches, there are two types of techniques: contact and noncontact procedures [1]. A variety of items are used to estimate distance in touch measuring. The main disadvantage of these methods is that the materials used can be corrosive. Laser reflection and ultrasonic reflection [2, 3] are examples of non-contact measurement methods that have been developed. While laser and ultrasonic techniques are faster, object reflectivity is critical for precisely measuring distance. The system will not function effectively if the object's reflectivity is low. In today's scenario, object detection and recognition is crucial.

Object detection and recognition are required in a wide range of computer science applications. A multitude of strategies or methodologies is available to achieve this purpose. Sensors are used in the majority of older systems for this reason. Machines can now detect and recognize borders in the same way that humans can. They use more than two cameras (stereovision) instead of eyes and in comparison to these, the recorded image is stored in a database, similar to how the human brain works. This technique outperforms the others in terms of real-time item detection and recognition.

Object detection and recognition are the two most researched and used fields in computer vision. Image retrieval, surveillance, manufacturing, automated car parking, and security are just a few of the applications that may be made with this technology. Other uses include space rovers [1], gesture recognition [2], and object identification for blind people. This allows those who have problems seeing what is in front of them to recognize what is there more easily. A variety of robots and devices have emerged in this field [3]. To recognize objects, a variety of gadgets use range sensors. As the distance among the obstacles is measured and the instrument, is used of range sensors for object detection. In contrast, stereovision is the retrieval of three-dimensional (3D) information with help of two or more two-dimensional (2D) images located at the same location, which aids in the creation of a disparity map that provides depth information.

Human vision and this technology have a lot in common. Two independent images concerned with the same point are obtained when more than two cameras two are situated horizontally from one another in stereovision. By comparing the relative depth data to a disparity map, the relative depth information of the obstacle can be identified. Several image-based distance measurement systems based on image analysis and pattern recognition tools have been created [6, 7] with the vision advanced technology. To be run, these solutions, on the other hand, require a lot of memory and a fast CPU.

A few studies have been published in recent years that use stereovision to determine object distance [8–10]. Stereovision is used to assess disparity or rich depth information of objects obtained from a pair of left and right image views acquired by a stereo camera system. Following that, the target distances are determined using depth information [2]. On the other hand, both the scientific community and the business community stress the need of researching this area. Distance measurement methods based on stereovision are computationally inefficient and unsuitable for real-time applications. We offer a simple and effective solution to these issues.

- A novel fuzzy correlation measure for detecting the same pixels between the left and right picture sequences is included in our stereo matching technique.
- The diagonal pixels in the panes are taken into account for matching correspondence.

Despite recent advancements in 3D object detection, the region concept continues to rely heavily on 2D object detectors. Sliding windows [4, 16, 31, 35] and 3D region proposal networks [27, 28] are commonly used to generate candidate 3D proposals based on image-based detection concepts. However, the 3D search computing complexity increases with resolution in a cubical manner for large scenes or real-time applications, making it computationally expensive. Methods used to project pointers on 2D images, on the other hand [3, 5], make surface and geometric quality, trade-offs that may be necessary in densely crowded areas. While there have been few attempts to train instantly from point features, PointNet [20, 22] highlighted as successful networks for processing points of 3D groups may be used to detect objects and semantically partition point clouds.

In their early work toward a comprehensive 3D object recognition channel [20], a 2D area proposal network creates bound package proposals from an RGB picture and raises them to a 3D frustum. PointNet is then used to segment the suggested frustum's point cloud, and the item's 3D modal bounding box is regressed. Even though their strategy boosts accuracy, the performer limits its effectiveness [21]. A 3D system that uses

Hough selection to estimate likely instances of items, followed by bound package detection [18], has recently enhanced this technique. Following feature extraction, the network only samples 1,024 points from a top cloud of 20,000 to 40,000 points.

13.2   Related Work

Stereovision and optical flow are the two most prevalent approaches for detecting obstacles using vision. Objects are identified according to motion patterns using the optical flow technique, which involves examining more than two photos obtained at different times (e.g., optical flow vectors). We can figure out the 3D structure of a scene by looking at it from two separate viewpoints. Stereovision was employed by Franke *et al.* [5, 6] to investigate a traffic problem in a city. Bohrer *et al.* [7] twisted the left and right views using stereovision and an inverse-perspective method to obtain zero disagreements at all ground plane positions. There are a few important points to remember. In their GOLD project, Bertozzi *et al.* employed a similar method to detect impediments in high-speed traffic [8, 9]. This paradigm removes the perspective effect from stereo views, resulting in two images that demonstrate the differences that occur when the original perception of a flat road is inaccurate, allowing the open area in front of the car to be detected.

Object segmentation was not taken into account when these programs were created. We developed a new technique for object segmentation using stereovision technology in this research. A high-quality disparity map was also produced using a proprietary area-based stereo matching method [36]. The complexity of object segmentation makes it a difficult task. Without a semantic understanding of the image, traditional image segmentation methods like region-growing and boundary detection methods are unable to achieve. For the automotive industry, some unique segmentation tactics have been devised. Following a car in a highway scene widely used pattern-based [9, 10] and symmetry-based [11] segmentation approaches. The 2D projection feature of the object is only considered by these segmentation methods, not its depth. Despite significant attempts to build 3D deep learning networks, research on 3D instance segmentation lags behind that on 2D instance segmentation. They use 3D feature learning to expand second feature learning for object detection and instance segmentation. The primary notable effort during this field was the SGPN [32], which allows the event of cluster proposals of objects by establishing modeling within the variety of a similarity matrix. As a result, the properties of points within the matrix happiness to an equivalent instance and distinctive object instances square measure virtually identical [12, 23]. Three-dimensional linguistics Instance Segmentation (3D-SIS) [9] is another technique that learns second options from multi-view RGB pictures and comes back to them onto matching 3D voxels. They use 3D feature learning to expand second feature learning for object detection and instance segmentation.

Joint Semantic-Instance Segmentation [17] is associate in nursing form for Joint Semantic-Instance Segmentation. Panoptic (semantic and instance) segmentation is addressed as one drawback in 3D whereas learning from purpose clouds. instead of analyzing the complete purpose cloud, they seek for matching 3D windows, that get fed into a degree network, that predicts linguistics category labels for the vertices among the window and embeds them into high-dimensional vectors.

The conditional random field is then applied to improve the results. They employ a push-pull embedding to establish instance segmentation, with Lpull attracting embedding to the centroids and Lpush keeping it away [24]. Lreg is a little force that pulls all centroids to the universe's center. One of the strategy's major disadvantages is that it necessitates running the network for each 3D window formed from the initial point cloud. As a result, for dense large-scale point clouds, this method could be computationally expensive. As far as we know, no existing solution can deal with all three issues (i.e., light variation, shadow interference, and multiple images). To fulfill the expanding public safety needs, new hardware components such as stereo or multi-camera systems have been added to existing surveillance systems to considerably improve system performance. A multi-camera system monitors a scenario from two or more angles and provides more data than a monocular camera system [27, 28]. The distance between the cameras distinguishes two types of multi-camera systems: broad baseline systems and short baseline systems. Wide baseline systems are frequently employed in current systems because they do not require prior system calibration and give wider viewing angles than short baseline systems. M2tracker [28] is a region-based stereo technique that uses 16 cameras to extract 3D object points directly, overcoming occlusion and producing the greatest overall performance for multi-object recognition and tracking in broad baseline settings. Planar homography is used by Khan and Shah [29] to match people's feet in different perspectives so that their ground plane locations can be determined even when they are obscured. Both of these methods rely on color to establish correspondence between separate cameras, which can be difficult when dealing with similar objects. [30] To overcome this challenge, a motion model is applied. Despite their relatively high processing costs, these broad baseline systems have a hard time producing a trustworthy correlation. Furthermore, these systems are difficult to generalize to public applications due to the use of specialized features or approaches. With little changes in multiple angles and short baseline camera systems, camera correlation can be accomplished quickly [12, 26]. The disparity in camera positions can be utilized to create a scene's depth map, which can then be separated into objects of interest. On the other hand, the depth map is vulnerable to noise, resulting in incorrect item recognition. Furthermore, for homogenous regions, disparity calculations frequently result in [31], which employs two additional skin-hue classification and face identification modules to detect and track the body and face independently, reducing noise. The rich depth map was created by Darrell *et al.* [32] using dynamic-range imaging and a lengthy learning procedure. The entire path is created offline using dynamic programming to reduce tracking issues. To solve the problem of homogeneous regions, Kollmitzer [33] used heterogeneous head detection. Because of the lack of microscopic head details, the head map is created as a flat zone. A scale-adaptive filter is used to determine the head's size before it can be retrieved. In any event, the tracking system is incapable of detecting a hidden head. A new tracking and reconstructing approach [34] for a single rigid object was recently devised, in which one stereo pair creates the 3D model sequentially and then predicts motion. Mozgov *et al.* [35] offer a human motion action-specific model for automating training sessions and learning 3D human postures for tracking connected body components that may be used to track linked body components. Due to the small object regions in the map, occlusion is a significant barrier for depth map segmentation. Additional modules (such as face or skin detection [31], augmentation [32], scale filtering [33], or a 3D model [34]) are frequently necessary to reduce the size of these systems. Optical flow and stereovision are the two most used methods for vision-based obstacle detection. The optical flow technique compares two or more photos taken at different times to segment objects based on motion patterns (e.g., optical flow vectors). We can figure out a scene's 3D structure by looking at it from two separate perspectives. Stereovision was adopted by Franke *et al.* [5, 6] to investigate a traffic problem in a city. To bend the left and right views, Bohrer *et al.* [7] combined stereovision and an inverse-perspective method, producing zero disparity at all ground plane positions. There are a few minor distinctions to be aware of. Bertozzi *et al.* [8, 9] used a similar technique to detect obstructions in high-speed traffic as part of their GOLD project. The perspective effect is removed from stereo views in this paradigm, resulting in two images that show the variations that arise when the underlying assumption of a flat road is incorrect, allowing the open space in front of the car to be detected [37].

When these programs were developed, object segmentation was not taken under consideration. during this analysis, we tend to used stereovision technology to make a replacement object segmentation technique. A proprietary area-based stereo matching methodology was accustomed generate a high-quality inequality map [25]. Object segmentation could be a difficult task due to its involution. Ancient image segmentation approaches like border detection and region-growing algorithms are tough to realize while not a linguistics comprehension of the image. Distinctive segmentation techniques are developed for the automotive trade. Segmentation strategies supported symmetry [9] and pattern [10, 11] were extensively used to follow an automotive in a very road scene. These segmentation approaches merely take under consideration the object's 2D projection feature and ignore its depth. Despite substantial efforts to construct 3D deep learning networks, 3D instance segmentation analysis lags behind that of second instance segmentation. The primary notable try during this field was the SGPN [32] that learns illustration within the style of a similarity matrix and creates cluster proposals of object instances [26]. As a result, the properties of points within the matrix that belong to identical instance and people that belong to totally different object instances are primarily identical. Three-dimensional linguistics Instance Segmentation (3D-SIS) [9] is another methodology that comes back to the second options from multi-view RGB footage onto matching 3D voxels. They extend second feature learning to 3D to discover objects and section instances.

13.3   Distance Measurement Using Stereo Vision

In stereovision, two images of the same scene are captured from slightly different angles by the left and right cameras in the same lateral plane [2]. As a result, practically every pixel on the same horizontal line in the left image corresponds to a pixel on the right image. As indicated in Equation (13.1), the disparity is described as the variation in coordinates between matched pixels.

$$d = x_L - x_R \tag{13.1}$$

As a result, the right image's pixel, x-R, corresponds to the left image's pixel, x-L. According to Equation (13.2), the disparity is inversely proportional to the object's depth or distance:

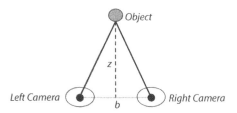

Figure 13.1 Stereovision dense depth estimation.

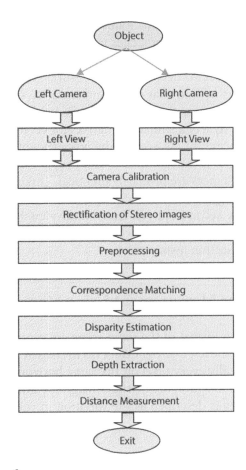

Figure 13.2 System flow.

$$z = \frac{b_f}{d} \tag{13.2}$$

where b is the base distance between the left and right cameras, and f denotes the camera lens' focal length. z represents the object's depth or distance from the camera.

Using the camera settings' triangulation geometry to assess the estimated disparity, stereoscopic vision may compute the 3D information or depth of points in images. As demonstrated in Figure 13.1, two images of the same object are produced by the left and right cameras seeing the same topic.

Figure 13.2 is a diagram of the planned system's pipeline.

13.3.1   Calibration of the Camera

To extract dense depth information from 2D image sequences, camera calibration is a method of identifying each camera's extrinsic and intrinsic properties. This study employs Zhang's camera calibration method, which is based on a 2D planar template [2].

13.3.2   Stereo Image Rectification

Any purpose on associate in nursing epipolar line in one image (the reference image) corresponds to the identical epipolar line within the alternative image in epipolar pure mathematics (i.e., target image). Rectification creates associate in nursing epipolar pure mathematics surroundings within which all identical points in each pictures should have identical coordinates. As a result, examination 2 images are as straightforward as looking out on identical epipolar line, cutting the search house from 2D to 1D. A stereo combine of pictures is corrected victimization the camera activity parameters. The corrected pictures area unit then used to construct the inequality map required to revive or recreate dense depth [2].

Preprocessing the nonheritable stereo image sequences improves the potency of the projected methodology. We tend to perform two operations within the preprocessing stage: (a) RGB to grayscale conversion as a result of a grayscale image needs less memory and interval than a color image, and (b) noise reduction as a result of the input image is also contaminated by noise, creating it troublesome to examine options or colors. For noise reduction, we tend to use a basic median filter; as a result in impulsive

(a)   (b)   (c)

Figure 13.3 Pre-processing methods. (a) RGB color image. (b) Grayscale image.
(c) Enhanced image.

noise settings, it is effective and fast. The impact of pre-processing on a
check image is seen in Figure 13.3.

13.3.3   Disparity Estimation and Stereo Matching

To determine disparity or depth, stereo matching compares the positions
of similar things in the left and right photo sequences. Global and local
techniques are used in stereo algorithms [13]. Global approaches [14–16]
minimize a global cost function with iterative systems to accomplish
disparity assignments. Although these methods yield precise and dense
disparity measurements, they are not suitable for real-time applications
because to their high processing costs. Local methods [17, 18], also known
as area-based methods, compute disparity at each pixel depending on the
photometric properties of nearby pixels.

Although slower than global processes, local procedures are suitable for many real-time applications. In this study, we provide a stereo
matching solution that is both computationally efficient and successful,
based on a local technique. Statistical measures like the Sum of Absolute
Differences (SAD), Sum of Squared Differences (SSD), or Normalized
Cross Correlations (NCC) are used in correlation matching to examine the
disparity or depth information of an item [19]. In the left image, the window costs are employed to calculate pixel correlation. Our stereo matching
algorithm makes the following assumptions:

(i)   In epipolar geometry, the matching pixels in two corrected
      stereo picture pairings are in both image sequences on the
      same horizontal scan lines.
(ii) Each pixel in a small window contributes to the neighbor-
      hood by having an intensity that is similar to that of its
      neighbors.

Based on these assumptions, we develop a fast stereo matching method that computes the window cost (similarity measure) for candidate pixels in the right image whose intensities differ by a threshold value from the intensity of the pixel in the target picture. Furthermore, rather than performing a traditional direct search on all pixels within a square window, our method simply performs correspondence matching on the center pixel's diagonal and horizontal neighbors, which speeds up processing without sacrificing accuracy [2]. (x+1, y), (x+1, y), (x+1, y+1), (x+1, y+1), (x+1, y+1), (x+1, y+1), (x+1, y+1), (x+1, y+1), (x+1, y+1), (x+1, y+1), (x+1, y+1), (x+1, y+1), (x+1, y+1), (x+1, y+1), (x+1, y+1), (x+1).

$(x-1, y+1)$	$(x, y+1)$	$(x+1, y+1)$
$(x-1, y)$	(x, y)	$(x+1, y)$
$(x-1, y-1)$	$(x, y-1)$	$(x+1, y-1)$

The following is the proposed stereo matching algorithm for Disparity Estimation:

1. For each potential pixel (x,y) in the left image, use a square window to look for a corresponding pixel on the same epipolar line in the right image within a search range.
   for $d' = -d_{max}$ to d_{max} do
   Calculate $W_c(x,y,d')$
2. Find d such that, $d = \text{argmax} W_c(x,y,d')$
3. Calculate the disparities of all pixels in the left image, and then repeat steps 1 and 2 for the right image.

13.3.4 Measurement of Distance

Once the disparity has been measured, the depth or distance of the object can be calculated using the estimated disparity and camera parameters. The second algorithm shows how to figure out distance.

1. For the pixel disparity d (x,y)
2. Calculate the depth or the distance between two points. $z = bf/d$.
3. Calculate the average distance by repeating steps 1 and 2 for each additional pixel.

13.4 Object Segmentation in Depth Map

13.4.1 Formation of Depth Map

A depth map can be created utilizing a transform from the XY plane to the XZ plane after acquiring 3D information from picture points. A depth map is a 3D scene observed from above, with lateral and longitudinal distances denoted by horizontal and vertical coordinates, respectively. A step-by-step guide to creating a depth map may be found as follows.

1. Create a map with a range resolution that corresponds to a rectangular region in real life.
2. Using (2), determine the 3D world coordinates of all picture points and ignore the road surface positions (3).
3. To locate the left places on the map, convert the world coordinates (X, Z) into map coordinates. Count how many dots there are in each rectangle on the map or one pixel.
4. Assign a number to each pixel's gray level to create the depth map.

By adding a gray-level threshold to the depth map, the binary depth map was constructed. This criterion is also used to exclude any depth map locations with fewer nonzero points from the disparity map. The road surface has been stripped of all lane markers and other road markings. Five dense clusters of dots were used to represent the five objects. The lateral and longitudinal orientations of these objects were well defined.

Because they all radiate from it, the disparity map shows all of the locations in the depth map. The object's breadth and thickness are defined by the volume of the point cluster. Due to the item's inability to be seen through in the deep direction, the thickness may be uneven in reality, leading to disparity analysis inaccuracies.

13.4.2 Density-Based in 3D Object Grouping Clustering

Using the normal region-growing process, the depth map's points were organized into discrete object entities. The eight orientation-related points are consolidated into a single entity. The procedure is as follows:

1. Select a seed point, group points from eight directions into a single object, and give each grouped point an object number.
2. Complete step 1 until all nonzero points are labeled.

Another method of object grouping is to use a Gaussian-based kernel to find the centroid point of each point cluster and then set a boundary condition to encompass the item. The kernel's shape is determined by the object we are looking for. For example, separating human objects requires a 1 m–by–1 m kernel. When segmenting items with a specified aspect ratio, this method works well.

The original image's placements inside the items are known after object grouping. The average values of all locations inside each item were then used to calculate the lateral and longitudinal distances of the individual things. The measurements are length and breadth. This value was used as a criterion to exclude fake objects with a small number of remapped points or small physical size. Because the size of an item's picture is inversely related to its distance due to perspective, this threshold value was dynamic and inversely proportional to the object distance. Furthermore, all segmented items' priority was decided by their longitudinal distance from the camera; the closer an object was to the camera, the greater its priority.

13.4.3   Layered Images Object Segmentation

Object segmentation is a technique used in-depth maps to segment objects and provides position and size information by integrating XZ data. The acknowledged height and width of things may be erroneous or unsatisfactory because of the impact of additional objects in the same position with different heights or noisy patches in the disparity image. More segmentation in the initial XY image is the most fundamental strategy for finer height and breadth. The system's goals also include classification and detection. Because object categorization is often based on its geometry shape, the XY information of things must be utilized for classification. From this vantage point, we must also examine the original photographs. The segmentation and categorization of objects in this image are difficult because the original image comprises a mixture of all components. To get around these issues, we proposed segmenting and classifying objects over many image layers. When each image layer has fewer elements, usually just one, object segmentation and categorization are easier and more reliable. In other words, the object distances from the initial segmentation stage are used to stack the original image. Because the disparity of the points within an object defines its distance, the disparity picture is originally overlayed based on the disparity ranges calculated. The original image may then be overlaid by indexing it with stacked disparity images. The layered grayscale photos, unlike the stacking disparity photographs, contain more information for segmentation and classification. In-depth maps, object segmentation is used to segment objects and provide position and size information by combining XZ data. The recognized height and width of things may be erroneous or unsatisfactory due to the influence of other objects in the same place with different heights or noisy patches in the disparity image. More segmentation in the initial XY image is the most fundamental strategy for achieving finer height and breadth. The system's goals also include classification and detection. Because object categorization is often based on its geometry shape, the XY information of things must be utilized for classification. From this vantage point, we must also examine the original photographs. The segmentation and categorization of objects in this image are difficult because the original image comprises a mixture of all components. To get around these issues, we proposed segmenting and classifying objects over many image layers. When each image layer has fewer elements, usually just one, object segmentation and categorization are easier and more reliable. In other words, the object distances from the initial segmentation stage are used to stack the original image. Because the disparity of the points within an object defines its distance, the disparity picture is originally overlayed based on the disparity ranges calculated. The original image may then be overlaid by indexing it with stacked disparity images. The layered grayscale photos, unlike the stacking disparity photographs, contain more information for segmentation and classification. In-depth maps, object segmentation is used to segment objects and provide position and size information by combining XZ data. Due to the impact of other objects in the same position with different heights or noisy patches in the disparity image, the recognized height and width of items may be incorrect or unsatisfactory. The most basic technique to get finer height and breadth is to do more segmentation in the initial XY image. The system's goals also include classification and detection. Because object categorization is often based on its geometry shape, the XY information of things must be utilized for classification. From this vantage point, we must also examine the original photographs. The segmentation and categorization of objects in this image are difficult because the original image comprises a mixture of all components. To get around these issues, we proposed segmenting and classifying objects over many image layers. When each image layer has fewer elements, usually just one, object segmentation and categorization are easier and more reliable. In other words, the object distances from the initial segmentation stage are used to stack the original image. Because the disparity of the points within an object defines its distance, the disparity picture is originally overlayed based on the disparity ranges calculated. The original image may then be overlaid by indexing it with stacked disparity images. The layered grayscale photos, unlike the stacking disparity photographs, contain more information for segmentation and classification. In-depth maps, object segmentation is used to segment objects and provide position and size information by combining XZ data. Due to the impact of other objects in the same position with different heights or noisy patches in the disparity image, the recognized height and width of items may be incorrect or unsatisfactory. The most basic technique to get finer height and breadth is to do more segmentation in the initial XY image. The system's goals also include classification and detection. Because object categorization is often based on its geometry shape, the XY information of things must be utilized for classification. From this vantage point, we must also examine the original photographs. The segmentation and categorization of objects in this image is difficult because the original image comprises a mixture of all components. To get around these issues, we proposed segmenting and classifying objects over many image layers. When each image layer has fewer elements, usually just one, object segmentation and categorization are easier and more reliable. In other words, the object distances from the initial segmentation stage are used to stack the original image. Because the disparity of the points within an object defines its distance, the disparity picture is originally overlayed based on the disparity ranges calculated. The original image may then be overlaid by indexing it with stacked disparity images. The layered grayscale photos, unlike the stacking disparity photographs, contain more information for segmentation and classification.

13.4.3.1   Image Layer Formation

The image points of the disparity map are sorted by disparity range to guarantee that all image points within the objects are included in the picture layer.

We will discuss how to make photo layers in the next paragraphs.

1. Determine the number of image layers and the disparity range for each image layer based on the number of recognized items.
2. Arrange the disparity picture points using disparity ranges as a guide. Search the original image for matched points using the sorted points as an index. The photo layer will be built using them. If N objects have been recognized by prior processing, then the relationship between distance and disparity

yields N equal groupings of dots in both the disparity and original images. The image points of the disparity map are sorted by disparity range to guarantee that all image points within the objects are included in the picture layer.

In the next paragraphs, we will go over how to create picture layers.

1. Determine the number of picture layers and the disparity range for each one using the number of recognized elements.
2. Using the disparity ranges, arrange the disparity image points. To find spots that are comparable to the original image, use the sorted points as an index. This is the point list that will be utilized to make the photo layer.

13.4.3.2   Determination of Object Boundaries

Various methods for estimating object contour exist, depending on the objective and limitations. In this study, we employed an edge-linking method to identify the geometry of the item. In the next paragraphs, the steps are outlined.

1. Get rid of the raw image's edge layers. A log-transformed image can likewise be used with the raw picture stacking method mentioned above.
2. Use a morphological "opening" technique on the edge picture after smoothing the object shape. To remove some dispersed noise points around the margins, the image is first degraded. A little piece with only two vertical pixels was chosen to serve as an erosion element. The dilation method improves the shape and length of an object by linking particular spaced edge points. As a result of these methods, the object should have a cleaner edge contour and certain noisy parts should be filtered out.
3. Join the associated places within a local neighborhood from eight distinct directions. The size of the neighborhood is an attempt to strike a balance. While a larger neighborhood scale is useful for bridging contour gaps, it may result in an erroneous link between noise sites and the scale. Meanwhile, count the number of connected points to figure out how long the contour will be. As a result of these procedures, an object edge contour that is long and continuous emerges.

It is worth mentioning that the connected edge contour will include a lot of interior points.

4. Continue with steps 3–4 until all of the points are connected to form a contour.

5. Set a limit for the length of the outlines you have found. This restriction is also configured by considering the perspective connection because the distance has been determined. Because the noise spots are the most likely source of the short edge contours, they have been removed. The edge contours' boundary points define the width and height of the confirmed items by forming a rectangular bounding box around them.

The proposed technique has been validated in a number of different scenarios in addition to the one provided here. According to statistical experimental data, object detection success rates reach 95% within a detection range of 4–50 m under optimum lighting conditions, and relative errors for distance and size estimations are less than 5% and 10%, respectively. For item categorization, precise measurements of object size are extremely useful. Thanks to our technology, preliminary classification by aspect ratio is now possible. This picture separation method uses a point-distributed model as well as statistical criteria to provide more exact categorization.

13.5   Conclusion

The complexity of the urban environment, where things to be recognized are diverse and intermingled with buildings, trees, traffic lights, and road signs, makes object segmentation a significant challenge for vision-based driver assistance systems. For the first stage of segmentation, the depth map (XZ plane) is used, which offers precise position and size data. The second stage of segmentation extracts smaller data from the stacked images (XY planes). This technique has been shown to reliably detect potential impediments and offer precise estimates of their size and position. To create dense and high-quality disparity images with rich information for further processing, a new area-based technique has been developed in detail. As a result, the depth map is made by translating image points to a scaled XZ plane. Using typical object grouping methods, objects on the depth map can be easily segmented. At first, the clever imposition was based on the separation of recognized things. The complexity of the urban environment, which contains a range of things to recognize as well as buildings, trees, traffic lights, and road signs, makes object segmentation a big issue for vision-based driver aid systems. To achieve this goal, this study presents a revolutionary stereovision-based object segmentation technique. Stereovision is a technique for translating 2D picture points into 3D coordinates in the real world. Object segmentation divides 3D data into two phases, which simplifies manipulation. The depth map (XZ plane) is used for the initial segmentation stage since it gives the precise position and preliminary size data. The second stage of segmentation derives finer size information from stacked images (XY planes). The method utilized in this study has been shown to detect potential impediments and provide accurate estimations of their location and magnitude. A novel area-based technique has been developed in detail to produce dense and high-quality disparity images with rich information for subsequent processing. As a result, the depth map is created by scaling the picture points to a scaled XZ plane. Using typical object grouping methods, you can easily segment the depth map. The first ingenious encroachment was based on the separation of identifiable things.

References

1. Garcia, M.A. and Solanas, A., Estimation of distance to planar surfaces and type of material with infrared sensors, in: *Proc. 7th Int. Conf. Pattern Recognition*, vol. 1, pp. 745–748, 2004.

2. Chowdhury, M., Gao, J., Islam, Md R., Distance Measurement of Objects using Stereo Vision. *Proceedings of the 9th Hellenic Conference on Artificial Intelligence*, 1–4, 2016, 10.1145/2903220.2903247.

3. Chowdhury, M., Gao, J., Islam, R., Extracting depth information from stereo images using a fast correlation matching algorithm. *Int. J. Comput. Appl.*, 42, 8, 798–803, 2020.

4. Culshaw, B., Pierce, G., Jun, P., Non-contact measurement of the mechanical properties of materials using an all-optical technique. *IEEE Sens. J.*, 3, 1, 62–70, Feb. 2003.

5. KlimKov, Y.M., A laser polarmetric sensor for measuring angular displacement of objects, in: *Proc. Eur. Conf. Lasers and Electro-Optics*, Sep. 8–13, 1996, pp. 190–190.

6. Gulden, P.G., Becker, D., Vossiek, M., Novel optical distance sensor based on MSM technology. *IEEE Sens. J.*, 4, 5, 612–618, Oct. 2004.

7. Caarullo, A. and Parvis, M., An ultrasonic sensor for distance measurement in automotive applications. *IEEE Sens. J.*, 1, 3, 143–147, Oct. 2001.

8. Peng, C.-C., *A Compact Digital Image Sensing Distance and Angle Measuring Device*, M.S. thesis, Opt. Sci. Center, National Central Univ., Chung Li City, Taiwan, R.O.C., 2001.

9. Lu, M.-C., Wang, W.-Y., Chu, C.-Y., Image-Based Distance and Area Measuring Systems. *IEEE Sens. J.*, 6, 2, 495–503, APRIL 2006.

10. Mustafah, Y.M., Noor, R., Hasbi, H., Azma, A.W., Stereo Vision Images Processing for Real-time Object Distance and Size Measurements. Presented at the *International Conference on Computer and Communication Engineering(ICCCE 2012)*, Malaysia, 2012.

11. Yu, M.Q., Araujo, H., Wang, H., Stereo-Vision Based Real time Obstacle Detection for Urban Environments. Presented at the *11th International Conference on Advanced Robotics*, 2003.

12. Hou, A.-L., Cui, X., Geng, Y., Yuan, W.-J., Hou, J., Measurement of Safe Driving Distance Based on Stereo Vision. Presented at the *Sixth International Conference on Image and Graphics*, 2011.

13. Zhang, Z., A flexible new technique for camera calibration. *IEEE Trans. Pattern Anal. Mach. Intell.*, 22, 11, 1330–1334, 2000.

14. Fusiello, A., Trucco, E., Verri, A., A compact algorithm for rectification of stereo pairs. *Mach. Vis. Appl.*, 12, 16–22, 2000.

15. Schastein, D. and Szeliski, R., A taxonomy and evaluation of dense two-frame stereo correspondence algorithm. *Int. J. Comput. Vis.*, 47, 7–42, 2002.

16. Tatsunori, T., Yasuyuki, M., Takeshi, N., Graph Cut based Continuous Stereo Matching using Locally Shared Labels. *CVPR*, 2014.

17. Yang, Q., Stereo Matching Using Tree Filtering. *IEEE Trans. Pattern Anal. Mach. Intell.*, 37, 4, 834–846, April 2015.

18. Muninder, V., Soumik, U., Krishna, G., Robust segment-based Stereo using Cost Aggregation. *BMVC*, pp. 1–11, 2014.

19. Chowdhury, M. and Bhuiyan, M.A., Fast Window based Stereo Matching for 3D Scene Reconstruction. *Int. Arab J. Inf. Technol.*, 10, 3, 209–214, July 2013.

20. Geiger, A., Roser, M., Urtasun, R., Efficient Large-Scale Stereo Matching, in: *Asian Conference on Computer Vision, (ACCV)*, 2010. [19] Lazaros, N., Sirakoulis, G.C., Gasteratos, A., Review of Stereo Vision Algorithms: From Software to Hardware. *Int. J. Optomechatroni.*, 2, 435–462, 2008.

21. Chowdhury, M., Gao, J., Islam, R., An efficient algorithm for stereo correspondence matching. *Int. J. Comput. Theory Eng.*, 9, 1, 69–72, 2017.

22. De-Maeztu, L., Mattoccia, S., Villanueva, A., Cabeza, R., Linear stereo matching, in: *IEEE international conference on computer vision (ICCV 2011)*, pp. 1708–1715, 2011.

23. Chowdhury, M. and Bhuiyan, M., Fast window based stereo matching for 3D scene reconstruction. *Int. Arab J. Inf. Technol.*, 10, 4, 209–214, July 2013.

24. Chowdhury, M., Gao, J., Islam, R., Fast stereo matching with fuzzy correlation. *IEEE Conference on Industrial Electronics & Applications (ICIEA 2016)*, Hefei, China, pp. 678–682, 2016.
25. Yang, Q., Stereo matching using tree filtering. *IEEE Trans. Pattern Anal. Mach. Intell.*, 37, 4, 834–846, 2015.
26. Geiger, A., Roser, M., Urtasun, R., Efficient large-scale stereo matching, in: *Asian conference on computer vision (ACCV)*, 2010.
27. Cai, L., He, L., Xu, Y., Zhao, Y., Yang, X., Multi-object detection and tracking by stereo vision. *Pattern Recognit.*, 43, 12, 4028–4041, 2010.
28. Chowdhury, M., Gao, J., Islam, R., Fuzzy logic based filtering for image de-noising, in: *IEEE international conference on fuzzy systems (FUZZ-IEEE 2016)*, Vancouver, Canada, pp. 2372–2376.
29. Suresh, A., Ajithkumar, N., Kalathil, S.T., Simon, A., Unnikrishnan, V.J., Mathew, D.P., Basil, P., Dutt, K., Udupa, G., Hariprasad, C.M., Menon, M., Balakrishnan, A., Ramachandran, R., Murali, A., Shankar, B., An Advanced Spider-Like Rocker-Bogie Suspension System for Mars Exploration Rovers, *Inventive Computation Technologies,* Springer International Publishing Switzerland, 2017.
30. Megalingam, R.K., Vishnu, S., Sasikumar, V., Sreekumar, S., Autonomous Path Guiding Robot for Visually Impaired People, in: *Cognitive Informatics and Soft Computing. Advances in Intelligent Systems and Computing*, vol. 768, Springer, Singapore, 2019.
31. Wattal, A., Ojha, A., Kumar, M., Obstacle Detection for Visually Impaired Using Raspberry Pi and Ultrasonic Sensors, in: *National Conference on Product Design (NCPD 2016)*.
32. Alexander, A. and Dharmana, M.M., Object detection algorithm for segregating similar coloured objects and database formation, in: *2017 International Conference on Circuit, Power and Computing Technologies (ICCPCT)*.
33. Kollmitzer, C., Object Detection and Measurement Using Stereo Images, in: *Multimedia Communications, Services and Security: 5th International Conference*, 2012.
34. Brad, R., Bebeselea-Sterp, E., Brad, R., A Comparative Study of Stereovision Algorithms. *Int. J. Adv. Comput. Sci. Appl. (IJACSA)*, 8, 11, 359–375, 2017.
35. Munro, P. and Gerdelan, A.P., Stereo Vision Computer Depth Perception, 2017.
36. Feng, W., Wang, Z., He, W., Xiao, H., Real-time SIFT-based object recognition system, in: *Mechatronics and Automation (ICMA), 2013 IEEE International Conference*.
37. Zin, T. and Thu, C.S.T., Implementation of Text to Speech Conversion. *Int. J. Eng. Res. Technol. (IJERT)*, 3, 911–915, March 2014.

14

Real-Time Depth Estimation Using BLOB Detection/Contour Detection

Arokia Priya Charles*, Anupama V. Patil and Sunil Dambhare

Dr. D. Y. Patil Institute of Engineering, Management and Research, Akurdi, Pune, India

Abstract

In this chapter, under the feature-based techniques, we propose to find the disparity by detecting the blobs in both the images and, using the moment calculations, the disparity between the pixels is calculated. We have applied algorithms both with background and without background for disparity calculations and depth estimation. The blob is found for the object of concern and the disparity is found between blobs of both the images. It is implemented in Java with multithreading. However, there are some limitations with the distance of the object that it can measure. This method can identify more than one object provided that there is no overlap of objects.

Keywords: Blob analysis, object detection, centroid, Hu moments, profile

14.1 Introduction

As of now, the methods were the object matching using similarity-based approaches such as region-based segmentation and clustering algorithms. This part of the thesis concentrates on the edge detection technique's discontinuity-based match procedure, and we propose that blob detection be used to detect the edge.

Object detection is the detection of real-life items in images/videos that belong to a variety of classes. It is the procedure for detecting the desired objects and removing the distracting background from the image. Object extraction is one of the most important processes/steps in object detection. To extract specific features of object from digital image, it is necessary

---

**Corresponding author*: prinnu@yahoo.com

R. Arokia Priya, Anupama V Patil, Manisha Bhende, Anuradha Thakare and Sanjeev Wagh (eds.)
Object Detection by Stereo Vision Images, (227–256) © 2022 Scrivener Publishing LLC

to perform segmentation process on original object. As a result of segmentation operation obtained image contains well differentiated object. However, the image may contain multiple objects. In addition, some objects may be unwanted. Using Connected Component or the Blob Extraction method, one can extract objects of interest from such an image.

A set/group of connected pixels sharing certain common property in a binary image is called a Binary Large OBject (BLOB). Binary objects of certain minimum size are of interest designated by the term "Large" and the objects below that certain size are generally noise. In computer vision, connected component categorization/labeling is adopted for detecting connected areas/regions in digital binary images, even if they are color images [2] or data of higher dimensionality [1]. When integrated into an image recognition system or human-computer interaction interface, connected component labeling can operate on a variety of information [3]. Blob extraction can also be deployed/applied on grayscale and color images, even though it is usually deployed/applied on the resultant binary image of a thresholding step. Blobs can be numbered, filtered, and tracked in a variety of ways. The methods in blob detection are targeted at differentiating areas/sections that vary in properties/characteristics like brightness or color, related to its neighbors/surroundings. Hence generally, a blob is a region/area in an image with all the points similar in characteristics/properties. Convolution is a most common method of blob detection. A blob is a group of connected pixels in an image that gives some common property.

These are bright on dark or dark on bright regions in an image. From pertinent input data, a graph with peaks and linking edges is made/created. Information for heuristic comparison is contained in the vertices and the edges indicate the connected neighbors. The vertices are labeled on the basis of their connectivity (4 or 8 connected) and their relative values of the neighbors by an algorithm. Subsets of the graph can then be created. The original data can then be recuperated for processing.

Of the two passes/runs, the algorithm performs on the image, and it records equivalences, assigns temporary labels in the first, and replaces the temporary labels with labels of its equivalence in the second. In the case of 8-connectivity, the pixel labels of Northeast, Northwest, North, and West are checked, and, in the case of 4-connectivity, the pixel labels of North and West are checked. The blob is to be detected from both the images, and the possibility of the real-time image could be with background and without background. This chapter highlights on both and the methods are discussed in the following part.

14.2   Estimation of Depth Using Blob Detection

Region matching methods took too long to complete the assignment, so we used the segmentation technique, which falls under the region based category, to separate the background from the foreground.

Algorithm for depth estimation without background (Figure 14.1):

1. For both the left and right images, load the input 2D image from the database.
2. Convert the input image to grayscale image.
3. The threshold image is applied with the connected components algorithm, i.e., BLOB that stands for Binary Large Object and refers to a group of connected pixels in a binary image and such algorithms are generally called as connected component analysis. Connected non-black pixels are isolated by individual blobs and array of information is provided.
4. The center of gravity is calculated in order to identify the object, and then, the disparity and depth are calculated using the usual approach.

Algorithm for depth estimation with background (Figure 14.2):

1. For both the left and right images, load the input 2D image from the database.
2. Load the background image (the image/scene without any objects/first frame) separately.

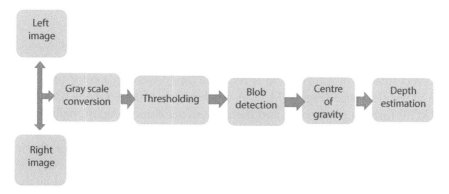

Figure 14.1 Process flow without background.

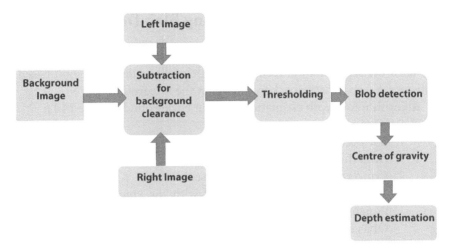

Figure 14.2 Process flow with background.

3. Remove the background image from the left as well as the background image from the right. This results in a left and right image with no background or a white background.

4. Now, perform thresholding on grayscale image to separate the foreground from background.

5. The threshold image is applied with the connected components algorithm, i.e., BLOB that stands for Binary Large Object and refers to a group of connected pixels in a binary image and such algorithms are generally called as connected component analysis. Individual blobs separate connected non-black pixels, and an array of data is presented.

6. The center of gravity is calculated in order to identify the object and, based on that, the disparity is calculated and the depth is estimated using traditional method.

14.2.1 Grayscale Conversion

Good amount of information is required for converting a color image to a grayscale image (Figure 14.1). A combination of Red, Green, and Blue (RGB) forms a pixel color, and their values are three dimensionally characterized in terms of lightness, chroma, and hue. The number of bits the device could support determines the quality of the color image (basic color, 8-bit; high color, 16 bit; true color, 24 bit; and deep color, 32 bit). The maximum number of colors supported by the device is determined by the number of bits. R, G, and B occupying 8 bit each (meaning combined RGB occupying 24 bit) supports 16,777,216 colors. The conversion of RGB (24 bit) values to grayscale (8 bit) is the conversion of color to grayscale, since 24 bit represents color and 8 bit represents grayscale luminance (ranging between 0 and 255). There are very many software applications/processing techniques that convert color to grayscale image.

14.2.2 Thresholding

The most basic approach of image segmentation is thresholding. Thresholding can be used to generate/create binary pictures from a grayscale image. When contrasted to a predefined/constant pixel value, every pixel with an image density is replaced by either a black or a white pixel, based on its intensity value (lower, black; higher, white).

$$\text{If } I_{i,j} < T \text{ then } I_{i,j} = 0$$

$$\text{else } I_{i,j} = 1$$

To take advantage of multithreading, we employed Net Beans and JAVA coding. It includes all of the tools Java developers need to create professional desktop, corporate, and mobile applications. The peaks, troughs, and curvatures of the smoothed histogram are taken into account in histogram shape-based algorithms. The thresholding is done based on which the photos are

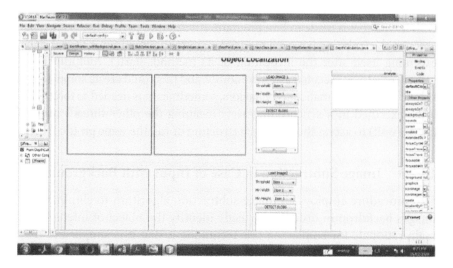

Figure 14.3 Interface for the image and threshold selection.

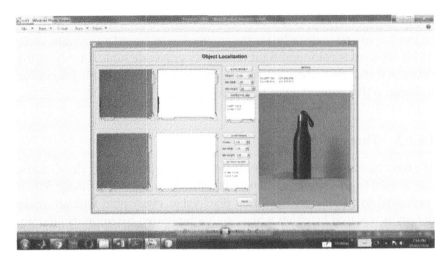

Figure 14.4 Thresholding option for segmentation.

segmented as background and foreground as in Figure 14.3 and Figure 14.4. A Java feature that maximizes CPU utilization is simultaneous/concurrent execution (multithreading) of two or more tiny programs (threads) of a program. Hence, threads are light-weight processes within a process. A class is constructed/created (an extension of Java language thread class), which overrides the "run ()" existing in the thread class. A thread begins its life inside run () method. An object of the new class is made and "start ()" is called to initiate the execution of the thread. Start () invokes the run () method on the Thread object. In Java language, an instance of the class "thread" represents each thread that is made in Java program. An instance of the class "runnable" executes the code that has been received on instantiation time. A thread starts executing itself after the invocation of its method. start(). Multithreading causes code to be executed asynchronously, and this could create some inconsistencies. To avoid malicious behaviors, sometimes, it is needed to force code to be executed in a synchronous way: meaning the other threads have to queue (wait) to access the same data structure or call the same protocol.

14.2.3   Image Subtraction in Case of Input with Background

This procedure employs an image subtraction algorithm to eliminate the image's backdrop in order to correctly identify the object of interest. The main rationale for employing this technique is that it is simple and may be used in limited real-time processing scenarios. It turned out to be a satisfactory solution. We evaluated a basic subtraction of the photos before looking for the optimal subtraction, assuming the camera was still [4]. In the case of a still camera, the background image should always be the same, particularly in applications such as security cameras. As the images are deemed to be static images, we must conduct some simple subtraction operations.

Any change in the picture that is taken will not give a background subtraction to be zero if there is a modification of the input image We have assumed that the photos are captured at regular intervals and that the subtraction occurs as a result. The reference frame is the background frame. The reference frames are consistent throughout. Any change in input, such as a person seen in the camera in the left image, is subtracted from the left background image, and the right image is subtracted from the right background image. Because the camera is a stereo vision camera, we will have two background images recorded in the memory/database.

14.2.3.1 Preliminaries

The emphasis is on selecting the optimum reference frame. The degradation of the frame to the "worst viewing frame" is undesirable since it will reduce the signal to noise ratio significantly.

The reference frame is thereafter convolved with the current frame for the matching procedure. This is done in order to achieve the best possible outcome.

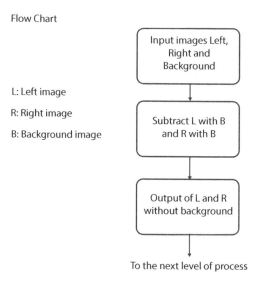

Flow Chart

L: Left image

R: Right image

B: Background image

Input images Left, Right and Background

Subtract L with B and R with B

Output of L and R without background

To the next level of process

14.2.3.2   Computing Time

This method would take much longer because it would have to process all pixels one by one. However, the actual cost of the calculations is substantially lower than first appears [5]. The calculation of the matrix consumes the majority of the computing time. MXN size will require MXN calculating time (where M is row and N is the column of image matrix). This method is time consuming for the CPU since it must perform two operations: one for the left picture and another for the right image. MXNX2 is the result of double the entire procedure. The remaining/balance of the operation takes approximately the same amount of time to compute. With a 2.5-GHz PC, and this way, we can process a 1000X750 frame in roughly 170 ms.

It gave a time consumption of (MXNX2)/2 = MXN

To reduce consumption time even more, the entire process was run on multicore CPUs with GPU.

14.3   BLOB

This operation is twofold: BLOB extraction and BLOB classification. As the name indicates, the first operation is to identify and separate the object that is of concern, and the second operation is to evaluate/analyze the separated/identified object.

14.3.1   BLOB Extraction

Isolating the BLOBs (objects) in a binary image is called BLOB extraction and it consists of a collection/group of pixels. The connectivity defines and identifies the connected pixels and their neighbors. The two most often applied types of connectivity: 4- and 8-connectivity.

The 4-connectivity, needing fewer computation, is much faster and hence used more frequently than the higher accurate 8-connectivity. The effect of the two different types of connectivity is illustrated in Figure 14.5 where the two blobs in case of 4-connectivity and one blob in case of 8-connectivity.

Algorithm

1. Read the black and white pixels in image
2. For y = 0 to height
      For x = 0 to width
            Find the pixels that are black
            Read till the next pixel is found

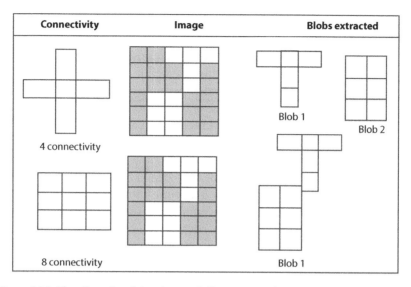

Figure 14.5 The effect of applying the two different types of connectivity: 4- and 8-connectivity.

        Mark the coordinates
      End for
    End for
3. Read all values, for value is 1 to 1
   Mark a rectangle
   Draw a rectangle
4. End for loop

14.3.2   Blob Classification

Blob classification is to classify the extracted objects in both the scenes and to find the object of our interest. In order that the objects are matched, we have used the concept of center of gravity.

Let b1, b2, b3, ..., bn be the number of objects, and H and W be the height and width, respectively.

To calculate COG,

$$COG = \sqrt{[(X2\ mid - X1\ mid)2 + (Y2\ mid - Y1\ mid)2]} \quad (14.1)$$

$$CX_i = W_i/2 \quad (14.2)$$

$$CY_i = H_i/2 \quad (14.3)$$

Hence, Cxi and CYi are the center of gravity points for respective objects.

Motion analysis has become indispensable/crucial in several vision systems, which is associated with time requiring examination, in the recent years. The rising interest in this research is in conjunction with the immense attentions of employing real-time application to control complex real-world systems such as in the case of traffic monitoring, airport surveillance, and face verification for ATM security. In achieving the realization of these diverse applications, motion detection is one of the most fundamental analysis tasks in the real-time process flow.

The objective of this extension of this idea is to implement a reliable and less computational process for real-time moving object extraction. Normally, background subtraction is employed to segment dynamic region from static region.

14.3.2.1   Image Moments

Blob as in Figure 14.6 and Figure 14.7 detection algorithm worked well by drawing a rectangle around every object and by finding the center of gravity. However, if the blob is outlined with always a rectangle or a square, then the center of gravity method works well. However, because it is stereo image there is a difference in the size of objects that are outlined which affects the center of gravity value. In turn, the center of gravity value is used to find the disparity of the pixels between two objects from both the left and right images.

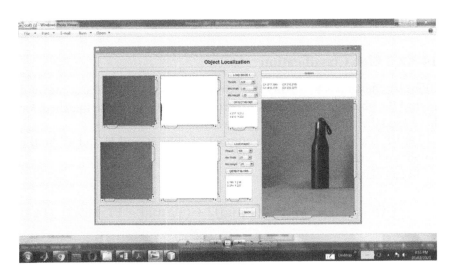

Figure 14.6 Blob for single object.

Figure 14.7 Blob detection for multiple objects.

It gives a huge difference in the disparity, and hence, the depth value is calculated using this disparity has huge error. If the distance of the object is increasing, then the error also increases. Hence, we thought of using the moments. An image moment is a property that describes an image's shape; things such as area, orientation, thickness, and skewness. We can use these properties to identify shapes in our image. The digital images are not continuous and are not noise-free in real applications, since they are rounded of in discrete co-ordinate by finite-precision pixels. Even more, noise gets into by several factors including camera system. Hence, errors are unavoidable in the computation of moment invariants. We can integrate functions to obtain moments. The general form for calculating the moment of a two variable function is as follows:

$$M_{ij} = \sum_{x=1}^{w} \sum_{y=1}^{H} x_i y_i f(x, y) dx dy \qquad (14.4)$$

where an image of width W and height H is denoted by f(x, y). When i = j = 0, the equation is simplified down to

$$M00 = \sum \sum (x, y) \qquad (14.5)$$

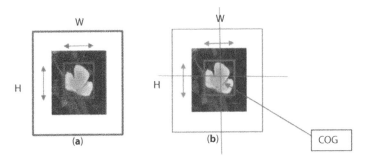

Figure 14.8 (a) Input image with H and W. (b) Center of gravity.

14.3.2.2   Centroid Using Image Moments

For the center of mass, the centroid is given by as shown in Figure 14.8

$$\bar{x} = M10 / M00 \tag{14.6}$$

$$\bar{y} = M01 / M00 \tag{14.7}$$

14.3.2.3   Central Moments

Central moments are very similar to the image moments, except that we subtract off the centroid from the x and y in the moment formula.

$$Mij = \sum_x \sum_y (x - \bar{x})(y - \bar{y})^j f(x, y) \tag{14.8}$$

Notice that the above central moments are translation invariant. In other words, no matter where the blob is in the image, if the shape is the same, the moments will be the same.

Central moments are translation invariant. However, that is not enough for shape matching. We would like to calculate moments that are invariant to translation, scale, and rotation so that the accuracy of the depth increases. So we used Hu Moments which are a set of seven numbers calculated using central moments [6] that are invariant to image transformations. All the seven moments were found to be invariant to scale, translation, and rotation. As far as image reflection is concerned, there is a change of sign in the seventh moment, while all other moments were invariant.

It was found [7] that the error decreases when the image size increases and the sampling intervals decrease but does not decrease monotonically in general. Besides quantization and noise pollution, transformations like scaling and rotation can also cause computational errors in moment invariants [8]. The image pixels either gets deleted or interpolated, depending on whether the image size is decreased or increased, respectively. Therefore, moment invariants may change as images scale or rotate [9].

Hu moments are used to find the distance between two shapes. The seven moments, invariant to scaling, translation, and rotation, are of great use as shown in Figure 14.9. The prevalent image geometric transformation technique normally involves translation, scaling, and rotation. Mapping of each pixel position from an input image to an output image is performed by the translation operator; sub-sample or interpolation mapping to shrink or zoom the image size is performed by scale operator; rotating each pixel by a specified angle and repositioning them in the output image (rotational mapping), which may create non-integer co-ordinates, is done by the rotation operator. Various interpolation methods like nearest-neighbor interpolation and bilinear interpolation, for instance, can be deployed to generate pixel intensity at every integer point. Rotation and scaling besides shifting the position of the pixels also change the image function unlike the translation which does only "shifting of the pixels" [10]. Hence, the errors in the moment invariants are primary caused by rotation and scaling only. Image function may change due to image scaling causing a corresponding change in the moment invariant. Thus, the study of the moment invariant and image scaling relationship becomes essential.

Shapes are closer in appearance for smaller distances and they are farther apart/away in appearance for larger distances. Euclidean distance computation is performed after shape matching and accordingly depth is found. So far, the baseline distance for all the images were kept as 50 mm almost same as that of the distance between two eyes. In the proposed system, the baseline is varied from 50 to 125 mm and the same algorithm is applied. For a base line of 50 mm, as the object distance increases, the error is less. For a base line of 75 mm, error percentage is more overall. We have done the analysis with various focal length and sensor sizes.

$$h_0 = \eta_{20} + \eta_{02}$$

$$h_1 = (\eta_{20} - \eta_{02})^2 + 4\eta_{11}^2$$

$$h_2 = (\eta_{30} - 3\eta_{12})^2 + (3\eta_{21} - 3\eta_{03})^2$$

$$h_3 = (\eta_{30} + \eta_{12})^2 + (\eta_{21} + \eta_{03})^2$$

$$h_4 = (\eta_{30} - 3\eta_{12})(\eta_{30} + \eta_{12})[(\eta_{30} + \eta_{12})^2 - 3(\eta_{21} + \eta_{03})^2] + (3\eta_{21} - \eta_{03})[3(\eta_{30} + \eta_{12})^2 - (\eta_{21} + \eta_{03})^2]$$

$$h_5 = (\eta_{20} - \eta_{02})[(\eta_{30} + \eta_{12})^2 - (\eta_{21} + \eta_{03})^2 + 4\eta_{11}(\eta_{30} + \eta_{12})(\eta_{21} + \eta_{03})]$$

$$h_6 = (3\eta_{21} - \eta_{03})(\eta_{30} + \eta_{12})[(\eta_{30} + \eta_{12})^2 - 3(\eta_{21} + \eta_{03})^2] + (\eta_{30} - 3\eta_{12})(\eta_{21} + \eta_{03})[3(\eta_{30} + \eta_{12})^2 - (\eta_{21} + \eta_{03})^2]$$

Figure 14.9 Moments.

Around a decade ago in computer-vision, the accuracy levels of the problems were getting saturated, and now with the advent and rise of deep learning techniques, the accuracy of the problems increased significantly. One of the major problems was that of image classification, which is defined as predicting the class of the image. Image localization, a little complicated problem, is the prediction of the class of location of the object in the image, by the system (object bounded by a box), where the image has a single object. The more complicated problem (this project) of object detection involves both classification and localization and calculating the depth of object from the camera. In this case, the input to the system will be a video stream from stereo camera or screen recorder, and the output will be a bounding box corresponding to every object in image along with their class. Using the same concept of blob detection the YOLO object detection technique is used to identify the object. The object that is been identified is uses multithreading since the input is a video and the frames are captured the same time in order to detect the contour.

Object size and distance measurement are very necessary for the navigation/localization of mobile autonomous system. Since most of autonomous systems nowadays are equipped with vision sensors or cameras, it is very beneficial that the vision information is utilized to obtained distance and size information that can be used to assist the system. Many researchers have worked on to determine the object-distance from a captured image. In the beginning, methods/protocols with single vision sensor/camera were proposed for determining the object distance. For instance, object distance measurement method with respect to variation in eye distance (distance between camera to person) using a single vision point/single camera was proposed by Rahman *et al.* Meanwhile, Wahab *et al.* proposed a monocular vision system that utilizes Hough transforms, and the object distance is determined using the relative object size. A variation in single camera approach was proposed by Kim *et al.*, wherein a rotating mirror was used along with the camera. In combination with a rotating mirror, the camera captures a sequence of reflected images which are then studied/analyzed to get the object distance. In a sequence of images, the pixel of an object point at a far distance moves at a higher speed. This phenomenon is used to determine the object distance in this method. Of late, many researchers have started to investigate the use of multi-vision sensors/multiple (stereo vision) cameras. For example, the measurement of safe driving distance of a vehicle by Lin *et al.* makes use of stereo vision camera, wherein the distance is determined from the disparity between the two frames captured by the stereo camera that is used. The distance measurement is based on the disparity of the front car in the two frames capture by the stereo camera.

An improvisation resulting in a more accurate disparity calculation was then proposed by Baek *et al.*, which can be effectively deployed for objects in a larger view area. Distance measurement has been the main focus/center of attention in most of the works reported in the literature. As we have stated before, the object size information is also very useful especially in a navigation and localization of an autonomous system. Moreover, the size information is very handy in short term object identification in autonomous systems.

In this work, a method to measure both object distance and object size using a stereo vision camera, which deploys a very fast algorithm enabling it to be used in real-time, is proposed. The objective of this research is to simulate the human eyes.

Computer vision is such kind of research field which tries to percept and represents the 3D information for world objects. Its essence is to reconstruct the visual aspect of image captured from both the cameras and to analyze actual depth by calculating disparity between two images; along with that, object detection is done in real time. The most important thing is that multiple objects are detected and depth is calculated for all the objects in the frame.

14.4   Challenges

The variable dimension of the output, which is produced by the varied number of objects that can be present in any given input image, is the key obstacle in this problem. For any generic machine learning activity, the model to be trained must have a fixed dimension of input and output. Another significant barrier to widespread implementation of object detection systems is the requirement for real-time (>30 fps) detection while maintaining accuracy. The more complicated the model is, the longer it takes to infer it, and the less complex the model is, the less accurate it is. The trade-off between accuracy and performance must be determined according to the application. The issue is one of classification. Because the task involves both classification and regression, the model must be learned simultaneously. This adds to the problem's complexity.

14.5   Experimental Results

In order to test the effectiveness of our approach, the result of experiment shows that our method can achieve detection of moving objects effectively in the indoor environment when taking place an illumination change. Real-time object detection using the video inputs were done single object

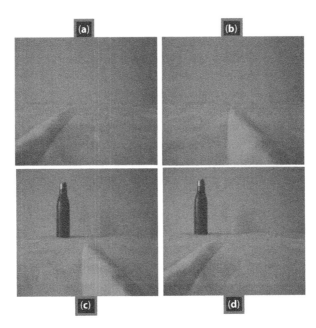

Figure 14.10 (a) Left: background image. (b) Right: background image. (c) Left: single-object image. (d) Right: single-object image.

Figure 14.11 (a) Left: background image. (b) Right: background image. (c) Left: two-object image (d) Right: two-object image.

and multiple objects are shown as in Figures 14.10 and 14.11. USB camera Logitech C270 HD—with the following specifications: maximum resolution, 720 p/30 fps; focus type, fixed focus; lens technology, standard; built-in mic, mono; FoV, 60°—is used. The video input from both cameras is taken.

There was an image frame lag between both the camera inputs as the code was executed sequentially and hence the frames with objects were not matching, sample pictures are shown as in Figure 14.12. It incurred as huge difference in the disparity and at times the frame itself was $(n+1)^{th}$ frame.

Figure 14.12 Input, left and right images, at different distances of objects from camera.

Hence, multithreading concept was used for image acquisition, and this gave a great result in terms of time consumption and the frame matching sample code shown in Figure 14.13.

From Figures 14.14 to 14.16, using centroid method as the object distance increases, since the moments do not take care of the scale, translation, and rotation invariant property, the centroid value calculated was not accurate. The accuracy kept on decreasing with the change in object distance. More the distant of the object less was the accuracy. This drawback was overcome by using the Hu moments as discussed earlier which helped in translation, scale, and rotation invariant.

As Hu moment shape descriptor will only be computed over the white pixels, our input images are converted to grayscale as it requires a single channel image. It is done to flatten our array to form our shape feature vector, which is further used to quantify and represent the shape of an object in an image.

In Figure 14.17 and Figure 14.18, the graph gives the Hu moments for the left and right images with the distances of the objects placed at three different distances. Till H4 moment, the left and right images do not show any change even with change in distances. However, from H5 onward, the values are opposite and hence proves that the there is a difficulty in finding a match. Hence, we have used only till H4 values to find the shape match between two same objects from two different images. Figure 14.19 shows actual output with one object. Figures 14.20 and 14.21 shows the plot with baseline of 50mm and 75mm. Figure 14.22 shows the call graph of functions used with the profiles in Figures 14.23 and 14.24.

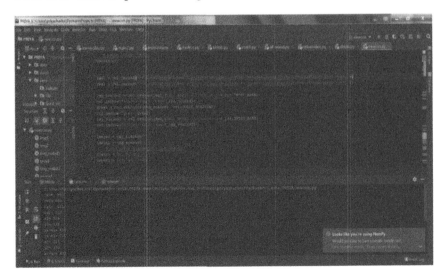

Figure 14.13 Code displaying the depth.

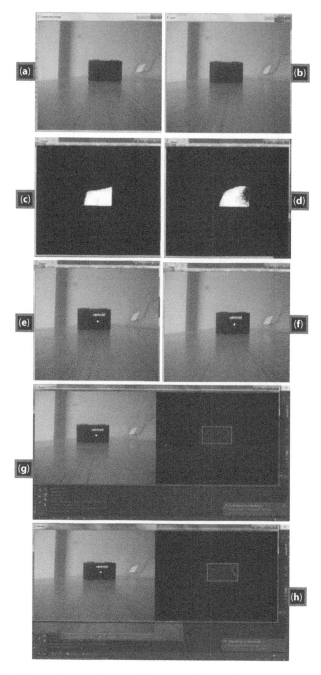

Figure 14.14 (a) Input image with actual distance = 30cm. (b) Grayscale image. (c, d) Segmented images, left and right. (e, f) Single object with centroid left and right images. (g) Blob, left. (h) Blob, right.

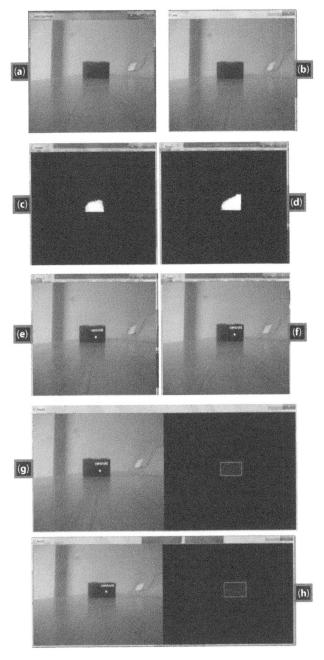

Figure 14.15 (a) Input image with actual distance = 60 cm. (b) Grayscale image. (c, d) Segmented images, left and right. (e, f) Single object with centroid, left and right images. (g) Blob, left. (h) Blob, right.

REAL-TIME DEPTH ESTIMATION   247

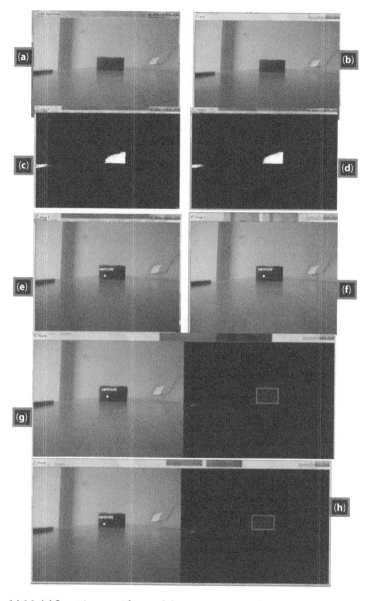

Figure 14.16 (a) Input image with actual distance = 110 cm. (b) Grayscale image. (c, d) Segmented images, left and right. (e, f) Single object with centroid, left and right images. (g) Blob, left. (h) Blob, right.

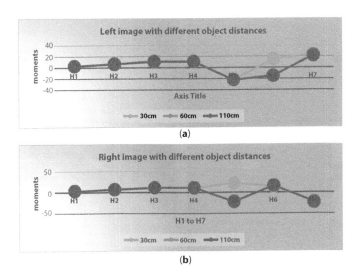

Figure 14.17 (a, b) Hu moments of left and right images with different distances of objects.

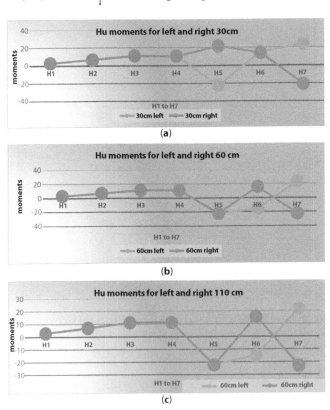

Figure 14.18 (a, b, c) Hu moments for 30-, 60-, and 110-cm distances.

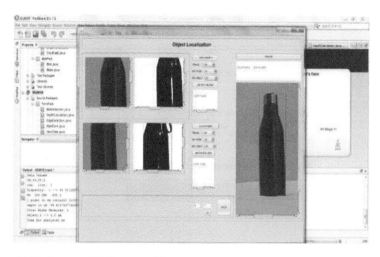

Figure 14.19 Input and blob detected image.

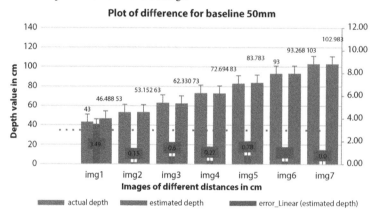

Figure 14.20 Baseline 50 mm.

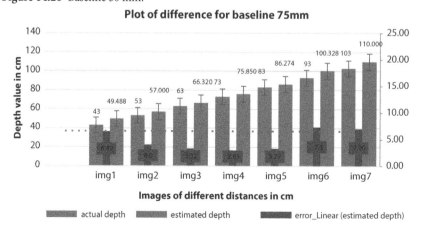

Figure 14.21 Baseline at 75 mm.

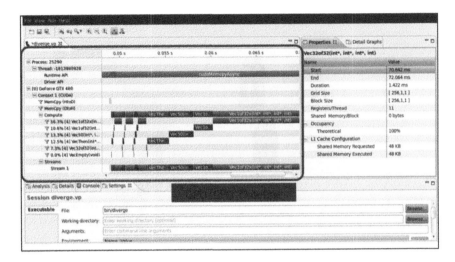

Figure 14.22 Call graph.

Profiler

File Edit Debug Window Help

Start Profiling Run this code:

Profile Summary

Generated 19-Sep-2018 15:18:25 using performance time.

Function Name	Calls	Total Time	Self Time*	Total Time Plot (dark band = self time)
onlysad	1	24.780 s	14.118 s	
uigetfile	2	6.740 s	0.002 s	
uitools\private\uigetputfile_helper	2	6.737 s	0.037 s	
FileChooser.FileChooser>FileChooser.show	2	6.509 s	0.001 s	
...gt.FileChooser.showPeerAndBlockMATLAB	2	6.048 s	0.003 s	
...ooser>FileOpenChooser.doShowDialog	2	5.991 s	5.991 s	
imshow	9	1.813 s	0.261 s	
initSize	5	1.198 s	0.082 s	
movegui	6	1.020 s	0.930 s	
imshowpair	1	0.855 s	0.003 s	
...eChooser>FileChooser.prepareDialog	2	0.460 s	0.035 s	
imhist	3	0.457 s	0.024 s	
imhist>plot_result	1	0.428 s	0.033 s	
imread	2	0.418 s	0.026 s	
...orks.mwswing.MJFileChooserPerPlatform (Java method)	16	0.347 s	0.347 s	
...leChooser>FileChooser.setPeerTitle	2	0.334 s	0.001 s	
stem	1	0.294 s	0.102 s	
newplot	23	0.278 s	0.045 s	
imagesci\private\readpng	2	0.274 s	0.088 s	
imfuse	1	0.226 s	0.005 s	
imadjust	1	0.197 s	0.009 s	
medfilt2	1	0.176 s	0.003 s	
mesh	2	0.175 s	0.077 s	
imagesci\private\pngreadc (MEX-file)	2	0.170 s	0.170 s	
imfuse>parse_inputs	1	0.147 s	0.071 s	
subplot	4	0.143 s	0.081 s	
padarray	3	0.143 s	0.022 s	
medfilt2>hPadImage	1	0.138 s	0.001 s	

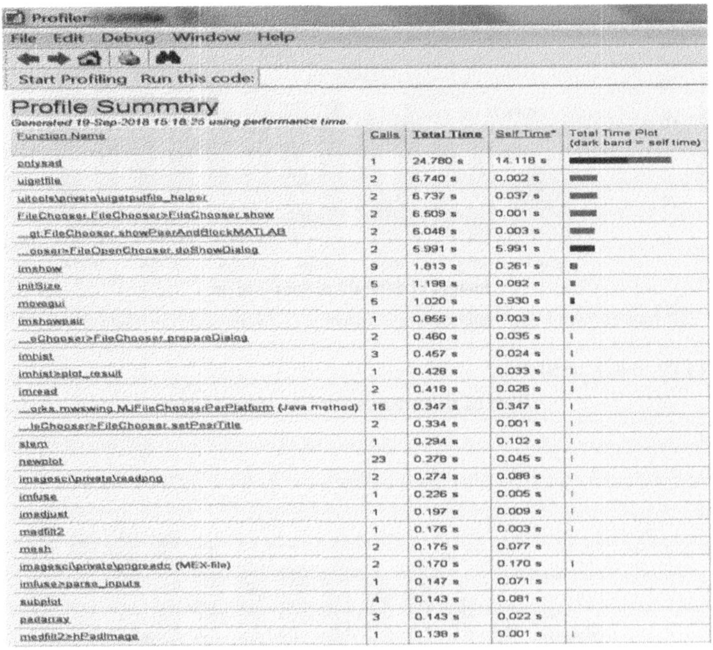

Figure 14.23 CPU profiler.

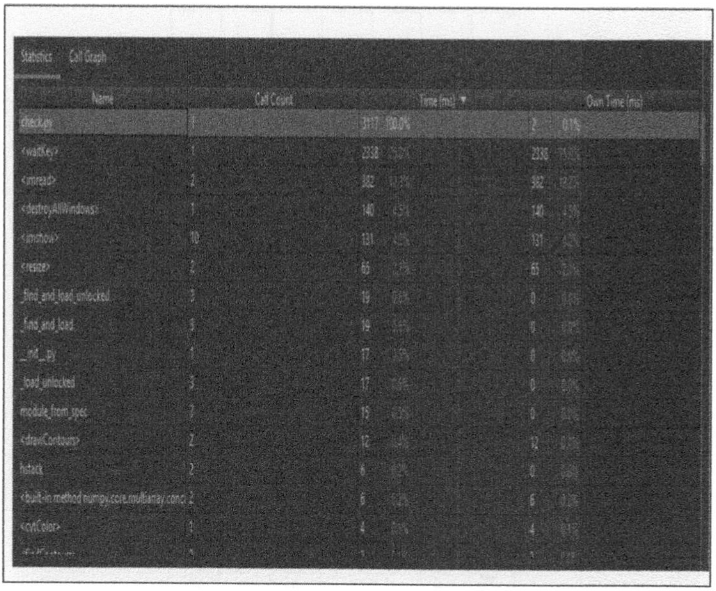

Figure 14.24 GPU profiler.

14.6 Conclusion

We calculate the computation of moment invariants shown in Table 14.1 for the distances from 30 to 110 cm in 3-cm increments in Lenovo ThinkPad W541 (20EF000NUS) Laptop: i7-4810MQ (up to 3.8 GHz). For the results of Hu moments for left and right images from the diagram, we can see that the relationship between the distance and the Hu moments is linear till H4, H5, H6, and H7 are inverse to each other. Therefore, we must use Hu matching only if the distance between both the cameras is to be increased beyond 50 mm as we tried for various distances like 50 and 75 mm. We extracted Hu moments from the shapes and computed the Euclidean distance between the shapes. Smaller Euclidean distances are more similar matches of objects. If the distance between the cameras is 50 mm, which is the distance between the eyes that are usually kept as the distance in case of robotic applications, then this Hu moment may not be required. However, if applications like cameras kept apart more than the eyes distance, then this can be of more useful as shown in Figure 14.25. Therefore, we must select an acceptable distance of cameras to balance computation and distance of object on the real application.

Table 14.1 Hu moment for input images.

Camera	Image distance	H1	H2	H3	H4	H5	H6	H7
Left	30 cm	2.830738	6.697409	11.51288	11.14912	22.4811	14.98563	23.66216
Right		2.84412	6.699054	10.83266	10.46468	21.70561	13.92455	−21.128
Left	60 cm	2.904562	6.799836	11.33158	11.24941	−22.5953	−15.3532	22.86372
Right		2.90746	6.789631	11.16153	11.08808	−22.2265	15.47345	−22.8211
Left	110 cm	2.889624	6.728495	10.91589	11.03215	−22.2199	−14.7468	22.10778
Right		2.909381	6.835905	11.07973	11.20078	−22.3462	15.65028	−23.1553

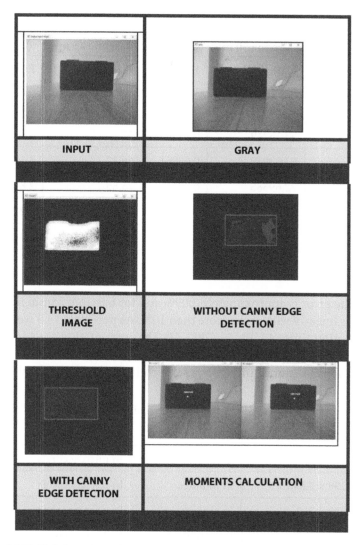

Figure 14.25 Blob detection using moments.

Our findings may be summarized as follows: (1) the moment invariants change as distance between the cameras increase, because images size decreases when the object distance increases and hence moments works much better in shape matching as the shape of the object would not be that significant. (2) Table 14.2 shows the distance of the objects using centroid methods for a baseline of 50 and 75 mm. The actual depth of objects as per measurements range from 43cm to 103cm. For baseline

Table 14.2 Depth using centroid (for baseline 50 and 75 mm).

Actual depth in cm	Baseline 50 mm		Baseline 75 mm	
	Estimated depth in cm	Error in cm	Estimated depth in cm	Error in cm
43	46.4876	3.4876	49.48	6.4876
53	53.15249	0.15249	57	4
63	62.33039	0.66961	66.32	3.32
73	72.69385	0.30615	75.85	2.85
83	83.78274	0.78274	86.27	3.274
93	93.26758	0.26758	100.3	7.328
103	102.983	0.017	110	7

50mm the error is approximately .009% and for baseline 75mm the error increases linearly with error more than 10%. As per Table 14.3 we can see the execution time of CPU vs GPU. (3) The computation time increases for calculating the Hu moments when the spatial resolution of images and the object distance increases as shown in Table 14.4 and Table 14.5.

Table 14.3 CPU vs. GPU of centroid matching.

Images	CPU	GPU
3,264 × 2,448	In minutes	In microseconds
4,288 × 2,848	In minutes	In microseconds
1,000 × 750	In seconds	In microseconds
1,000 × 664	In seconds	In microseconds

Table 14.4 Computation time for Hu matching for image size of 1,000 × 750.

Object distance	CPU	GPU
30 cm	9.9 s	0.63 μs
60 cm	10.464 s	0.78 μs
110 cm	14.3 s	0.94 μs

Table 14.5 Depth using Hu (for baseline 50 and 75 mm).

Actual depth in cm	Baseline 50 mm		Baseline 75 mm	
	Estimated depth in cm	Error in cm	Estimated depth in cm	Error in cm
43	45.38	2.38	47.3	4.3
53	53.6	0.6	55.88	2.88
63	63.82	0.82	65.10	2.1
73	74.49	1.49	75.7	2.7
83	84.9	1.9	86.1	3.1
93	95.672	2.672	101.4	8.4
103	104.531	1.531	113	10

(4) This does not work for a greater number of blobs especially if the objects overlap. From the experimental studies, we find that the choice of image spatial resolution and the distance between the cameras are very important to keep invariant features. To decrease the computation time of moment invariants, the image spatial resolution must be lower in case of CPU. However, the resolution can be too high in case of GPU, because the computation will remarkably increase as the resolution increases. Hence, an appropriate resolution is to be chosen to get an uncompromising balance between computation and resolution in real application.

References

1. Samet, H. and Tamminen, M., Efficient Component Labeling of Images of Arbitrary Dimension Represented by Linear Bintrees. *IEEE Trans. Patt. Anal. Mach. Intell.*, 10, 4, 579, 1998.
2. Michael, B., Dillencourt, H.S., Tamminen, M., A general approach to connected-component labeling for arbitrary image representations. *J. ACM*, 39, 2, 253, 1992.
3. Chen, W., Maryellen, L.G., Bick, U., A Fuzzy C-Means (FCM)- Based Approach for Computerized Segmentation of Breast Lesions in Dynamic Contrast-Enhanced MR Images. *Acad. Radiol.*, 13, 1, 63–72, 2006.
4. Desa, S.M. and Salih, Q.A., Image subtraction for real time moving object extraction. *Proceedings. International Conference on Computer Graphics, Imaging and Visualization*, Penang, Malaysia, July 2004.

5. Alard, C. and Lupton, R.H., A method for optimal Image subtraction. *J. Astrophys.*, 503, 325 331, August 10, 1998.

6. Huang, Z. and Leng, J., Analysis of Hu's moment invariants on image scaling and rotation. *2010 2nd International Conference on Computer Engineering and Technology*, pp. 16–18, April 2010.

7. Salarna, G., II and Abbott, A.L., Moment invariants and quantization effects. *1998 IEEE Computer Society Conference on Computer Vision and Pattern Recognition*, Santa Barbara, CA, USA, pp. 157–163, 1998.

8. Teh, C.H. and Chin, R.T., On Image Analysis by the Methods of Moments. *IEEE Trans. Patt. Anal. Mach. Intell.*, 10, 496–513, 1988.

9. Gonzalez, R.C. and Woods, R.E., *Digital Image Processing*, 3rd, Pearson International edition, London, UK, 1992.

10. Hu, M.K., Visual pattern recognition by moment invariants. *IEEE Trans. Inf. Theory*, 8, 2, 179–187, 1962.

Index

Printed and bound by CPI Group (UK) Ltd, Croydon, CR0 4YY

27/10/2024

14580178-0001